EXTREMES

EXTREMES

How to Keep Your Virtues
from Becoming Vices

ROBERT EATON

DESERET
BOOK

Salt Lake City, Utah

Library of Congress Cataloging-in-Publication Data

Eaton, Robert I.
   Extremes : how to keep your virtues from becoming vices / Robert Eaton.
      p.   cm.
   Includes bibliographical references and index.
   ISBN 978-1-59038-957-7 (paperbound)
   1. Virtues.   2. Vices.   3. Church of Jesus Christ of Latter-day
Saints—Doctrines.   4. Mormon Church—Doctrines.   I. Title.
   BV4630.E28 2008
   241'.049332—dc22   2008016073

Printed in the United States of America
Publishers Printing, Salt Lake City, UT

10   9   8   7   6   5   4   3   2   1

In memory of
CLAYTA BERNICE HATHAWAY EATON

CONTENTS

ACKNOWLEDGMENTS

I am grateful to many different individuals for their support and constructive feedback, which helped make this a better book. John Hilton III, Jeremy Oswald, and Max Checketts provided valuable, detailed, and comprehensive feedback on all of the manuscript or major portions of it. John Thomas, Steve Dennis, Steve Eaton, Henry J. Eyring, and Henry C. Eyring provided very useful comments on specific chapters. Joel Wakefield came up with a title for the book that we nearly used, but he got outvoted. Elizabeth, Jonathan, Rebecca, and Danielle Eaton provided useful feedback and assistance along the way. As always, I appreciate the patience of my wife, Dianne, with my endless writing, particularly when I could be spending my time in ways that might have been a more immediate blessing to our family and her.

I am once again grateful to Cory Maxwell for his encouragement, support, and thoughtful suggestions. I also very much appreciate the efforts of the entire Deseret Book team, including Jay Parry, my editor; Richard Erickson, the art director; Tonya Facemyer, the typographer; and Derk Koldewyn, an editorial assistant.

While I have tried to give credit in the endnotes for specific ideas

I have gleaned from others, I have invariably been enlightened and influenced by my students in ways that I have not been able to remember or acknowledge in endnotes. I appreciate the diligence with which they study the gospel and the insights I gain as I teach them at BYU–Idaho each semester.

I am also grateful for the remarkable body of work from General Authorities, auxiliary leaders, and other Latter-day Saint writers. My life and my writing have both been blessed by their insights.

Finally, notwithstanding the help from all the individuals I have mentioned here, I give the credit to Heavenly Father for inspiring me with any worthwhile ideas and take responsibility myself for the rest.

THE SWINGING PENDULUM

Few endeavors in life are more harrowing than helping a child learn to drive, particularly without the benefit of a passenger-side brake. Even the most basic skills that experienced drivers take for granted sometimes require training and explanation. With my first child, I anticipated helping her learn to cope with such challenges as merging into traffic and making left-hand turns on busy streets. However, I quickly realized I needed to begin with much more basic principles: "Stay on the road! *Our* side of the road!"

One aspect of staying on the road that proved particularly challenging for this daughter was the simple problem of overcorrection. Assisted by subtle promptings from her patient father—"Honey, honnney, honnnney! You're going off the road!"—my daughter would occasionally fix the problem so quickly and definitively that I found myself even more alarmed as we darted toward the opposite side of the road.

For all of us who are trying to stay on the strait and narrow path that leads home to Heavenly Father, there is power in recognizing that Satan is eager to get us off the road any way he can. And for virtually every byway on the left, there is a corresponding byway to the right. Indeed, our very effort to avoid some temptations may unwittingly cause us to steer into others. For example, while slothfulness beckons some to the left, the compulsion to climb the career ladder at all costs beckons others to the right. Pride may siphon off some sojourners to one side of the path, while lack of self-esteem diverts others to the opposite side. And even though each exit in the pair leads in a completely different direction, Satan succeeds whenever he entices us to leave the strait and narrow path—regardless of the direction.

Like beginning drivers, some of us may even repeatedly veer from one side of the narrow path to the other, passing quickly over the course we ought to be on before swerving to the other side. Satan initially whispers to sinners that they have no real need to repent, only to change his tune when we finally realize we really have gone too far. With rationalization having run its course, Satan swings the pendulum to the other extreme, telling transgressors they have gone so far that they can never hope to be forgiven. Both rationalization and hopelessness are lies—contradictory lies—but both serve the adversary's purposes quite effectively.

The premise of this book is simple, but I have found it to be powerful in teaching and living the gospel: "Almost any virtue taken to excess," warned Elder Quentin L. Cook, "can become a vice."[1] Water, for example, is good, even essential. But too much can be fatal. There is danger both in dying of thirst and in drowning. Similarly, many of Satan's tactics have complementary counterparts; at either extreme of his swinging pendulum, there is spiritual danger. Recognizing this can help us identify our own spiritual weaknesses and help us resist the extremes at which virtues become vices. In each chapter, I address a pair of countervailing temptations and discuss how we can find appropriate balance in walking a course between the two extremes.

Most of us find it much easier to recognize and resist some temptations than others. When we understand that detours from the narrow path often come in corresponding pairs, we can better identify the particular temptations to which we are more susceptible. If being too easy on ourselves is not a problem for us, for example, maybe being too hard on ourselves is. If we are not tempted to be too permissive in our parenting, is it possible that we naturally list toward being too controlling?

Prophets have long recognized that some of us seem more drawn to certain detours than others. President Ezra Taft Benson taught: "Each of us has his or her own battlefield. The tactics which the enemy will use against us will vary from time to time. He will seek to exploit our weak spots, so we must be alert to the devil's devious designs—the subtle sins and clever compromises as well as the obvious offenses."[2]

Elder Dallin H. Oaks similarly urged us to be aware of our spiritual weaknesses: "I seek to remind each of us of the mortal susceptibilities and devilish diversions that can unite to produce our spiritual downfall. . . . If we are wise, we will know our weaknesses, our spiritual Achilles' heels, and fortify ourselves against temptations in those areas."[3] Recognizing Satan's ability to pervert almost any virtue in either direction—"sometimes by diluting that which is good, sometimes by camouflaging that which is evil"[4]—should help us remember that for each sinful diversion that has little natural appeal to us, there is bound to be a more tantalizing detour nearby on the other side of the road.

When we understand that detours from the narrow path often come in corresponding pairs, we can better identify the particular temptations to which we are more susceptible.

Remembering the adversary's ability to pervert virtues into vices can also help us guard against spiritual overcorrection. In his seminal sermon on this subject, "Our Strengths Can Become Our Downfall," Elder Oaks reminded us, in effect, that even as we vigilantly avoid drifting off the path to the right, we may find ourselves drifting to the left: "But weakness is not our only vulnerability. Satan can also attack us where we think we are strong—in the very areas where we are proud of our strengths. He will approach us through the greatest talents and spiritual gifts we possess. If we are not wary, Satan can cause our spiritual downfall by corrupting us through our strengths as well as by exploiting our weaknesses."[5]

When we recognize that many detours come with their own extreme counterparts, we can be more cautious not only in our own course corrections but also in helping others navigate. When we address only one-half of a pair of complementary temptations, we certainly help those who struggle with that particular weakness. But we may also sometimes unwittingly compound the problems of those who struggle with a countervailing temptation. For example, troubled by some underachieving students, I may wish to talk with my class about the temptation to approach education lackadaisically. However, if I address only that issue—forgetting that a few students in my class may actually be trying too hard—I may exacerbate the problem for those students who are already anxious overachievers. Similarly, Elder Oaks noted that a "call for repentance that is clear enough and loud enough to encourage reformation for the lax can produce paralyzing discouragement for the conscientious. This is a common problem. We address a diverse audience each time we speak, and we are never free from the reality that a doctrinal under-dose for some is an overdose for others."[6]

Wise teachers and leaders can avoid confusion and over-correction by at least acknowledging danger at both extremes, even as they address the predominant problem for their audience.[7] Notice how King Benjamin addressed both slackers and sprinters in his comments about pacing ourselves in the marathon of life: "And see that all these things are done in wisdom and order; for it is not requisite that a man should run faster than he has strength. And again, it is expedient that he should be diligent, that thereby he might win the prize; therefore, all things must be done in order" (Mosiah 4:27). To those who might be inspired by his counsel on helping the poor, King Benjamin encourages wisdom and prudence so they don't burn themselves out in a burst of charitable fireworks. To those at the other extreme, who might be overwhelmed to the point of paralysis, King Benjamin preaches diligence and focus on the ultimate reward. With one verse, the prophetic king succinctly recognizes and cautions against two overreactions his listeners might have to his sermon.

As we strive to stay on the strait and narrow path and help others do the same, our safety lies, in the words of Elder Mark E. Petersen, in "preserv[ing] a good balance of thought and action, and avoid[ing] the extremes which never fail to develop unhappiness and misery."[8] President Gordon B. Hinckley echoed that admonition when he said: "Grow with balance. . . . I want to plead with you to keep balance in your lives. . . . Beware of obsession. Beware of narrowness."[9] As we become aware of dangerous and often competing extremes that lie on both sides of our path, we can walk with balance along the course that leads home to Heavenly Father.

Finally, in the very spirit of balance and perspective that I am advocating, I should note the potential pitfalls of my model. First, while a swinging pendulum may be a useful way to categorize many of the temptations we encounter in life, it doesn't really work for every sin. Some temptations simply do not seem to have any real flipside. Because this model is not doctrine itself but simply a way to help organize and understand doctrines, we should not be troubled by the fact that the model is incomplete or imperfect.

Second, focusing on the fact that a temptation may have a conceptual counterpart may lead us to mistakenly see symmetry in the seriousness and frequency of the sins in question. For example, when it comes to chastity, the adversary has successfully persuaded a few to miss out on the blessings of marriage and family by convincing them that lifelong celibacy is desirable. But he is far more successful in persuading people to walk the much more perilous path of promiscuity. Thus, even as I identify pairs of temptations in the chapters that follow, I do not mean to suggest that both extremes are equal in magnitude or appeal.

The final potential pitfall in this approach is that it can be misinterpreted as a defense of mushy mediocrity. It is not. After warning against letting our strengths become our weaknesses, Elder Oaks reminded us of the importance of living wholeheartedly:

> The Savior said that if we are "lukewarm," he "will spue [us] out of [his] mouth" (Rev. 3:16). Moderation in all things is not a virtue, because it would seem to justify moderation in commitment. That is not moderation, but indifference. That kind of moderation runs counter to the divine commands to serve with all of our "heart, might, mind and strength" (D&C 4:2), to "seek . . . earnestly the riches of eternity" (D&C 68:31), and to be "valiant in the testimony of Jesus" (D&C 76:79). Moderation is not the answer.[10]

Similarly, my idea in writing this book is not to advocate spiritual sauntering. Once we are on the strait and narrow path, we must, indeed, forge ahead with all our hearts, minds, and strength (albeit, as King Benjamin would remind us, at a marathoner's pace rather than a sprinter's). But recognizing the cleverness with which the adversary has created detours can help us avoid slipping off the path and then overcorrecting if we do.

In any event, what follows is an application of this principle in numerous contexts. The list of examples is not intended to be comprehensive, but illustrative. My hope is that it will be of use to all of us both in identifying our own opportunities for improvement and in helping others stay on the path that leads home to Heavenly Father.

Notes

1. Quentin L. Cook, "Looking beyond the Mark," *Ensign,* Mar. 2003, 40–42.

2. Ezra Taft Benson, "In His Steps," *Ensign,* Sept. 1988, 2.

3. Dallin H. Oaks, "Our Strengths Can Become Our Downfall," *Ensign,* Oct. 1994, 12.

4. Ibid.

5. Ibid.

6. Dallin H. Oaks, "Sin and Suffering," *Ensign,* July 1992, 74.

7. This book addresses the phenomenon of countervailing extremes only in a spiritual context, but even business and political leaders can benefit from this analysis. During my brief corporate career, I remember well the tendency for consultants or new corporate leaders to focus on fixing a problem—such as moving too slowly in making corporate decisions—only to swing the pendulum too far in the opposite direction and create corollary problems that were just as great—such as making hasty, ill-informed decisions. Recognizing potential harms at both extremes can help any kind of leader steer a steady, measured course in correcting problems, rather than veering wildly back and forth as people realize the proverbial pendulum has swung too far.

8. Mark E. Petersen, *The Way to Peace* (Salt Lake City: Bookcraft, 1969), 248.

9. Gordon B. Hinckley, *Teachings of Gordon B. Hinckley* (Salt Lake City: Deseret Book, 1997), 32.

10. Oaks, "Our Strengths Can Become Our Downfall," 19.

CHAPTER 1

THE COMPLACENTLY CONFIDENT AND THE DEJECTEDLY SELF-CRITICAL

Few questions are more fundamental than how we are progressing spiritually and how we view our eternal potential. Perhaps one of the adversary's most dangerous and effective psychological tricks, then, is how he distorts our views of ourselves, our growth, and our possibilities. He leads many of us to become spiritually stagnant, losing the drive to draw nearer to the Savior because we assume all is well, not only in Zion but in our own lives. Feeling we've already arrived, we stop climbing. He convinces others that they don't measure up spiritually and never will. Ironically, the result is often the same. Whether we're blissfully ignorant about our need to progress or hopelessly misled about our capacity to progress, we give up the battle to become better.

BEEN THERE, DONE THAT

I confess that I'm not a big fan of the phrase, "Been there, done that." For starters, even when the phrase is used accurately, it conveys an attitude of curt dismissal rather than empathy. It usually minimizes rather than acknowledges others' experiences. "You've been on crutches for six weeks? Been there, done that!" meaning, "Hah, that's no big deal at all, really, because I've done that exact thing."

What irks me even more, though, is that people often use the expression inaccurately. I was once in a meeting in which a group of lawyers from various companies were getting to know each other by sharing their backgrounds. Once everyone else had spoken, the lawyer with the most seniority took his turn. "Well, as I listen to everything you folks have said," he began, "my thought is, 'Been there, done that.'" He was a nice man and a decent lawyer, and he definitely had more experience than anyone else in the room. But frankly, he had neither been there nor done that when it came to the accomplishments of several of his new colleagues. By oversimplifying the experiences of others, he assumed there really wasn't much he hadn't done in the legal profession or much that he could still learn or much that others could uniquely offer—a perception that was far from accurate.

One would think that with its bastion of returned missionaries who served in foreign lands, no college in the country would be better suited to train its students linguistically than Brigham Young University. Yet ironically, according to Dilworth Parkinson, a professor of Asian and Near Eastern languages at BYU, the proficiency of returned missionaries often serves as one of the greatest obstacles to students developing genuine fluency in a foreign language. Why? Because they are under the misimpression that they have already arrived. Having become fluent in their own eyes, they see no need to invest additional time learning to speak a language they naively believe they have already mastered. "When a student becomes satisfied with what he knows, when he feels he 'knows the language,' he almost immediately ceases to make progress."[1] *Been there, done that,* they say, in effect, when it comes to studying the language further. (I plead guilty to succumbing to this very mistake myself when deciding whether to take additional German courses at BYU after my mission.)

Professor Parkinson labels this mentality "returned-missionary syndrome." "Missionaries become fluent and proficient in their language in a very limited sphere. Unfortunately, many of them decide somewhere deep within their souls that they know enough that they don't need to know any more. They come home and enter our classes and don't make progress; they already know enough. They are seemingly oblivious to all the things they don't know."[2]

I encountered this phenomenon myself as a zone leader. I challenged district leaders to encourage the missionaries in their districts to learn three to five new German words each day. One of the district leaders informed me rather dismissively that he'd studied German for several years before coming on a mission and that he'd already learned thousands of German words. "There may be a few off-the-wall words I haven't learned already," he said with a straight face, "but I seriously doubt there are very many useful ones I don't already know." He was serious.

This district leader could have benefited from Professor Parkinson's insights: "Being reminded of the huge gulf between one's own language abilities, no matter how advanced, and those of a native speaker appears to be a prerequisite for further progress."[3] In fact, even in our mother tongues, most of us still have plenty of room for growth.

After I returned home from my mission, I decided to try the same experiment in English. I fell short of learning three to five words a day, but I was astonished at just how many words I learned—in my own native language—whose meaning I hadn't fully understood. At one point, I even exchanged lists of new words on a weekly basis with a boss who was a fellow attorney. I learned that (1) I had plenty of room for improvement in my mastery of the English language and (2) without realizing lesson #1, I was unlikely to improve my vocabulary much.

A related challenge occurs when speakers master just enough of a new language to communicate passably. Able to handle such basic tasks as buying food or asking for directions, they lose the drive to improve any further. I was surprised to meet many immigrants on my mission whose German was worse after twenty years than most missionaries' was after twenty weeks. Those immigrants had reached a comfort zone in which they knew enough to barely get by linguistically in their new country, and they were content to remain on that plateau. Similarly, many missionaries are not as naively arrogant about their language abilities as the district leader in my story, but they lose their motivation to improve once they reach a level where they can basically understand and be understood.

Professor Parkinson insightfully applies this same analysis to our spiritual growth. "We are not yet *native* speakers of the gospel. Even though we may have developed some gospel fluency, there is a huge gulf between where we are now and where we could and should be."[4] As Paul taught the Corinthians, "If any man think that he knoweth any thing, he knoweth nothing yet as he ought to know" (1 Corinthians 8:2). Whether we are ignorant of our true position in relation to God or just comfortably content with the status quo despite our awareness of our imperfections, we stop progressing spiritually. We love to apply Nephi's warning in 2 Nephi 28 to those outside the Church who reject the Book of Mormon—and it certainly does apply. But could not his warnings also be for us as members if we say, in essence, "I've got enough light and knowledge already, thanks"?

Whether we are ignorant of our true position in relation to God or just comfortably content with the status quo despite our awareness of our imperfections, we stop progressing spiritually.

"Wo be unto him that shall say: We have received the word of God, and we need no more of the word of God, for we have enough! . . . for unto him that receiveth I will give more; and from them that shall say, We have enough, from them shall be taken away even that which they have" (2 Nephi 28:29–30).

How do we overcome the "been there, done that" mentality of

those afflicted with returned-missionary syndrome or the malaise of those who figure they've journeyed far enough? Let me offer two suggestions.

First, part of the remedy for those of us who naively believe we've arrived spiritually is to realize just how much room we really have to grow—and what our true station is in relation to God. Some have climbed to the top of a spiritual foothill and foolishly believe they have conquered the mountain. Only as we raise our sights—often by immersing ourselves in the scriptures and becoming acquainted through experience with God's power and glory—do we realize the height of the peaks we have yet to climb. Moses had just such an experience when he personally beheld God's glory and then fell to the earth in a crumpled heap when that glory was withdrawn, leading him to declare that "man is nothing, which thing I never had supposed" (Moses 1:10). When we seek God's help to see both our ultimate potential and our present station more clearly, we become more humble even as we draw closer to realizing that potential. Thus, although Moses became one of the most powerful men to walk the earth, he did not forget the source of his power and was "very meek, above all the men which were upon the face of the earth" (Numbers 12:3).

Second, we can leave room in our hearts for what Elder Neal A. Maxwell has called "divine discontent." In some ways, it is easier to have a yearning drive to improve our situation when we hit rock bottom than when we are doing relatively well, spiritually speaking. Yet those who would be truly great spiritually are never content with being merely good. Instead, they take their lead from Abraham, who was already a happy "follower of righteousness" (Abraham 1:2) when he became "filled with divine discontent," according to Elder Maxwell.[5] Abraham described this pivotal season of his life in this way: "Finding there was greater happiness and peace and rest for me, I sought for the blessings of the fathers, and the right whereunto I should be ordained to administer the same" (Abraham 1:2). Father

Abraham did not mistake the spiritual plateau he'd reached for the mountaintop the Lord had prepared for him.

Similarly, those who heard King Benjamin's transforming address at the tower were a self-selected congregation of believers willing to show up to a temple—sacrifices in hand—to listen to the counsel of their royal prophet. Fortunately, they did not yield to the temptation to dismiss his address as inapplicable to them: "This would have been so good for my neighbor to hear; he insists on walking without God. But King Benjamin's singing to the choir when it comes to me. Been there, done that." Instead, they made room in their hearts for a divine discontent that led them to fall to the ground and plead for the atoning blood of Jesus Christ to cleanse and transform their hearts.

NOT CELESTIAL MATERIAL

At the other end of this spectrum, many good followers of Christ are acutely aware of both God's high expectations and their own shortcomings. Unfortunately, when they focus on the chasm between who they are and what God has asked them to become, they are often filled with paralyzing despair rather than energizing drive. "When comparing one's personal performance with the supreme standard of the Lord's expectation," observed Elder Russell M. Nelson, "the reality of imperfection can at times be depressing. My heart goes out to conscientious Saints who, because of their shortcomings, allow feelings of depression to rob them of happiness in life."[6] Concluding that they are simply not "celestial material," such Saints run the race of life with heavy burdens and little hope. Elder David S. Baxter of the Seventy noted that "such feelings of personal inadequacy can prove debilitating. If we allow them to persist, the weight of the world will press down on us, and we will be held back from achieving our potential."[7]

Is there any hope for disciples who are persistently and naturally pessimistic about their eternal potential? Actually, hope is the perfect place to begin our analysis of this extreme.

Plowing in Hope

There's a natural temptation to guard against disappointment by making sure we don't get our hopes up. Indeed, some might argue that it's better to assume we're not celestial material and then let God pleasantly surprise us on Judgment Day than it is to assume we're doing great and then be disappointed.[8] Such individuals might wonder what's wrong with walking without hope, as long as we stay on the strait and narrow path.

For starters, it's hard to make much progress on a hike if we've lost all hope of reaching our destination. Consider the plight of a family who is hopelessly behind on their mortgage payments and comes across an extra $20. With little hope of escaping foreclosure, why not order pizza instead of giving the bank another $20? Perhaps that's one reason that many families in financially desperate situations spend more money on short-term indulgences than families with more money but longer-term financial goals. For example, my wife and I couldn't help but notice when we lived in an apartment while saving for a house that virtually everyone in the apartment complex drove more expensive cars than our old sedan, even though I earned a decent salary as an attorney at a large Seattle law firm. Many other tenants had no hope of saving for a house, so they poured what funds they had into the priciest car they could buy, with eager help from accommodating lenders. With a house out of reach, they spent for the moment.

Spiritually, those who lose hope of eternal rewards are often more vulnerable to seeking short-term pleasures. As Elder Maxwell noted: "Loss of hope almost inevitably sends selfishness surging as many, resignedly, turn to pleasing themselves."[9] Indeed, Moroni indicates that without hope, we will never make enough progress to return home to Heavenly Father: "Man must hope, or he cannot receive an inheritance in the place which thou hast prepared" (Ether 12:32).

Perhaps this is because hope "maketh an anchor to the souls of men, which would make them sure and steadfast, always abounding in good works, being led to glorify God" (Ether 12:4). By contrast, when the Nephites lost hope altogether, they drifted aimlessly in sin, buffeted about by their carnal desires—"even as chaff is driven before the wind, or as a vessel is tossed about upon the waves, without sail or anchor" (Mormon 5:18). When Paul admonished us to "plow in hope" (1 Corinthians 9:10), he must have known that those who have little hope of reaping a fruitful harvest eventually give up on plowing, planting, and tending their crops altogether.

Trusting in Christ

At first blush, pointing out to a despairing, overwhelmed person that having hope is critical to her eternal welfare may not seem like the best motivational move. "Great," she might think. "That's just one more reason I don't qualify as celestial material: I have no hope." Without further doctrinal discussion, simply encouraging disheartened Saints to have hope may be about as effective—and offensive— as telling someone who suffers from migraine headaches that she should just stop having them. The fact is that many live in very challenging and trying circumstances. Elder Jeffrey R. Holland reminded us, "Christ knows better than all others that the trials of life can be very deep and we are not shallow people if we struggle with them."[10]

Few prophets can identify more with those who feel surrounded by despair than Mormon and Ether, both of whom witnessed the horrific unraveling and undoing of their people. That is why they are able to teach about faith, as Elder Maxwell was able to teach about adversity, "with authenticity."[11] When Mormon implored his people and us to have faith, he was writing not from book knowledge but from the heart-wrenching, soul-stretching personal experience of a man who knew how important it was to hope on when all reason to hope seemed lost.

So how did they do it? Two passages shed some light on how they and we can find hope when darkness crowds in around us. In describing hope as the anchor to our souls, Ether added this illuminating modifier: "which hope *cometh of faith*" (Ether 12:4; emphasis added). Although we often think of hope as preceding faith—and in some senses, it can—Mormon taught that faith precedes hope, serving as its very foundation: "Without faith there cannot be any hope." Indeed, the inevitable result of real faith in Christ is a genuine, motivating hope in salvation: "If a man have faith he must needs have hope." What kind of hope will such individuals have? "Hope through the atonement of Christ and the power of his resurrection, to be raised unto life eternal, and this because of your faith in him according to the promise" (Moroni 7:41–42).

If we find ourselves running low on hope for eternal life, it might be because we are also short on faith in Jesus Christ.

In other words, if we find ourselves running low on hope for eternal life, it might be because we are also short on faith in Jesus Christ. In fact, according to Mormon, it's impossible to exercise such faith without beginning to be filled with greater hope for our own prospects of eternal life. Thus, when the Savior commands us to be of good cheer, according to Elder Holland, "such counsel is not a jaunty pep talk about the power of positive thinking, though positive thinking is much needed in the world. . . . But even as the Lord avoids sugary rhetoric, He rebukes faithlessness and He deplores pessimism. He expects us to believe!"[12]

Faith in Jesus Christ and His redeeming grace is the key, then, to cultivating real hope. When we realize that it is ultimately "by grace that we are saved, after all we can do" (2 Nephi 25:23), it is much easier to be filled with hope than if we labor under the misconception of those who zealously go about "to establish their own righteousness" (Romans 10:3)—as if heaven were some graduate school to which they had to gain admittance based solely on their own outstanding resumés. As discussed in the chapter on cheap grace and misplaced self-reliance (see page 131), foolishly believing we must earn salvation all on our own is a depressing and ultimately debilitating thought. But when we understand we can be perfected through the grace of Christ and we begin to rely "wholly upon the merits of him who is mighty to save" (2 Nephi 31:19), our hopes soar.

Of course, some of us are better at exercising such faith in the abstract or for others than we are at exercising it for ourselves. As Stephen Robinson has observed, we may believe *in* Christ without believing *Him* when He promises that our sins will be forgiven and forgotten if we truly repent.[13]

I recently played in a fundraising "best-ball" golf tournament in which all four players on a team hit their shots but only the best shot counted. In addition, players were allowed to purchase up to two mulligans (do-over shots) apiece, which they were free to use anywhere on the course. Finally, each team was given about ten feet of string, which they were told could be used to move the ball anywhere on the course. Once any portion of the string was used to move the ball—whether it was six feet or six inches—that portion of string had to be cut off and could not be used again. But the ten feet of mercy was ours to use to improve our score in any way we could.

We eventually realized that the wisest use of the string was to place the ball in the hole when our best shot had come up a few inches short. Then, by cutting off just a few inches of our string, it was as if we had made the putt, and we saved an entire stroke. Using each player's best shot, the generous string, and the purchased mulligans, we found ourselves collectively getting scores none of us ever dreamed of shooting individually under the normal rules of golf. In disbelief, one of our foursome asked, "Are you sure we're really allowed to use the string like this?"

We were. In fact, our team finished only in the middle of the pack. But it was hard to believe that so much generous discretion was really allowed. Similarly, even though we may take all the steps we need to in order to repent and be forgiven of our sins, some of us wonder at times, "Can I really be forgiven, despite all the things I've done? Does the Atonement really work like this?" When applied to ourselves individually, the Atonement seems almost too good to be true.

In fact, in what I consider perhaps the classic example of Satan's nimble approach of perverting virtues into vice, the same adversary who often begins by telling us we have no need to repent of our sins at all changes his tune dramatically once the Spirit convinces us of our need to change. Instead of telling us we're not so different from other normal people, he now whispers that the Atonement may work for others, but certainly not for someone like us. He harnesses our guilt and inflates it so that it becomes a debilitating burden of doubt rather than an inspiring agent of change. We've fallen off the white horse and landed in the mud, he says, so we may as well just stay and play in it.

Such a lack of faith in the Savior's power to wash us clean holds some of us down as we constantly look back at past sins. "To you who have sincerely repented yet continue to feel the burden of guilt, realize that to continue to suffer for sins when there has been proper repentance and forgiveness of the Lord is prompted by the master of deceit," taught Elder Richard G. Scott. "Lucifer will encourage you to continue to relive the details of past mistakes, knowing that such thoughts can hamper your progress. Thus he attempts to tie strings to the mind and body so that he can manipulate you like a puppet to discourage personal achievement."[14]

Recognizing that his son Corianton was beginning to move away from the fallacy of thinking he had no need to repent, Alma warned him against swinging to the other extreme of despondency and despair: "And now, my son, I desire that ye should let these things trouble you no more, and only let your sins trouble you, with that trouble which shall bring you down unto repentance" (Alma 42:29). In other words, the purpose of guilt is to prompt us to repent, not merely to cause us to suffer. Alma knew that Satan would try to pervert the purpose of Corianton's guilt so that it actually became counter-productive, halting his spiritual progress rather than aiding it.

Paul was certainly another prime candidate for such devilish manipulations. Not only had he consented to the death of Stephen—holding the clothes of his executioners—but he had "breath[ed] out threatenings and slaughter against the disciples of the Lord," seeking authorization to bind Saints in Damascus and drag them to Jerusalem (see Acts 7:58; 8:1; 9:1). How easily might Paul have replayed such scenes endlessly in his mind, wondering whether God could ever really forgive him. With such a background, Paul's advice to the Philippians is poignantly instructive for all of us whose memory of past sins threatens to impede our future progress: "This one thing I do, *forgetting those things which are behind, and reaching forth unto those things which are before,* I press toward the mark for the prize of the high calling of God in Christ Jesus" (Philippians 3:13–14; emphasis added).

Focus More on Direction Than Location

When dieting, traveling, or hiking, we are sometimes tempted to quit when we realize how far we have to go. "The adversary deploys derision to discourage us with feelings of worthlessness," observed Elder Baxter. "He would have us look at how far we have yet to travel and the challenges en route, in the desire that we might give up in a state of discouragement and hopelessness."[15] At such times, I find it helpful to focus more on my direction than my location. As long as I'm consistently moving closer to my goal—even if I am still far away—I find reason to continue with some degree of confidence.

We may mistakenly believe that we must become perfect in this life all on our own if we are to be admitted back into God's presence. But according to Elder Bruce R. McConkie, when we yoke up with Christ and head in the right direction, we can expect to ride His coattails the rest of the way to perfection and eternal life.

Nobody becomes perfect in this life. Only the Lord Jesus attained that state, . . . but we must become perfect to gain a celestial inheritance. . . . Becoming perfect in Christ is a process. . . . As members of the Church, if we chart a course leading to eternal life; if we begin the processes of spiritual rebirth, and are going in the right direction; if we chart a course of sanctifying our souls, and degree by degree are going in that direction; . . . then it is absolutely guaranteed—there is no question whatever about it—we shall gain eternal life.[16]

More recently, Elder M. Russell Ballard offered similar words of comfort to those who are tempted to drop out of the race of life because they feel they can't run fast enough:

To you who feel harried and overwhelmed and who wonder whether you ever will be able to run fast enough to catch the departing train you think you should be on, I suggest that you learn to deal with each day as it comes, doing the best you can, without feelings of guilt or inadequacy. . . . No one can do everything. When you have done the best you can, be satisfied and don't look back and second-guess, wondering how you could have done more. Be at peace within yourselves. Rather than berate yourself for what you didn't do, congratulate yourself for what you did. . . . Remember, our Heavenly Father never expects more of us than we can do.[17]

STRIKING THE BALANCE

The first time my wife and I went cross-country skiing, we learned on some groomed trails in Washington's Cascade Mountains. After spending a few hours becoming comfortable on the largely flat terrain of the beginner trails, we decided to try our luck on what proved to be much more challenging intermediate trails. Neither of us had learned to downhill ski at that point, and this track featured several hills—each with a rather sharp turn at the bottom of the narrow trail. Dianne and I fared almost identically, navigating our way successfully along the trail and even down the hills until we reached the sharp turns, where we inevitably and often spectacularly crashed.

"Wow," I said as we returned to the car. "I think we did pretty well for our first time ever cross-country skiing. We nearly handled the intermediate trail."

"Are you kidding?" my wife replied. "We wiped out on every single hill."

It's not hard to guess which one of us is too hard on herself spiritually and which one is too easy. Whether by nature or nurture or both, when it comes to how we view our abilities and our spiritual progress, members of the Church often view ourselves as disparately as my wife and I viewed our cross-country skiing experience. Consequently, some of us need to be told we're doing much better than we think, while others need to be slapped upside the head by the Spirit occasionally to see just how much room we have for improvement.

The trick is trying to figure out which is the case for each of us personally and presently. That is why Elder Maxwell taught that "it is left to each of us to balance contentment regarding what God has allotted to us in life with some divine discontent resulting from what we are in comparison to what we have the power to become. Discipleship creates this balance on the straight and narrow path."[18]

Differentiating between "divine discontent and the devil's dissonance"[19] is no small feat. I recall counseling as a bishop with someone who had committed a serious sin and did not yet feel forgiven. "My friends tell me that my problem is that I just can't forgive myself," he suggested, and much of the time I would have agreed with precisely that counsel. But I was not so sure in this case, and as we talked further, I soon learned why. "I know what we did was wrong, but it did bring us closer together." This individual did not yet feel fully forgiven because he had not yet fully repented. What would have been the right counsel for many individuals would have been counter-productive in this case, because forgiveness and peace cannot come without a truly broken heart and contrite spirit.

Am I too hard on myself or too easy? It may vary from day to day and attribute to attribute, but God knows—and He's willing to tell me. As we seek personal guidance from the Lord, through the Spirit He will give us the customized direction we need. If we ask, many who struggle with feelings of inadequacy will receive comforting reassurances that they're doing much better than they think. A few may learn that their despair is a result of unresolved sins from which they need to repent. And if we have the courage to ask where we stand, many of us will receive gentle chastisements nudging us to improve in specific areas.

When we invite constructive feedback—whether divine or human—it's much easier to receive than when criticisms are uninvited. Asking for such direction is a sign of both humility and spiritual maturity. When one of my colleagues was teaching at one of the largest institutes of religion, he received a classroom visit from his boss. As my friend was talking with his supervisor after class, he thanked him for visiting his class and asked, "Do you have any suggestions for me on how I could improve my teaching?" The administrator seemed to get choked up, so my friend offered to discuss the matter another time, if that would be better.

"No, no," replied the man charged with overseeing the teaching at the institute. "It's just that this is the first time in all my years with seminaries and institutes that anyone has asked me for feedback like that."

My friend's story pricks me because it reminds me how slow I am to seek such corrective counsel myself. Based on experience, my impression is that Heavenly Father is eager to share constructive feedback with me. In fact, I have found that there is no better way for me to get clear answers when I pray than to ask, "What wouldst thou have me do differently or become that I am not?" I remember kneeling with the intent to ask that very question one day and receiving a distinct answer before I had even begun my prayer. I suspect the Lord has a long list of ways to help me become better, but He's willing to share most of them only when I ask. Yet He never reveals them to me in a way that leaves me depressed or despondent.

Finally, just as seeking personal revelation can help us avoid both extremes, so can focusing more on the Savior's life, teachings, and Atonement. As we better understand both the redemptive and transformative power of the Atonement, despair gives way to hope. But as we focus on how Jesus lived and what He has asked us to become, we will realize there's much progress yet to be made. Ironically then, both for those who naively think they've arrived and for those who foolishly believe they can never arrive, coming more fully unto Christ is the best way to make sure we travel with Him to heights unattainable on our own.

Notes

1. Dilworth B. Parkinson, "Line upon Line," *BYU Magazine,* Summer 2004, 45.

2. Parkinson, "Line upon Line," 45.

3. Parkinson, "Line upon Line," 45.

4. Parkinson, "Line upon Line," 46; emphasis in original.

5. Neal A. Maxwell, "I Will Arise and Go to My Father," *Ensign,* Sept. 1993, 67.

6. Russell M. Nelson, "Perfection Pending," *Ensign,* Nov. 1995, 86.

7. David S. Baxter, "Overcoming Feelings of Inadequacy," *Ensign,* Aug. 2007, 10.

8. Some might even cite the parable of the Pharisee and the publican to support this view. However, there is a significant difference between concluding we have no chance of obtaining eternal life and the publican's prayer, in which he acknowledges his unworthiness but pleads for mercy (see Luke 18:10–13).

9. Neal A. Maxwell, "Hope through the Atonement of Jesus Christ," *Ensign,* Nov. 1998, 62.

10. Jeffrey R. Holland, "An High Priest of Good Things to Come," *Ensign,* Nov. 1999, 37.

11. Bruce C. Hafen, *A Disciple's Life: The Biography of Neal A. Maxwell* (Salt Lake City: Deseret Book, 2002), 562.

12. Holland, "An High Priest of Good Things to Come," 37.

13. Stephen E. Robinson, *Believing Christ: The Parable of the Bicycle and Other Good News* (Salt Lake City: Deseret Book, 1992), 8.

14. Richard G. Scott, "The Path to Peace and Joy," *Ensign,* Nov. 2000, 26.

15. Baxter, "Overcoming Feelings of Inadequacy," 13.

16. Bruce R. McConkie, "Jesus Christ and Him Crucified," *1976 Devotional Speeches of the Year* (Provo, Utah: Brigham Young University, 1977), 399–400; as quoted in Jan Underwood Pinborough, "Keeping Mentally Well," *Ensign,* Sept. 1990, 50.

17. M. Russell Ballard, "Be an Example of the Believers," *Ensign,* Nov. 1991, 95.

18. Neal A. Maxwell, "Becoming a Disciple," *Ensign,* June 1996, 18.

19. Neal A. Maxwell, "Notwithstanding My Weakness," *Ensign,* Nov. 1976, 14.

Chapter 2

Shallow-Rooted Palms and Doubters

In the process of deciding what we believe, we are often pushed and pulled by crosswinds of doubt and thoughtlessness. On the one hand, in this age of rampant skepticism and cynicism some find it difficult to walk forward in faith. They may perceive flaws in Church leaders or encounter challenging doctrines or struggle to reconcile the scriptural record with sound science. Yet those who soak their souls in doubts often end up sinking. At the opposite end of the spectrum, others may casually arrive at their beliefs with little conscious thought, assuming the Church is true simply because those around them believe it is. Like a palm tree that has not had to develop deep roots to find water, such people may discover their grounding is too shallow to weather storms of doubt in more difficult times.

In this chapter, I discuss how we can find the right balance between being Doubters or Shallow-Rooted Palms (names I choose to characterize the extremes of these two dispositions, not to condemn those who struggle with such tendencies). To progress spiritually, some Saints may need to do more to doubt less. On the other hand, others may not develop deep spiritual roots until they fertilize their faith with questions. And whichever extreme is more tempting to us individually, we are all better off as we identify our own natural tendencies and try to better understand those whose tendencies are different from our own.

SHALLOW-ROOTED PALMS

As I teach hundreds of BYU–Idaho students each year, I occasionally encounter students from good families and good wards who are cruising along the gospel path mostly on borrowed light. The good news is that they are on the right path. The bad news is that they are at far greater risk of being blown off course than they might imagine.

> *Leaning on the testimony of parents, friends, or leaders may not be a bad way to start our gospel journey, but it rarely provides enough staying power to finish the journey well.*

Why? First, a mere working assumption that the Church is true will not provide the spiritual grounding necessary to withstand the mightiest whirlwinds the adversary can muster. If we draw our light largely from friends, family, and local leaders, we will find ourselves in darkness upon the departure or spiritual demise of those whose light we are borrowing. Second, if we lack a healthy spiritual curiosity, we are unlikely to gain the valuable insights and knowledge that come to those who are appropriately inquisitive.

Shallow Roots and Severe Storms

Elder Joseph B. Wirthlin has spoken of beautiful palm trees that "are lovely to look at but will not stand up in a heavy wind because they are not well anchored." Such trees often develop nothing more than shallow roots because they are so close to water. "Contrast this with giant oak trees that have deep root systems that can extend two and one-half times their height. Such trees rarely are blown down regardless of how violent the storms may be."[1] Spiritually, especially when gospel waters lie near, we may sometimes develop nothing more than shallow roots to reach the conclusion that the restored gospel of Jesus Christ is true. Conversely, those who have paid a price to gain a testimony for themselves tend to be much more firmly "grounded and settled," in the words of Paul (Colossians 1:23).

To switch metaphorical gears, those who have shallow roots in the gospel tend to live largely on borrowed light. Leaning on the testimony of parents, friends, or leaders may not be a bad way to start our gospel journey, but it rarely provides enough staying power to finish the journey well. Church leaders have thus warned repeatedly that we "will not be able to travel through life on borrowed light."[2] Perhaps one reason for this is that more turbulent times are almost invariably ahead. To the Saints assembled in the Salt Lake Valley, Elder Heber C. Kimball explained:

> Let me say to you, that many of you will see the time when you will have all the trouble, trial and persecution that you can stand, and plenty of opportunities to show that you are true to God and his work. This Church has before it many close places through which it will have to pass before the work of God is crowned with victory. To meet the difficulties that are coming, it will be necessary for you to have a knowledge of the truth of this work for yourselves. The difficulties will be of such a character that the man or woman who does not possess this personal knowledge or witness will fall. If you have not got the testimony, live right and call upon the Lord and cease not till you obtain it. If you do not you will not stand.
>
> . . . The time will come when no man nor woman will be able to endure on borrowed light. Each will have to be guided by the light within himself. . . . If you don't have it you will not stand; therefore seek for the testimony

of Jesus and cleave to it, that when the trying time comes you may not stumble and fall.[3]

Embracing parents' beliefs may come easily when children live at home, but remaining true to the faith becomes much more trying when young children one day become young adults living on their own. For instance, it is one thing for youth living in a home with no cable television to refrain from watching inappropriate programming. But it's much more challenging for a college student living away from home with access to a nightly panoply of pornography to remain disciplined. Even for adult members of the Church, remaining true to the faith may be easier in a season of goodwill than when the Church passes through some of the "tight places" through which prophets have warned we have yet to pass.[4] All of us are better able to withstand the temptations and mockery we are bound to encounter along the strait and narrow path if we are led by more than just borrowed light. "We can rely on the faith and testimony of others only so long," warned President Thomas S. Monson. "Eventually we must have our own strong and deeply placed foundation, or we will be unable to withstand the storms of life, which *will* come."[5]

> *We are all eventually forced to decide whether we belong to the Church of Jesus Christ because it is His church or our social club.*

Thus, our goal for our children, our students, and ourselves is not begrudging, temporary compliance to God's commandments, but lasting obedience born of independent conviction. When we obey because we want to rather than because we are supposed to, our obedience continues even when the scaffolding of family, friends, callings, and missions is removed.[6] Such steadiness will undoubtedly be necessary, because virtually all members of the Church are required at some point in our spiritual odyssey to walk a tightrope without the complete social safety net that gives us confidence when we begin our journey. If we hitch our star spiritually to the testimonies of others rather than knowledge from God, we may find ourselves in the wrong universe if our spiritual mentors go astray. And whether we move or missionaries are transferred or fallible friends and leaders disappoint us or a new ward is not welcoming, we are all eventually forced to decide whether we belong to the Church of Jesus Christ because it is His church or our social club. If our membership is built upon the unsure foundation of good friends and casual conviction, our activity rate is destined to fall. "Those who seek or are satisfied to stop with an intellectual conviction live in a spiritual habitation built upon the sand," warned Elder Dallin H. Oaks. "For them and for their children—if that is all the inheritance their children obtain—that habitation is forever vulnerable."[7]

Finally, enduring to the end requires not only fortitude, but wisdom. Saints who are like palm trees may not only lack the strength to stay the course but the capacity to find the correct course for themselves when their spiritual mentors aren't around to help them. Elder Bruce C. Hafen described the need for developing such independence in these terms:

> We need to develop the capacity to form judgments of our own about the value of ideas, opportunities, or people who may come into our lives. We won't always have the security of knowing whether a certain idea is "Church approved," because new ideas just don't always come along with little tags attached to them saying whether the Church has given them the stamp of approval. . . . We must develop sufficient independence of judgment and maturity of perspective that we are prepared to handle the shafts and whirlwinds of adversity and contradiction as they come to us. When those times come, we cannot be living on borrowed light.[8]

The Benefits of Spiritual Curiosity

Recognizing the importance of faith, some leaders and parents may wish to suppress any doubts and questions that bubble to the surface in the hearts and minds of those in their charge. They may even teach that questions are incompatible with faith. Elder Cecil O. Samuelson tackled this issue head-on in an insightful devotional address he gave at Brigham Young University before becoming its president:

> Some seem to believe that faith and questions are antithetical. Such could not be further from the truth. The Restoration itself was unfolded by the proper and necessary melding of both. The Prophet Joseph Smith had both faith and questions. Indeed, the passage of scripture that led Joseph to the Sacred Grove experience includes both a question and the promise of an answer based on the asker's faith.
>
> I marvel each time I consider the wonderful way in which the Prophet Joseph Smith used proper questions not only to enhance his knowledge but also to enlarge his faith.[9]

One of the principal reasons Joseph Smith received so many illuminating answers is that he asked so many searching questions.

The scriptures underscore Elder Samuelson's position both explicitly and implicitly. President Boyd K. Packer taught that "no message appears in scripture more times, in more ways than, 'Ask, and ye shall receive.'"[10] This doctrine applies not just to temporal blessings but also to the divine gift of spiritual understanding: "If thou shalt ask," the Lord has promised, "thou shalt receive revelation upon revelation, knowledge upon knowledge, that thou mayest know the mysteries and peaceable things" (D&C 42:61).[11] Fortunately for all of us who benefit from his revelatory legacy, Joseph Smith understood this doctrine well: one of the principal reasons he received so many illuminating answers is that he asked so many searching questions. Understanding that he lacked wisdom and believing that the Lord would give wisdom to him liberally (see James 1:5), Joseph asked and the Lord answered. Indeed, the Doctrine and Covenants is, in large part, a transcript of some of Joseph's question-and-answer sessions with the Lord.

Is there room in this doctrine for asking the Lord questions about our doubts? Elder Howard W. Hunter thought so. He said that those who "engage in the great conflict of resolving doubts" would "emerge from the conflict into a firmer, stronger, larger faith because of the struggle. They have gone from a simple, trusting faith, through doubt and conflict, into a solid substantial faith which ripens into testimony."[12]

Such spiritual curiosity blesses the lives not only of novices but of seasoned Saints as well. One of the most inspiring facts about the revelation we now celebrate as section 138 of the Doctrine and Covenants is its place in the chronology of Joseph F. Smith's life: He received it on October 3, 1918—nearly eighty years after his birth and just over six weeks before his death on November 19, 1918. At a time when he could have been excused for coasting comfortably with the knowledge he had already attained, this disciple prophet "sat in [his] room pondering over the scriptures" (D&C 138:1). As with Nephi and Joseph Smith before him, such contemplative curiosity led to sublime revelation (see 1 Nephi 11:1, D&C 76:15–19).

The negative corollary of this doctrine is that if we do not ask, we generally will not receive. The Savior told His disciples in the Americas that if those who had been with Him during His Jerusalem ministry did not specifically ask for a knowledge of their branch of scattered Israel, such knowledge would be kept from them for the time being (see 3 Nephi 16:4). Similarly, Lehi's sons present a study in contrasts when it comes to seeking to better understand their father's richly symbolic dream. Nephi knew that his father's teachings "were hard to be understood, save a man should inquire of the Lord" (1 Nephi 15:3). Thus, although he believed his father's vision, he importuned God to gain an independent and deeper understanding of his father's dream, that he "might see, and hear, and know of these things, by the power of the Holy Ghost" (1 Nephi 10:17). On the other hand, Laman and Lemuel declined to ask, assuming God wouldn't make such things known to them anyway (1 Nephi 15:9).

We can only guess how different the result would have been for Adam if, instead of obeying and explaining, "I know not, save the Lord commanded me," he had refused, saying, "I will not, unless the Lord explains Himself."

In sum, asking appropriate questions and even grappling honestly with genuine doubts can lead to spiritual strength and deeper insights—strength and insights that do not come to those who do not ask and wrestle. Such enhanced wisdom and fortitude results in greater spiritual staying power than we can ever get by coasting along on casually obtained convictions.

DOUBTERS

Properly used, fire is an extraordinarily versatile and useful element. It can warm cold homes, light dark paths, and refine precious metals. Unchecked and abused, however, fire can also inflict sweeping and permanent damage. Similarly, when we address our honest doubts and questions patiently and with faith, they can actually help fuel our spiritual growth. But if we allow our doubts to overwhelm us or lean on them as excuses, they can swallow us up in negativity that may permanently damage not only our souls, but also those of our family and friends. As Elder Marion D. Hanks taught: "Doubting, if it motivates us to move in the right direction and begin to search, can be constructive. But doubting can immobilize and enervate and destroy. We need to search and teach in the context of faith."[13]

Hurting Ourselves

When I have encountered difficult doctrines or historical details, I have on occasion sensed myself slipping into a dangerous posture: chin up, arms folded, and feet no longer moving. It becomes quite tempting in such circumstances to say, in effect, "I'm not going anywhere until I get some answers here." Contrast such an attitude with Nephi's willingness to leave Jerusalem first and seek further light and knowledge later, or Adam's sacrifice in the absence of an explanation for what must have been a counterintuitive commandment. We can only guess how different the result would have been for Adam if, instead of obeying and explaining, "I know not, save the Lord commanded me" (Moses 5:6), he had refused, saying, "I will not, unless the Lord explains Himself." As a general rule, divine explanations follow rather than precede obedience.

Our willingness to proceed despite doubts is especially important at certain critical junctures in our lives, given President James E. Faust's reminder that some "of our important choices have a time line. If we delay a decision, the opportunity is gone forever. Sometimes our doubts keep us from making a choice that involves change. Thus an opportunity may be missed."[14] In other words, if we are not careful, like the children of Israel we may forfeit the privilege of entering lands of promise by succumbing to "doubts and fears."[15]

One key to avoiding such missed opportunities is to seek to maintain the light we have already received, even as we grapple with areas of intellectual darkness. Elder Robert D. Hales compared this challenge to riding a bicycle with an old-fashioned generator light. Only when the wheel is spinning does the light shine brightly. If the rider slows, the light dims, and if he stops, the light goes out altogether. "The generation of spiritual light comes from daily spiritual pedaling. It comes from praying, studying the scriptures, fasting, and serving—from living the gospel and obeying the commandments."[16] Indeed, the best prescription for resolving doubts is often immersing ourselves in the service of the Lord. "As you exercise your time and talents in service," President Gordon B. Hinckley promised, "your faith will grow and your doubts will wane."[17]

Finally, it's important to note that we are rarely asked to forge ahead blindly, although we are often asked to walk in faith. Surely Nephi had some spiritual inkling that his father was a man of God when Lehi shared the Lord's command for the family to leave Jerusalem. What he desired and received later was to "know of the mysteries of God," which resulted not only in a confirmation of the decision to leave Jerusalem, but also in a revelation about the blessed nature of his family's destination (see 1 Nephi 2:16, 20). Just as he would later creep into Jerusalem *with* knowledge that he should but *without* a detailed explanation of why, Nephi probably left Jerusalem being "led by the Spirit, not knowing beforehand" everything he would like to know about the journey (1 Nephi 4:6).

Hurting Others

Even if we manage to play with the fire of doubt without doing significant damage to ourselves, we should not be surprised if our children or others in our charge are burned as they follow our example. I once met a member who complained that only half of his adult children had remained active in the Church—a fact he attributed mostly to the community in which they had been raised. As we chatted over the course of a couple of hours, however, I could not help but notice that virtually every comment he made about the gospel was negative. It is one thing to challenge our children and others in their thinking in order to strengthen their testimonies; it is quite another to lace every conversation with doubt and criticism of the Church and its leaders.

President Hinckley observed that there are some "who spend their time digging out and writing about what they regard to be weaknesses which really are of no consequence. With doubt concerning [the Church's] past, they have no vision concerning its future."[18] Whether we are scholars, parents, friends, teachers, or leaders, what we emphasize in our gospel conversations is crucial, since our words may profoundly affect the beliefs of others. Elder Jeffrey R. Holland's counsel for parents in this regard applies to some degree to all of us who care for the Lord's children in some capacity:

> In this Church there is an enormous amount of room—and scriptural commandment—for studying and learning, for comparing and considering, for discussion and awaiting further revelation. . . . But no child in this Church should be left with uncertainty about his or her parents' devotion to the Lord Jesus Christ, the Restoration of His Church, and the reality of living prophets. . . .
>
> Parents simply cannot flirt with skepticism or cynicism, then be surprised when their children expand that flirtation into full-blown romance. . . . No, we can hardly expect the children to get to shore safely if the parents don't seem to know where to anchor their own boat. . . .
>
> I think some parents may not understand that even when they feel secure in their own minds regarding matters of personal testimony, they can nevertheless make that faith too difficult for their children to detect. . . .
>
> To lead a child (or anyone else!), even inadvertently, away from faithfulness, away from loyalty and bedrock belief simply because we want to be clever or independent is license no parent nor any other person has ever been given. In matters of religion a skeptical mind is not a higher manifestation of virtue than is a believing heart, and analytical deconstruction in the field of, say, literary fiction can be just plain old-fashioned destruction when transferred to families yearning for faith at home. And such a deviation from the true course can be deceptively slow and subtle in its impact.[19]

In sum, being sensitive to the dangers of uncritical acceptance of gospel truths, we may swing to the other extreme of becoming drenched in doubt. Such spiritually waterlogged Saints risk not only becoming bogged down in their own spiritual progress, but dragging down those whom they love and serve.

STRIKING THE BALANCE

So how do we strike the proper balance between cultivating a healthy spiritual curiosity without allowing our doubts to lead us into broad paths? Where is the line between invigorating inquiry and dangerous doubting? For starters, we might choose to err on the side of tolerance when dealing with others' doubts and caution when dealing with our own.

Cutting Others Slack

When we hear friends or loved ones or youth openly express doubts, they may be taking an important step along the road to resolving those doubts and gaining greater spiritual strength. Thus, rather than condemn them for being open about their questions, we may wish to embrace them in fellowship as we help them address their concerns. As Elder Maxwell observed, there is a great danger in taking an unduly harsh and judgmental approach to individuals at such critical times in their lives:

> Too often, a young person's outward *non-compliance* with Church standards, or his seemingly confrontive questions, or his expressed doubts get him quickly labeled. The results can be distance and, sometimes, disaffiliation. True love does not like labels! However youth define their problems, for them, these problems are real; canned answers will not do! One wonders how many prodigals felt *put* off before they *went off*.[20]

One way to attain this more merciful mentality is to remember that, as President Faust observed, "almost everyone has—at one time or another—some private questions. That is part of the learning process."[21] Indeed, President Hinckley admitted that as a young college student himself, "I began to question some things, including perhaps in a slight measure the faith of my parents."[22] As he might have said with typical understatement, he turned out all right—and so will many disciples who struggle with doubts.

Stricter Scrutiny for Ourselves

With our own doubts we may want to engage in a more searching introspective analysis. To begin with, we might ask ourselves what motivates our doubts. As Church leaders have acknowledged in comments already cited in this chapter, good members may encounter honest doubts. Indeed, in the course of our gospel study, I can't help but think the Lord would almost be disappointed if some of His most counterintuitive commands did not give us pause at times. Whether it was the command for ancient Israel to utterly destroy their enemies or the authorization of plural marriage or the withholding of the priesthood from blacks, sincere Saints may have honest doubts about certain divine directives. Such genuine questions that arise in the normal course of spiritual growth are completely understandable. If we are not careful, however, at least two other motives may cause us to become fixated on such doubts or even to flaunt them.

First, most of us can comfortably cope with a minor gap between how we aspire to live and how we actually live—and almost all of us live with such a gap. But if our actual conduct deviates more significantly from the standards we profess, our emotional discomfort (or what psychologists call our "cognitive dissonance") increases. The bigger that gap between our beliefs and our behavior becomes, the more difficulty most of us have explaining it away and dealing with the emotional discord. Thus, we tend not to meet many members of the Church who live largely in sin but still attest to the importance of adhering to the standards set forth by the Savior. Instead, one of two things tends to happen: we either raise the level of our behavior by repenting, or we lower the level of our standards by changing our beliefs.

How we believe we should live

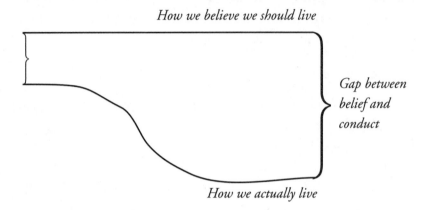

Gap between belief and conduct

How we actually live

Consequently, when the gap between how we are living and how we believe we ought to be living is great, unless we repent we become very vulnerable to any arguments that call our beliefs into question. Through the lens of sin, existing doubts are magnified and new doubts suddenly appear.

Elder Russell M. Nelson illustrated this principle with a telling letter from a member who struggled to maintain his testimony while battling serious sin: "The guilt and failure I feel make it almost impossible for me to repent. I am losing my faith. The sins were first; the doubts followed. The order is important because sin needed doubt. When I doubted my faith, sins lost their meaning and guilt its bite. Doubting began, then, as a means of anesthesia. It served to diminish the guilt that was literally tearing me apart. Before long, however, the doubts thrived independent of the needs that conceived them."[23] There can be little question that sin is a breeding ground for doubt.

A second suspect motive for our doubts emerges when airing them results in acceptance and popularity in certain circles. For example, although voicing doubts in my current position as a professor of religion at BYU–Idaho would be a bad move professionally and socially, flaunting doubts about my faith would have been a good social move for me at law school or most law firms. For some, the pressure to fit in can be intense, and for others such desires can even mutate into an appetite for the fame someone is always willing to accord (however fleetingly) those who publish their doubts in books and op-ed pages.

C. S. Lewis wrote bitingly of such unworthy motivations for spiritual skepticism when he imagined a postmortal exchange between two ministers who had both struggled with doubts during their earthly lives, albeit with widely different results: one succumbed completely to his doubts, while the other eventually resisted them and embraced faith. The faithless cleric protests when his friend— essentially on leave from heaven in order to persuade his colleague to repent and escape hell—informs him that his apostasy has kept him from heaven.

> "Do you really think people are penalised for their honest opinions? Even assuming, for the sake of argument, that those opinions were mistaken."
>
> "Do you really think there are no sins of intellect?"
>
> "There are indeed, Dick. There is hidebound prejudice, and intellectual dishonesty, and timidity, and stagnation. But honest opinions fearlessly followed—they are not sins."
>
> "I know we used to talk that way. I did it too until the end of my life when I became what you call narrow. It all turns on what are honest opinions."
>
> "Mine certainly were. They were not only honest but heroic. I asserted them fearlessly. When the doctrine of the Resurrection ceased to commend itself to the critical faculties which God had given me, I openly rejected it. I preached my famous sermon. I defied every chapter. I took every risk."
>
> "What risk? What was at all likely to come of it

except what actually came—popularity, sales for your books, invitations, and finally a bishopric?"

"Dick, this is unworthy of you. What are you suggesting?"

"Friend, I am not suggesting at all. You see, I *know* now. Let us be frank. Our opinions were not honestly come by. We simply found ourselves in contact with a certain current of ideas and plunged into it because it seemed modern and successful. At College, you know, we just automatically started writing the kind of essays that got good marks and saying the kind of things that got applause. When, in our whole lives, did we honestly face, in solitude, the one question on which all turned: whether after all the Supernatural might not in fact occur? When did we put up one moment's real resistance to the loss of our faith?"[24]

Of course, many Latter-day Saints who struggle with doubt and even air their doubts publicly are not motivated by such ulterior motives. Indeed, the cultural risks for them (at least in the mainstream of LDS society) are much greater than they were for Lewis's apostate pastor. But the pull still exists at the fringes of LDS culture and in the academic and cultural mainstream outside the Church. Just as there are always some young men who will laugh at an irreverent aside in priesthood meeting, there are always some cynics who will laud the "candor" and "courage" of those who publicly register their doctrinal differences with the Church.

If one key to avoiding counterproductive doubting is to keep our motives pure, another is to be true to truths that have already been revealed to us. For example, I may be personally perplexed by the Savior's decision to refrain (with a few notable exceptions) from teaching His gospel to the Gentiles during His earthly ministry. But because I have received spiritual confirmation of the divinity of Jesus Christ and the truthfulness of the New Testament generally, the question I should ask the Lord is *why* He would direct such a stagger-step approach in spreading the gospel—not *whether* the ban on teaching the gospel to the Gentiles was divinely directed. The first question implicitly builds on answers I have already received while seeking further knowledge. The second question implicitly rejects answers I have already received to questions I have already asked.

Remembering and honoring the framework of truth that has already been revealed to me helps keep my rebelliousness in check when I struggle to comprehend less significant matters. Even as I struggle to improve my understanding of certain doctrinal details, I can exercise continued faith in the ultimate truths I already understand. Like Nephi, who knew that God loved His children even though he didn't know "the meaning of all things" (1 Nephi 11:17), I might declare, "I can't answer all your challenges to the Book of Mormon, but I know that it is the word of God." Or as President James E. Faust humbly testified, "I do not claim to have an absolute understanding of all of the principles of the gospel, but I have come to know with certainty the divinity and authority of this Church."[25]

Similarly, having received a divine witness of certain eternal truths, we can avoid engaging in activities and associations that invite doubt rather than build faith. Elder Maxwell cautioned against window-shopping for doubt: "Why are a few members, who somewhat resemble the ancient Athenians, so eager to hear some new doubt or criticism? (See Acts 17:21.) Just as some weak members slip across a state line to gamble, a few go out of their way to have their doubts titillated. Instead of nourishing their faith, they are gambling 'offshore' with their fragile faith."[26]

Early in his career, a friend of mine discovered some fellow seminary teachers with whom he could comfortably discuss his political views and even candidly share his doctrinal questions. Soon he began joining them for an occasional breakfast, where they could talk freely together. Over time, however, my friend noticed that these breakfast conversations did much more to undermine his faith than to bolster it, and he became increasingly uncomfortable participating in them. As diplomatically as possible, my colleague wisely withdrew from the informal breakfast club. Years later, as some members of the group drifted further away from the gospel and left their teaching positions, my friend realized the Lord had blessed him in prompting him to leave an environment that invited doubt.

One final step in keeping our doubts from becoming counter-productive relates to how and when we air them. I hesitate to criticize anyone for publicly sharing doubts, since we admire Martin Luther, Roger Williams, and Joseph Smith for doing just that. Thus, for those who genuinely reach a final conclusion that their previously held religious beliefs were flawed, I certainly would not advocate a self-imposed gag order. On the other hand, there is something perplexing about those who still claim some desire to identify themselves with the Church of Jesus Christ but feel impelled to publicize their differences with the Church.

Elder James E. Faust commented on the spiritual risks of taking such public stands:

> I cannot help wondering if a member of the Church does not place himself in some spiritual peril when publicly disparaging the prophetic calling of Joseph Smith, or his successors, or any of the fundamental, settled doctrines of the Church.
>
> When a member expresses his private doubts or unbelief as a public chastisement of the leadership or the doctrine of the Church, or as a confrontation with those also seeking eternal light, he has entered upon sacred ground."

Hearkening back to a danger previously discussed, Elder Faust noted that "those who complain about the doctrine or leadership of the Church but who lack the faith or desire to keep God's commandments risk separating themselves from the divine source of learning."[27]

Finally, while both extremes described in this chapter pose real spiritual dangers, if I were to err, I would prefer to err on the side of believing too easily than the side of doubting too much. As President Hinckley implored, "To all who may have doubts, I repeat the words given Thomas as he felt the wounded hands of the Lord: 'Be not faithless, but believing.'"[28]

Notes

1. Joseph B. Wirthlin, "Deep Roots," *Ensign,* Nov. 1994, 75.

2. James E. Faust, "The Voice of the Spirit," *Ensign,* Apr. 1994, 8.

3. Orson F. Whitney, *Life of Heber C. Kimball,* 3d. ed. (Salt Lake City: Bookcraft, 1945), 449–50.

4. See, for example, Ezra Taft Benson, "Valiant in the Testimony of Jesus," *Ensign,* May 1982, 64.

5. Thomas S. Monson, "How Firm a Foundation," *Ensign,* Nov. 2006, 62; emphasis in original.

6. I am indebted to Elder David Bednar for the concept of missions serving as scaffolding.

7. Dallin H. Oaks, "Nourishing the Spirit," *Ensign,* Dec. 1998, 10.

8. Bruce C. Hafen, "On Dealing with Uncertainty," *Ensign,* Aug. 1979, 65.

9. Cecil O. Samuelson Jr., "The Importance of Asking Questions," Brigham Young University devotional address, Nov. 13, 2001, http://speeches. byu.edu/reader/reader.php?id=767.

10. Boyd K. Packer, "Reverence Invites Revelation," *Ensign,* Nov. 1991, 21.

11. See also Matthew 21:22; 1 Nephi 10:19; Enos 1:15; Mormon 9:21; Moroni 7:26; D&C 29:6; 88:63–64.

12. Howard W. Hunter, in Conference Report, Oct. 1960, 108; as quoted by Robert D. Hales, "The Importance of Receiving a Personal Testimony," *Ensign,* Nov. 1994, 22.

13. Marion D. Hanks, "An Attitude—The Weightier Matters," *Ensign,* July 1981, 68.

14. James E. Faust, "Choices," *Ensign,* May 2004, 52.

15. Gordon B. Hinckley, "Stay the Course—Keep the Faith," *Ensign,* Nov. 1995, 71.

16. Robert D. Hales, "Out of Darkness into His Marvelous Light," *Ensign,* May 2002, 71.

17. Gordon B. Hinckley, "He Is Risen, As He Said," *Ensign,* Apr. 1983, 7.

18. Hinckley, "Stay the Course—Keep the Faith," 71.

19. Jeffrey R. Holland, "A Prayer for the Children," *Ensign,* May 2003, 85–86.

20. Neal A. Maxwell, "Unto the Rising Generation," *Ensign,* Apr. 1985, 9; emphasis in original.

21. James E. Faust, "Lord, I Believe; Help Thou Mine Unbelief," *Ensign,* Nov. 2003, 19.

22. Quoted in Sheri Dew, *Go Forward with Faith: The Biography of Gordon B. Hinckley* (Salt Lake City: Deseret Book, 1996), 46–47.

23. Russell M. Nelson, "A More Excellent Hope," *Ensign,* Feb. 1997, 60.

24. C. S. Lewis, *The Great Divorce* (New York: McMillan Publishing Co., 1946), 39–40.

25. James E. Faust, "It Can't Happen to Me," *Ensign,* May 2002, 48.

26. Neal A. Maxwell, "'Answer Me,'" *Ensign,* Nov. 1988, 32–33.

27. James E. Faust, "The Abundant Life," *Ensign,* Nov. 1985, 8.

28. Gordon B. Hinckley, "Be Not Faithless," *Ensign,* Apr. 1989, 2.

CHAPTER 3

RIGID PLANNERS AND WINGERS

It's difficult to know which is worse—the teacher who is so good on his feet that he simply wings his lesson with no preparation (Wingers) or the teacher who is so prepared that she will not be derailed from her detailed lesson plan no matter how great the need or the prompting (Rigid Planners). In the leadership context, Wingers are creative, energetic, and spontaneous—but disdain such organizational trappings as outlines, agendas, and calendars—while Rigid Planners are so prepared and organized that they can become inflexible spiritual androids, marching forward as if programmed to ignore all unanticipated situations and stimuli. If they were navigators, Wingers would travel without a map or directions, simply following their hunches and trusting their memory (and certainly not asking for directions if lost). Rigid Planners would have printouts of detailed directions from the Internet, but would be unable to deal with a major traffic jam or natural disaster that would lead a prudent traveler to change course.

Of course, ideal disciples and teachers recognize the strengths and dangers of both extremes. Whether personally or by enlisting the aid of others, they are prepared but flexible, organized but open to last-minute promptings, diligent yet joyful in their service.

RIGID PLANNERS

Walking in Faith

One of the great drawbacks of being a planning perfectionist is being unwilling to move without a detailed plan of action in place. Planning before acting is a reasonable default policy, but if we make total preparation an absolute prerequisite to action, we'll often be stuck in preparation purgatory. Nephi's best plans to retrieve the brass plates failed. Only when he was willing to walk in faith, being "led by the Spirit, not knowing beforehand the things which [he] should do" did he finally succeed (1 Nephi 4:6). Had Nephi refused to proceed without a detailed plan of action that night, he would have gained neither the plates nor the spiritual growth that came from literally going forward in faith.

> *Planning before acting is a reasonable default policy, but if we make total preparation an absolute prerequisite to action, we'll often be stuck in preparation purgatory.*

Joseph Smith, too, was often given commandments and even visionary blueprints with no practical means in sight for achieving them. Had he waited until such divinely mandated projects were feasible, the Saints would never have built the Kirtland and Nauvoo Temples. Because we "receive no witness until after the trial of [our] faith" (Ether 12:6), we should realize that, in our planning, the Lord will often reveal only the next step of our journey rather than the distant scene[1]—or sometimes the distant scene without a detailed route showing how to arrive there. If we refuse to move until we see the entire path lit, we will often remain frozen, like a frightened child holding a lantern but separated from his goal by seemingly impenetrable darkness. Elder Boyd K. Packer reminded us that we exercise faith and find spiritual knowledge in the very "moment when [we] have gone to the edge of the light and stepped into the darkness to discover that the way is lighted ahead for just a footstep or two."[2]

Some of our sweetest spiritual experiences come in precisely such moments, when we "go forward," as the Lord admonished the trembling children of Israel on the banks of the Red Sea (Exodus 14:15). When Israel went "forward in faith," Elder Dallin H. Oaks noted, "what seemed impossible . . . occurred."[3] With their backs against a watery wall and their enemies upon them, Moses received the revelation he needed to save his people.[4] Interestingly, the Lord later chose this eleventh-hour example of inspiration to epitomize the revelatory process: "Now, behold, this is the spirit of revelation; behold, this is the spirit by which Moses brought the children of Israel through the Red Sea on dry ground" (D&C 8:3).[5] In doing so, perhaps God was reminding us, as Elder Oaks taught, that "revelation comes most often when we are on the move."[6]

Elder Russell M. Nelson experienced an application of this principle when a faith-filled patriarch pressed him to perform heart surgery under circumstances where none of the established procedures promised any real hope of success. After receiving a spiritual confirmation to perform the surgery—but before being shown what to do once cutting the man open—Elder Nelson went forward in faith. Once inside the man's chest, Elder Nelson saw in his mind a detailed diagram of exactly how to proceed—thus saving the man's life and pioneering a cardiac procedure that has since blessed the lives of many other heart patients.[7]

Most of us will not be required to retrieve brass plates, build temples without any money in the bank, walk through seas, or perform pioneering heart surgery. However, we may well be prompted to take uncharted detours from our best-laid plans—detours that test our faith. For my wife and me, such a test of faith came when, after happily practicing law and working as an executive for several years, I persistently felt called in a different direction professionally.

We tried to prepare for making such a career change as prudently as possible. However, when much prayer and fasting led us to conclude that the time had come for me to try to begin teaching seminary and institute, the Lord seemed intent on testing our willingness to walk in faith. It became clear that to have any real chance of being hired by the Church Educational System, I needed to be observed in a daily teaching setting, which would have been impossible while serving as a bishop and traveling frequently as an executive. The Lord simultaneously provided a way and a test, when a change in duties at work gave me the option to take a severance package that would provide several months' pay. Unfortunately, no one in CES had ever observed me teaching, so I had no earthly promise or assessment of my chances of obtaining the job I dreamed of getting. Having the safety net of a decent severance package in place made our decision far from Abrahamic. Yet the Lord seemed intent on orchestrating the change in a way that gave our family an opportunity to take a fairly big hop of faith.

This exercise of faith was particularly impressive and especially difficult for my wife. She naturally leans more toward the Rigid Planner end of the spectrum, someone who wants everything well mapped out before starting the journey. But she recognized the promptings of the Spirit and the hand of the Lord in orchestrating the opportunity for me to teach religion for a living. Even when shown only a single step instead of the distant scene, my wife and I knew from experience that we were always happier going where the Lord wanted us to go than staying where we might have been naturally inclined to stay.

Compassionately Changing Course

Another challenge with well-laid plans is that we become so fixated on planning and preparing that tactical means threaten to become the end themselves, obscuring our vision of our real goal. For example, I vividly and shamefully remember spending one Sunday morning conscientiously polishing my talk for sacrament meeting, only to realize after Church that I had perfected a Mother's Day sermon while utterly and ironically failing to celebrate and serve my wife that morning.

Perhaps it was similar preoccupation with priestly preparation and public commitments that led the priest and the Levite to pass by the half-dead man in Christ's parable of the Good Samaritan (see Luke 10:30–32). Surely one of the lessons we should draw from this story is that opportunities to serve others are often thrust upon us rather than planned by us in advance; they tend to intrude inconveniently upon our scheduled, hectic lives. Indeed, if we served only when doing so fit our schedule, we would miss out on many of our most meaningful chances to minister to others. "Think of all the opportunities you will have to serve at inconvenient times," Elder Vaughn J. Featherstone observed. "I promise you that most of the service you render to the Lord will come at times not convenient to you."[8] Among other things, parents so intent on accomplishing tasks listed in their daily planners may well miss out on some of the best teaching moments with their children, which so often require spontaneity.

> *Opportunities to serve others are often thrust upon us rather than planned by us in advance; they tend to intrude inconveniently upon our scheduled, hectic lives.*

No story demonstrates this principle more vividly than the Savior's visit to Lehi's descendants after His resurrection. After a very long day of teaching—simply allowing 2,500 Saints to touch His hands, feet, and side "one by one" must have taken several hours[9]—the Savior planned to depart to visit the lost tribes of Israel (3 Nephi 17:4). He had already taught these New World Israelites more than they could understand (3 Nephi 17:2–3). Yet when "he cast his eyes round about again on the multitude, and beheld they were in tears, and did look steadfastly upon him as if they would ask him to tarry a little longer with them," He changed His plans (3 Nephi 17:5). "Behold, my bowels are filled with compassion towards you," the Savior announced (3 Nephi 17:6). One of the most extraordinary chapters in all scripture, 3 Nephi 17 is the record of healing, praying, teaching, and blessings that were apparently not on the original itinerary. When we serve out of compassion rather than mere obligation, our service is often spontaneous rather than scheduled—and sublime rather than merely dutiful.

This truth about teaching moments applies not only to teachers, but to disciple-students as well. The famous episode involving the Savior, Mary, and Martha dramatically demonstrates the importance of flexibility and spontaneity in spiritual matters. Before analyzing that story, however, it is important to remember just what we know about Martha.

The sister of Mary and Lazarus, Martha was clearly one of the greatest stalwarts among the Savior's followers. Although we know Jesus loves us all, John singles out Martha, Mary, and Lazarus as disciples Jesus loved (see John 11:5). The Master ate at Martha's house more than once (see Luke 10:38; John 12:1–3), demonstrating the trust He must have had in this dedicated disciple. In her plea to raise her brother from the dead, Martha demonstrated extraordinary spiritual assertiveness and knowledge (see John 11:21–29); indeed, her faith helped facilitate the miracle that followed. On the one occasion we read in the Bible of Jesus weeping, his tears were undoubtedly not for Lazarus (as the Jews assumed), but for the temporary anguish He knew Mary and Martha had to suffer in order for Him to be able to perform this pivotal miracle in such a definitive fashion (see John 11:4–7, 15, 35–36).[10]

So when Christ teaches Martha a lesson in Luke 10, He is offering graduate-level disciple instruction to one of His most dedicated followers. Yet the fact remains that He clearly offers Martha some gently corrective instruction from which we can all learn. Martha had generously received Jesus—and presumably the disciples traveling with Him—into her house (see Luke 10:38). While she was busily engaged in serving the Savior (apparently out of earshot), her sister, Mary, "sat at Jesus' feet, and heard his word" (Luke 10:39). Understandably frustrated that she was left alone with the burden of serving her guests, Martha asked Jesus to encourage Mary to help. To the "cumbered" Martha (Luke 10:40), Jesus responded simply: "Martha, Martha, thou art careful and troubled about many things: But one thing is needful: and Mary hath chosen that good part, which shall not be taken away from her" (Luke 10:41–42).

Whether or not Jesus was criticizing Martha's choice of activities for herself,[11] he was, at a minimum, chiding Martha for begrudging Mary's choice of activities. Martha had become so focused on getting things done that she had failed to see, as her sister did, what a precious learning opportunity it was to sit at the feet of the Son of God and be taught by Him. Christ not only defended Mary's decision to listen and learn, but He also noted that the conscientious Martha was "careful" (which could have been translated "worried") and "troubled about many things" (Luke 10:41), while only "one thing is needful" (Luke 10:42). Such phrases suggest that Martha was not only busily readying a meal but had perhaps become so anxious and weighed down by her temporal tasks that she was not able to perceive the unprecedented spiritual opportunity in her front room. Rather than preparing food with "singleness of heart" in this Sabbath-like setting (D&C 59:13), Martha may have been troubled about such nonessential matters as putting on an impressive spread.

Applying the lessons from this encounter to our lives, Elder Dallin H. Oaks concluded: "This scripture reminds every Martha, male and female, that we should not be so occupied with what is routine and temporal that we fail to cherish those opportunities that are unique and spiritual."[12] Elder Neal A. Maxwell added: "Martha-like anxiety . . . can also deprive us of special experiences if we are too 'cumbered about much serving.'" Not only is "conscientiousness . . . not an automatic guarantee that we will choose the 'good part,'"[13] but if we are not careful, misdirected conscientiousness may actually detract from our ability to do those things that are most important.

While any spiritual slacker would be better off in Martha's shoes on Judgment Day, the Savior was helping this stalwart disciple rise to an even higher level. We can only speculate as to what Martha herself learned from the exchange, but it is interesting to note that when Jesus later came to Bethany after Lazarus's death, Martha, "as soon as she heard that Jesus was coming, went and met him: but Mary sat still in the house" (John 11:20). On this later occasion, it was Martha rather than Mary who dropped what she was doing so that she could importune the Savior before He had even arrived at her home.

Customizing Answers and Actions

A third drawback of rigidly planning and preparing is that we might mistakenly assume that whenever we assiduously prepare a talk or a lesson or an answer, we have created the definitive document, to which we should slavishly adhere and which we can simply recycle whenever the need arises. Parents and leaders who become more experienced may encounter a problem with which they have dealt repeatedly before—and thus assume they know exactly what to say or do. If we are not careful, experience can then become the enemy of inspiration, for we may look to what we have done in the past rather than looking to God for customized inspiration for the present. In my last few months serving as a bishop, I had to make a much more conscious effort to seek the guidance of the Lord than I did in my first six months, when I was desperate for divine direction. Jacob's counsel about being learned might apply similarly to being prepared: to be prepared is good *if* we continue to seek and be open to inspiration from God (see 2 Nephi 9:28–29).

Any of us with the inclination to rely exclusively on our careful preparation may be the target audience for this advice from the Lord for His missionaries: "Neither take ye thought beforehand what ye shall say; but treasure up in your minds continually the words of life, and it shall be given you in the very hour that portion that shall be meted unto every man" (D&C 84:85). If we lazily fall back on past experience or rely solely on previous preparation, we may not fervently seek direction from the Lord *in the moment* that might apply uniquely to the situation in which we find ourselves.

Similarly, when we are so prepared that we are merely reading our words[14] or reciting those written by others, we may find it more difficult to recognize and act upon promptings of the Spirit to change our approach. Elder Oaks explained that our desire to follow the Spirit should make us "willing to put aside all our preparation and follow the Spirit's direction."[15] President Gordon B. Hinckley acknowledged the limitations of well-prepared but mechanically delivered presentations when he said, "We must . . . get our teachers to speak out of their hearts rather than out of their books, to communicate their love for the Lord and this precious work, and somehow it will catch fire in the hearts of those they teach."[16]

As missionaries, my companions and I tried to employ a number of different door approaches, without necessarily deciding in advance exactly what we would say. I will never forget how one older German man was about to close the door on us when my companion, Dell Brown, offered an inspired follow-up question about the resurrection. Herr Pose opened the door wide, explaining that if he hadn't believed in the resurrection, he wouldn't have been able to cope with the loss of his wife. I attribute Brother Pose's subsequent baptism largely to my companion's flexibility in responding to the Spirit—something that simply wouldn't have happened had he had programmed himself to say the same thing to every person at every door. Elder Brown was clearly doing door approaches in the same way leaders of the Church in the Book of Mormon conducted meetings: "And their meetings were conducted by the church after the manner of the workings of the Spirit, and by the power of the Holy Ghost; for as the power of the Holy Ghost led them whether to preach, or to exhort, or to pray, or to supplicate, or to sing, even so it was done" (Moroni 6:9).

WINGERS

Doing Our Part

Some teachers and leaders are able to perform remarkably well on the fly. Unfortunately, some then use their improvised success to justify laziness—even citing the Lord's injunction to take no "thought beforehand what ye shall say" (D&C 84:85) as scriptural justification for their lack of diligence. Such a selective use of the words of this verse ignores the following phrase, which enjoins us to "treasure up in [our] minds continually the words of life" (D&C 84:85). Elder Oaks summarized the Lord's complete instruction in this way:

> We should be in constant general preparation by "treasuring up" in our minds the teachings of the gospel, and when invited to give a talk or to present a lesson, we should make specific preparations. Most of the time we will carry through with our preparations. But sometimes there will be an authentic impression to leave something out or to add something. We should make careful preparation, but we should not be exclusively bound to that preparation. . . .
>
> In short, the Lord's instruction to teach by the Spirit does not relieve us in the slightest degree from the necessity of making personal preparation.[17]

Even with his talks delivered from prepared manuscripts, President Henry B. Eyring has demonstrated the approach Elder Oaks described. When asked on one occasion how he went about preparing his talk for general conference, Elder Eyring explained that he had written 100 pages before finally receiving his errand from the Lord.[18] No one could ever justifiably accuse President Eyring of winging it.

President Eyring's example reminds us that preparation is usually part of the price to be paid for receiving inspiration. As the Lord reminded Oliver Cowdery, we should not expect to approach the Lord cavalierly and receive revelation: "Behold, you have not understood; you have supposed that I would give it unto you, when *you took no thought save it was to ask me.* But, behold, I say unto you, that *you must study it out in your mind;* then you must ask me if it be right, and if it is right I will cause that your bosom shall burn within you; therefore, you shall feel that it is right" (D&C 9:7–8; emphasis added).

Caring Enough to Do Our Best

As a missionary, I once attended a sacrament meeting in Hannover, Germany, where a very conscientious member made a single comment in a talk that has remained with me ever since: "If I appear somewhat nervous to you today," he said, as well as I can recollect, "it is because I take the privilege of speaking to you seriously." This disciple was not nervous because he was unprepared or because he worried about how others would perceive him or his talk; he was nervous because he cared, because he knew what he said that day mattered.

Can some teachers or leaders perform their callings well enough to get by without doing much preparation? Perhaps—but getting by really isn't the goal. Occasionally, a loved one or friend of someone I teach or for whom I have stewardship will share words of concern about their friend or loved one. With such additional knowledge, I almost always find myself ratcheting up the level of my preparation for a class or visit that might otherwise become routine. When we remember that our efforts matter—whether in a Primary class, a home teaching visit, a sacrament meeting talk, or a presidency meeting—we find ourselves taking our preparation more seriously.

Elder Oaks described the standard for dedicated disciples in the teaching setting in this way: "We must study the scriptures. We must study the teachings of the living prophets. We must learn all that we can to make ourselves presentable and understandable to our children, our students, and our investigators. . . . All of this and much more is part of preparation. And preparation is a prerequisite to teaching by the Spirit."[19]

Moreover, "when [we] are in the service of [our] fellow beings, [we] are only in the service of [our] God" (Mosiah 2:17). Thus, when we serve others haphazardly, we serve God haphazardly. All those who choose to "embark in the service of God"—not just as full-time missionaries—are commanded to serve Him with all their "heart, might, mind and strength" if they hope to "stand blameless before God at the last day" (D&C 4:2). To serve God in such a manner requires exerting ourselves emotionally, intellectually, and even physically. We are each expected to learn our "duty, and to act in the office in which [we are] appointed, in all diligence" (D&C 107:99). Only then, when we teach and serve diligently, does the Lord's grace attend us in our efforts (see D&C 88:78).

Petitioning Prophets and Sending Spies

Some who drift toward the Winger end of the spectrum may actually do so out of spirituality rather than laziness. Their great faith may lead them to believe that tactical tools are not necessary when we rely on the Lord. They may even believe that preparation evidences a lack of faith. However, Captain Moroni's example helps us recognize that stalwart disciples look to the Lord for guidance while simultaneously using all the resources available to them.

When Moroni's men rebuffed Zerahemnah and the Lamanites, the Lamanite army fled into the wilderness. Needing to know exactly where his enemy was, Moroni took a belts-and-suspenders approach: "But it came to pass, as soon as they had departed into the wilderness *Moroni sent spies* into the wilderness to watch their camp; **and Moroni**, also, *knowing of the prophecies of Alma, sent certain men unto him*, desiring him that he should inquire of the Lord whither the armies of the Nephites should go to defend themselves against the Lamanites" (Alma 43:23; emphasis added).

Moroni had both the prudence to use the resources at his disposal and the faith to seek direction from the Lord through His prophet. Even after receiving revelatory reconnaissance, Moroni continued to use his spies to get further intelligence about the Lamanites' location. Given the importance of his cause, Moroni "thought it no sin that he should defend [his people] by stratagem; therefore, he found by his spies which course the Lamanites were to take" (Alma 43:30). Similarly, although we can seek direction from the Lord in our righteous endeavors, we can simultaneously use the intellectual and other resources God has given us to solve our problems.

Building Temples and Building Towers

Some Wingers may be tempted to use the fact that the Lord occasionally gives us impractical, faith-stretching, and faith-building commands—such as the directives to build the Kirtland and Nauvoo Temples—as justification for pursuing outlandish, unrealistic goals. What's more, Wingers may undertake audacious projects not so much in a calculated, diligent sort of way, but in creative fits and bursts. Absent clear inspiration to do so, Wingers with dreams would do well to remember the parable of the tower: "Which of you, intending to build a tower, sitteth not down first, and counteth the cost, whether he have sufficient to finish it? Lest haply, after he hath laid the foundation, and is not able to finish it, all that behold it begin to mock him, Saying, This man began to build, and was not able to finish" (Luke 14:28–30).

From the Joseph Smith Translation, we know that the Savior employed this parable to help those considering following Him make sure they did not do so unless they were "able to continue" (JST, Luke 14:31). However, the parable has practical applications beyond deciding whether to follow the Lord. Elder Russell M. Nelson characterized the Lord's counsel in this verse as stressing "preparation before embarkation."[20] Similarly, in discussing how to provide for one's family, Elder M. Russell Ballard wrote of the possibility of starting a business to increase one's income. While the visionary Winger might want to pursue the dream of starting a business based solely on a lifelong wish, Elder Ballard advocated a more cautious, pragmatic approach: "We must be wise, however, and analyze all factors and seek sound counsel from an attorney, accountant, banker, and most importantly, from a businessman who is successfully managing his own company. After developing a plan, we should pray for guidance; and when we receive an inward assurance that we should begin our own business, then we should do it." Elder Ballard then cited the Lord's counsel about building towers as support for this approach.[21]

> *Prayerful analysis of the practicality of our pursuit can spare us the heartache of fruitlessly beginning construction of a dream castle that will only bankrupt us in the end.*

In sum, while the Lord sometimes inspires us to engage in audacious undertakings akin to building the Kirtland Temple, unless we have received such divine directives, we would be wise to follow the Lord's counsel about building towers in our lives by carefully calculating the costs to make sure our dreams are feasible. Whether we are considering an extraordinary ward activity, a drastic career change, or an unprecedented family trip, prayerful analysis of the practicality of our pursuit can spare us the heartache of fruitlessly beginning construction of a dream castle that will only bankrupt us in the end.

STRIKING THE BALANCE

In leading, teaching, or living the gospel, some of us would become more effective if we became more diligent, more organized, and more conscientious. On the other hand, some of us are so scheduled and prepared that there is little room for the Spirit to alert us to unanticipated opportunities or needs. "Daily goals and plans are extremely important in bringing order to our lives, in helping us to establish priorities, and in assisting us to use our time most efficiently," observed Elder Spencer J. Condie, "but we must be cautious that we do not 'look beyond the mark' (Jacob 4:14) and become so caught up in maintaining efficient schedules that we have too little time for compassionate detours in our lives."[22]

One reason that presidencies and councils can be such an effective synergistic tool is that Wingers and Rigid Planners can temper each other's extreme tendencies, creating a more balanced result. But each of us can become more effective individually when we recognize the extreme to which we naturally drift and guard against its dangers. We are at our best in our callings, our families, and our classrooms when we balance careful planning with faith-fueled action, diligent preparation with spiritual spontaneity, wholehearted service with joyful ministering, rigorous analysis with inspired creativity, and audacious ideas with practical perspective.

Notes

1. See "Lead, Kindly Light," *Hymns of The Church of Jesus Christ of Latter-day Saints* (Salt Lake City: The Church of Jesus Christ of Latter-day Saints, 1985), no. 97.

2. Boyd K. Packer, "The Candle of the Lord," *Ensign,* Jan. 1983, 54.

3. Dallin H. Oaks, "Reach Out and Climb!" *New Era,* Aug. 1985, 6.

4. While Moses appears not to have known in advance exactly how the Lord would save Israel from such dire straits, he may have been given a patriarchal premonition of what was to come when the Lord promised him that he would "be made stronger than many waters; for they shall obey thy command as if thou wert God" (Moses 1:25).

5. I am indebted to Mark Beecher for this insight.

6. Dallin H. Oaks, "Sharing the Gospel," *Ensign,* Nov. 2001, 9.

7. Russell M. Nelson, "Sweet Power of Prayer," *Ensign,* May 2003, 7–8.

8. Vaughn J. Featherstone, "Why Now? Why Me?" *New Era,* Jan.-Feb. 1984, 7.

9. If each person were allowed 10 seconds for such an encounter, for example, the activity described in 3 Nephi 11:15 alone would have taken 416 minutes, or nearly seven hours. In addition, the Savior preached at least the words contained in the remainder of 3 Nephi 11 and 3 Nephi 12–16.

10. For an excellent discussion of this miracle—and Martha's conversation with the Savior that preceded it—see Jo Ann H. Seely, "From Bethany to Gethsemane," in *From the Last Supper Through the Resurrection: The Savior's Final Hours,* Richard Neitzel Holzapfel and Thomas A. Wayment, eds. (Salt Lake City: Deseret Book, 2003), 40–42.

11. "The rebuke would not have come had Martha not prompted it. The Lord did not go into the kitchen and tell Martha to stop cooking and come listen. Apparently he was content to let her serve him however she cared to, until she judged another person's service. . . . Martha's self-importance, expressed through her judgment of her sister, occasioned the Lord's rebuke, not her busyness with the meal" (Catherine Corman Parry, "'Simon, I Have Somewhat to Say unto Thee': Judgment and Condemnation in the Parables of Jesus," in *Brigham Young University 1990–91 Devotional and Fireside Speeches* [Provo, Utah: 1991], 116; as quoted in Dallin H. Oaks, "'Judge Not' and Judging," *Ensign,* Aug. 1999, 12).

12. Dallin H. Oaks, "Spirituality," *Ensign,* Nov. 1985, 61.

13. Neal A. Maxwell, "Wisdom and Order," *Ensign,* June 1994, 42.

14. Obviously, there are some situations, such as general conference sessions, where logistical or even spiritual considerations require speakers to prepare and adhere to written remarks.

15. Dallin H. Oaks, "Teaching and Learning by the Spirit," *Ensign,* Mar. 1997, 10.

16. Gordon B. Hinckley, *Teachings of Gordon B. Hinckley* (Salt Lake City: Deseret Book, 1997), 619–20.

17. Oaks, "Teaching and Learning by the Spirit," 10.

18. President Eyring made this comment on September 17, 2004, in response to a student question in a Teachings of the Living Prophets class at BYU–Idaho.

19. Oaks, "Teaching and Learning by the Spirit," 10.

20. Russell M. Nelson, "The Five A's of Stewardship," *Ensign,* Apr. 1972, 24.

21. M. Russell Ballard, "Providing for Our Needs," *Ensign,* May 1981, 86.

22. Spencer J. Condie, *In Perfect Balance* (Salt Lake City: Deseret Book, 1993), 23.

CHAPTER 4

SPRINTERS AND SAUNTERERS

Pace matters—whether we're running a race, getting in shape, completing a challenging project, or living the gospel of Jesus Christ. Some of us lack the sense of urgency that would lead us to pursue spiritual progress with the intensity we need. We saunter through life, taking plenty of time to smell the roses, but never really getting anywhere. Others of us are periodically filled with a zest that hurtles us along the track so fast that we burn out long before reaching the finishing line. And some of us may find ourselves veering wildly between the two extremes, sauntering for a season, sprinting to regain lost ground, and then sauntering again because we're out of emotional gas. In this chapter, I discuss how we can strike the best balance between being Sprinters and Saunterers.

SPRINTERS

There's nothing quite like watching a movie like *Rocky* to get me out of my chair and onto the road to fitness. Unfortunately, with the soundtrack still ringing in my ears, I'm tempted to climb out of bed the next morning before the crack of dawn, down a few raw eggs, jump rope, run several miles, and climb the biggest set of stairs around—only to collapse at the top, unable to exercise for days to come. The same sort of thing happens in health clubs throughout the country during the first week of January each year, and it captures the essential problem of those who sprint when running the marathon of life: they burn out. "Sometimes we may reward our breathlessness with a respite that turns into a permanent repose," cautioned Elder Neal A. Maxwell.[1]

Like a child who quits playing the piano after a week because she can't yet play any sonatas, Sprinters often lack the staying power to see the long-term rewards of sustained spiritual striving.

Yet the desire to sprint is a natural response to the realization that there is a need to run. For instance, a trip to a shantytown in a Third World country may lead a sympathetic Church member to empty out a savings account and send it to organizations who help the world's homeless—leaving him unable to pay the mortgage on his own home. A rousing sermon or scripture—much like an inspiring movie—can get us so pumped up that we try to do all our family history the following week. Yet Elder David A. Bednar advised us that "as we become more spiritually mature and increasingly steadfast and immovable, we are less prone to zealous and exaggerated spurts of spirituality followed by extended periods of slackness."[2]

What's the problem with such well-motivated spurts of spirituality? First, we often fail to make the progress we wish we could make when we begin our sprint. We may spend hours in efforts to invite less-active members to Church, only to have none of them attend services on Sunday. We may vow in a single week to attend the temple, establish better relations with the neighbors, help a visiting teaching sister with her garden, solve a vexing genealogical puzzle, spend quality time with the children, and master the book of

Isaiah—only to find that we've fallen woefully short of our goal at week's end. Sprinters tend to want to see immediate results and become frustrated when they don't. Thus, like a child who quits playing the piano after a week because she can't yet play any sonatas, Sprinters often lack the staying power to see the long-term rewards of sustained spiritual striving.

Second, even when Sprinters do make progress—and they sometimes will see remarkable short-term gains—they are often exhausted by the effort they have invested to reap such rewards. A fired-up follower of Christ may choose to read the Bible in one week, no matter what the costs. If she succeeds, she will undoubtedly enjoy some great benefits from such scripture study. But she will also suffer some negative repercussions from having neglected familial, employment, or academic duties. Exhausted from the sprint, she may find herself setting aside her scripture study altogether for several months, much worse off than if she had simply studied the Bible for thirty minutes each day. And as Elder Bednar noted, "a single scripture-reading marathon cannot produce the spiritual growth of steady scripture study across many months."[3]

The Sprinter in this example may also have lost her job or failed a class or forgotten a child. When we sprint by focusing our energies completely on one aspect of our lives, we usually do so at the cost of other important areas. Elder M. Russell Ballard warned against just such imbalance when he cautioned those who "become so energetic in their Church service" that they "complicate their service with needless frills and embellishments that occupy too much time, cost too much money, and sap too much energy. . . . As a result of their focusing too much time and energy on their Church service, eternal family relationships can deteriorate. Employment performance can suffer. This is not healthy, spiritually or otherwise."[4]

Third, Sprinters are occasionally (but not always) motivated in less noble or productive ways than those who manage to plod along more slowly but steadily. For example, the young man who wants to court a spiritually mature young woman may suddenly display a burst of speed in order to quickly become worthy of the woman he loves. Whether he gets the girl or not, however, his changes probably won't last if he is not inspired by higher motives than romance alone. Similarly, even when our motives are more pure, our resolutions to change are less likely to succeed when they are inspired by singular spiritual sensations, such as a great youth conference, than when prompted by daily scripture study or seminary attendance. While such one-time events can serve as catalysts to meaningful spiritual growth, without the support of sustaining habits such as scripture study and prayer, our hasty commitments to change dramatically may result only in short-term gains that soon evaporate.

In many ways, making long-term spiritual improvement is like losing weight: those who chip away at their goal by adhering to a reasonable diet and increased exercise are much more likely to reach their ultimate goal of sustained weight loss than those who sprint toward it by starving themselves. The scriptures amply demonstrate that dramatically quick turnarounds are possible, but as President Ezra Taft Benson warned, "We must be cautious as we discuss these remarkable examples. Though they are real and powerful, they are the exception more than the rule. For every Paul, for every Enos, and for every King Lamoni, there are hundreds and thousands of people who find the process of repentance much more subtle, much more imperceptible. Day by day they move closer to the Lord, little realizing they are building a godlike life."[5]

I can still vividly remember a childhood friend who began carrying his Book of Mormon to junior high every day after joining the Church; he privately confided that he hoped to be the prophet one day. Unfortunately, he did not remain active in the Church long enough even to serve a mission.

Fourth, spectacular dashes tend to distract us from the long-distance training we really need to be doing. We may placate our conscience with a singular dramatic donation to someone in need, losing sight in the process of the importance of paying a consistent, unspectacular tithing and steadily making other offerings.

Ultimately, as the Preacher said, the race is rarely "to the swift, nor the battle to the strong" (Ecclesiastes 9:11). Instead, the prize usually goes to those who run diligently, but not faster than they have strength (see Mosiah 4:27). In sum, as Elder Bednar explained, "A spurt may appear to be impressive in the short run, but steadiness over time is far more effective, far less dangerous, and produces far better results."[6]

Finally, such cautions are relevant not only as we try to pace ourselves, but as we extend callings and work with others in leadership positions. Elder Ballard counseled: "For Church members to be able to balance their lives, Church leaders must be sure they do not require so much from members that they have no time to accomplish their personal and family goals."[7] Whether we impose a Sprinter's pace on those who serve with us or we instinctively recommend the most capable (and perhaps already overworked) person in our organization for a calling without truly seeking to know the Lord's will, we may generate the very problems for others that sprinting can create for ourselves.

SAUNTERERS

While burning out in a flash is a distinct danger for some, laziness is apparently a much bigger problem for most natural men and women, given how many times the Lord reminds us to be diligent. In fact, as Elder Bednar noted, while God's work is to "bring to pass the immortality and eternal life of man" (Moses 1:39), our work is defined by the Lord in Doctrine and Covenants 11:20: "Behold, this is your work, to keep my commandments, yea, *with all your might, mind and strength*" (emphasis added).[8]

There's nothing leisurely about that mission statement. For all those who are serious about embarking in God's service, the charge is to be dedicated disciples every day rather than weekend spiritual warriors. We are to serve with all the emotion, intellectual energy, and physical power we can muster—with "all [our] heart, might, mind and strength, that [we] may stand blameless before God at the last day" (D&C 4:2). Such a charge doesn't leave much room for prolonged gospel vacations.

The Scriptural Case for Diligence

The scriptures command us to be diligent and commend those who are, whether in

- keeping the commandments generally (1 Nephi 4:34; Alma 7:23; 37:20; 38:10; D&C 6:20);
- magnifying callings (Jacob 2:3; 5:61; 5:75; Jarom 1:11; Moroni 8:6; 9:6; D&C 88:78, 84);
- teaching our children gospel truths (Deuteronomy 4:9; 6:7); or
- engaging in secular pursuits (Proverbs 22:29; 27:23).

The scriptures make it eminently clear that diligence is a virtue and idleness is a vice. The Lord repeatedly commands His people in general not to be idle (see, for example, D&C 42:42; 88:124). To those "sent to preach my gospel" He gives a particular commandment: "Thou shalt not idle away thy time" (D&C 60:13). And after calling all sluggards to attention, the author of Proverbs warns us that if we plan on a life of sleeping in, our expectations shouldn't be too high: "Yet a little sleep, a little slumber, a little folding of the hands to sleep: So shall thy poverty come as one that travelleth" (Proverbs 6:9–11).

Consistency Over Speed

Of course, diligently keeping the commandments doesn't mean that we must always be running at a spiritual sprint. The meaning of *diligence* has more to do with the consistency of our effort than the impressiveness of our speed. The 1828 *Webster's Dictionary* defines *diligent* as being, among other things, "constant in effort or exertion to accomplish what is undertaken; . . . prosecuted with care and constant effort."[9] Undoubtedly, Heavenly Father's hope for us, like the hope Lehi had for Laman and Lemuel, is that we become "firm and steadfast, and immovable in keeping the commandments" (1 Nephi 2:10).

Stretching Our Capacity

Perhaps we need such frequent and forceful reminders to be diligent not only because we naturally list toward laziness, but also because we underestimate our own abilities. Personally, I am often unaware of my capacities until they are stretched and discovered by necessity or serendipity. Participating in school basketball showed me I could push myself (or, to be more accurate, Mr. Powell and Mr. Book could push me) much further and harder than I had ever imagined. My first full-time job working for an uncle at age fourteen taught me how to work an eight-hour day. Both my mission and college showed me that when I needed to, I could consistently put in much, much more than a forty-hour week of work.

Of course, stretching ourselves secularly doesn't always translate into spiritual growth, but it can if we connect the dots. It was in law school that I made the connection between enlarging my secular capacity and increasing my spiritual capacity through diligence. As I participated in an appellate advocacy competition (sort of a debate tournament for law students), I poured myself into preparing like I never had before for any other academic event. I managed to memorize large chunks of prepared remarks as I got ready to be grilled by a panel of mock judges. After realizing some success from such preparation, I was asked to give a talk in Church. I began to prepare in the usual way, which had always seemed more than adequate. Yet my preparation paled compared to the effort I'd invested in the law school contest. Then at some point a stinging question came to my mind: Why had I prepared so much more for the law school contest than for the talk? Was I more concerned about impressing my classmates and the visiting judges than I was about pleasing my Heavenly Father?

None of the possible answers was acceptable. Having discovered a greater capacity to prepare for any kind of oral presentation, I began doing much more to get ready for most talks and lessons I gave in Church. As I began applying the same kind of diligence in the spiritual context that I did in the secular context, I found that my dedication in callings improved considerably.

Keeping Our Eye on the Prize

So how do we muster the focus and energy to avoid becoming spiritual sluggards? Several years ago on Halloween we took our children trick-or-treating, including our daughter Elizabeth, who was not quite two at the time. We strolled pleasantly along for the first few houses, with Elizabeth struggling to keep up with her older sisters. Then somewhere between perhaps the third and fourth house, a light went off in her little toddler brain. It must have seemed too good to be true, but the pattern was unmistakable: whenever she knocked on a door and opened her bag, people put candy in it. Filled with a new sense of purpose for this cold, evening walk, she uttered a single word twice before dashing off after her sisters: "Hurrwwwy! Hurrwwwy!" Without any encouragement from us, she virtually ran from door to door for the rest of the evening.

Those serving because they want to bless the lives of others are both more diligent and more effective than those who drag themselves out the door simply because they feel they ought to.

Elizabeth's change of heart demonstrates the difference between how we tend to perform when doing something we are supposed to do—something we feel *compelled* to do—and how we perform when doing something we really want to do—something we feel *impelled* to do. From missionaries to Mutual leaders, those serving because they want to bless the lives of others are both more diligent and more effective than those who drag themselves out the door simply because they feel they ought to.

How do we move from merely going through the gospel motions to living with a self-imposed sense of urgency? For starters, the better we understand the eternal rewards promised for diligence, the more we move like Elizabeth. And just as wide-eyed children understand they have only one night to create a candy stash for the year, remembering that our conduct during this brief mortal test has everlasting consequences can help us pick up our pace. Once we truly understand that, much like Elizabeth on Halloween, we don't need constant reminders to keep things moving.

This is particularly true because the prize we seek is infinitely greater than a bulging bag of candy. Note the extraordinary blessings promised or given as a result of diligence in each of these scriptures:

- Spiritual knowledge is "the gift of God unto all those who diligently seek him" (1 Nephi 10:17; see also 1 Nephi 10:19; Alma 17:2; 40:3; D&C 88:63).
- Oliver Cowdery was promised that if he would be "faithful and diligent in keeping the commandments of God" the Lord would "encircle [him] in the arms of [His] love" (D&C 6:20).
- Having "faith and [being] diligent before" God are the prerequisites to being "crowned with blessings from above, yea, and with commandments not a few, and with revelations in their time" (D&C 59:4).
- Joseph Smith was promised that "if he [would] be diligent in keeping my commandments he [would] be blessed unto eternal life" (D&C 18:8).
- Nephi, the son of Helaman, was promised eternal blessings, including being made "mighty in word and in deed, in faith and in works"—all because he

had served God with "such unwearyingness" (Helaman 10:5).

Focusing on such eternal rewards can help us find our inner drive, just as it did Paul. Speaking of eternal blessings awaiting the diligent, Paul wrote, "For which cause we faint not; but though our outward man perish, yet the inward man is renewed day by day. For our light affliction, which is but for a moment, worketh for us a far more exceeding and eternal weight of glory" (2 Corinthians 4:16–17).

Moving Up the Motivational Totem Pole

But even understanding the eternal blessings that come from earthly diligence may not be enough to motivate us in the most difficult of times. In his masterful sermon on motives, Elder Dallin H. Oaks acknowledged that since "we are imperfect beings, most of us probably serve for a combination of reasons, and the combinations may be different from time to time as we grow spiritually. But we should all strive to serve for the reasons that are highest and best." And while hope of eternal reward is certainly better motivation than looking good for our friends or hoping to network, taught Elder Oaks, it's still not the highest or most powerful motivator. "If our service is to be most efficacious, it must be accomplished for the love of God and the love of his children."[10]

Several years later, Elder Oaks illustrated this point with a self-deprecating story about his own service and motives as a younger man:

> I was assigned to visit a less-active member, a successful professional many years older than I. Looking back on my actions, I realize that I had very little loving concern for the man I visited. I acted out of duty, with a desire to report 100 percent on my home teaching. One evening, close to the end of a month, I phoned to ask if my

companion and I could come right over and visit him. His chastening reply taught me an unforgettable lesson.

"No, I don't believe I want you to come over this evening," he said. "I'm tired. I've already dressed for bed. I am reading, and I am just not willing to be interrupted so that you can report 100 percent on your home teaching this month." That reply still stings me because I knew he had sensed my selfish motivation.[11]

Perhaps it's not coincidence that our service is both most effective and most enjoyable when we serve out of love rather than duty. Elder Oaks's conclusion about effective missionaries is applicable to all who labor to help others in God's kingdom: "The most effective missionaries, member and full-time, always act out of love."[12]

When we serve out of lesser motives (including even the hope of eternal reward), we are more likely to run out of gas when the road gets steep. It's much easier to get up off the couch to help someone we love than it is if our main focus is gaining a greater reward for ourselves in the hereafter. And even when we get up off the couch and do manage to serve people out of a sense of responsibility or hope of reward rather than real love, we are much less likely to make a difference with the service we provide. Perhaps when the Savior taught that all His commandments "hang" on the first two great commandments—loving God wholeheartedly and loving others—He was suggesting, in part, that our obedience generally depends on just how much we love God and His children (see Matthew 22:37–40). As the Savior taught, if we love Him, we will keep His commandments (see John 14:15).

On the other hand, spiritual sauntering and haphazard obedience reveal ingratitude for what He has done for us. "We would be the most ungrateful and unworthy people that ever lived," taught President Wilford Woodruff, "if, after receiving such wonderful manifestations of His goodness, we slackened in our diligence or failed in our obedience and devotion to Him and His great cause."[13]

Striking the Balance

So where and how do we draw the line between sprinting and sauntering? How do we serve God with all our heart, might, mind and strength without burning out?

Developing the Drive and Discipline to Pick Up the Pace

Since it's always easier to slow down than to speed up—and since the bulk of scriptures urge us to diligence—we might start by making sure we really are keeping up a steady pace. For those of us who tend to saunter more than sprint, let me share five additional keys to increasing the consistency and urgency with which we serve the Lord.

Study the doctrine. President Packer has repeatedly reminded us that the "study of the doctrines of the gospel will improve behavior quicker than talking about behavior will improve behavior."[14] The better we understand how much Heavenly Father and Jesus Christ have done for us and how much they expect of us, the more we will want to serve them. So when our pace lags, few things are as helpful as deepening our doctrinal understanding.

Remember the time is short. Quickening the pace is especially important for us as we labor in the final lap of this world's history. As a race or contest nears its end and competitors pick up the pace, athletes who want to win have no choice but to match their opponents' intensity. Our adversary is fully aware of how little time remains. John the Revelator warned that "the devil is come down unto you, having great wrath, because he knoweth that he hath but a short time" (Revelation 12:12). Not surprisingly, then, the Lord's counsel to those who run for Him when time is short is to pick up the pace: "Go to, and labor in the vineyard, with your might. For behold, this is the last time that I shall nourish my vineyard; for the end is nigh at hand, and the season speedily cometh; and if ye labor with your might with me ye shall have joy in the fruit which I shall lay up unto myself against the time which will soon come" (Jacob 5:71).

Fill life's cracks. Elder Henry B. Eyring, speaking at a Church Educational System fireside in 2001, taught young adults some principles that apply to all of us:

> Too often we use many hours for fun and pleasure, clothed in the euphemism "I'm recharging my batteries." Those hours could be spent reading and studying to gain knowledge, and skills, and culture. For instance, we too often fail to take advantage of the moments we spend waiting. . . . You could just have a book and paper and pencil with you. That will be enough. But you need determination to capture the leisure moments you now waste.[15]

Work with faith. Packing more into life's empty spaces is a good start for many of us, but some have already arrived at a point where there appears to be no more room, even with creative packing. And when we work alone, we may well have reached our limits.

Yet when we are in the service of our God, there is no need to work alone. Indeed, counseled Elder Eyring in that same CES fireside, we can view the "problem of crowded time" as "an opportunity to test [our] faith." Noting that God is truly all-powerful, Elder Eyring gave us this promise: "When we put God's purposes first, He will give us miracles. If we pray to know what He would have us do next, He will multiply the effects of what we do in such a way that time seems to be expanded."[16] So many of the tasks in our day do not require a set amount of time; they require only as long as it takes to get the job done. And whether we are preparing a lesson, figuring out how to take down the trampoline, trying to get the snow blower started, solving a trigonometry problem, or writing an appellate brief, we can perform any task more quickly and effectively with the Lord's help than we can alone.

I remember having many good things I hoped to accomplish one Saturday, including cutting down some ornamental grass that grows in groupings in front of our house. My wife had spent thirty minutes on each of three or four clumps she had pruned the day before. She'd trimmed half the clumps and felt overwhelmed, so I volunteered to cut down the rest, even though my day already looked full. I offered a prayer that somehow, I might be unusually productive so that I could get to more things on my list than I otherwise would. I had been tediously snipping off strands of ornamental grass with the clippers for only five minutes when our neighbor approached from across the street with an inspired offer. "You know, I've got an electric hedge trimmer that might work a little better. Would you like to borrow it?"

We gladly accepted the offer and were almost embarrassed to see that we could cut through an entire clump in seconds. At the outset of the day, it had been difficult to imagine cutting down the clumps any more quickly than my wife had. But when the Lord answered my prayer through our neighbor, I had to laugh about the fact that we hadn't even thought of looking to borrow such a tool sooner.

When we exercise faith, we may discover that one way the Lord amplifies our efforts is by inspiring us to, in the words of Elder Ballard, "be innovative. As we work to magnify our callings, we should seek the inspiration of the Spirit to solve problems in ways that will best help the people we serve." When we do this, noted Elder Ballard, rather than expanding our efforts we tend to simplify them.[17] Spiritually speaking, we may be tackling some problems with clippers when electric hedge trimmers are available if we will only seek the Lord's help.

Have done with lesser things. A very good friend of mine, Mark Beecher, does a version of the rocks and sand object lesson with an important twist. In its usual form, this object lesson consists of trying to fill a jar first with sand, then small rocks, and finally with large rocks, some of which will not fit. The exercise is then repeated in reverse order, and students learn that there's room for everything in our lives as long as we put in the big rocks first. My friend then modifies the object lesson by providing too much sand and too many rocks, so that even when he places the largest objects in the jar first, there's still not quite enough room in the jar for everything. God can magnify our efforts and amplify our productivity, as Elder Eyring noted, but such blessings may require us first to leave some of our favorite leisure activities out of our jars altogether.

One way to serve our Creator more, then, is to indulge ourselves less. "Rise up, O men of God! Have done with lesser things," urges the hymn.[18] Some activities may be unworthy of us altogether, while others—including many of my favorite recreational activities such as basketball and golf—are not inherently evil. Yet if I have enough time in my week to play golf regularly but not to attend the temple, I may need to choose different priorities.

Developing the Discipline to Slow Down and Cut Back

A few remarkable Church members have mastered all such suggestions and moved beyond diligence to imbalanced overzealousness. While Sprinters' intentions are noble, they could benefit from developing a different kind of discipline—the discipline to slow down and cut back. Here are four suggestions to help spiritual Sprinters guard against the kind of imbalance against which Elder Ballard warned.

> *One way to serve our Creator more is to indulge ourselves less.*

Set limits and say no. Unless I set limits, any task I enjoy or consider important can easily consume me. That's why in my professional career I have almost always had to choose a time to go home—bus schedules helped force such decisions when I worked in Seattle—and then go home, even though my work was unfinished.[19] In a demanding calling or job (including the world's most demanding job, being a parent), one's work is never finished at the end of the day. In a world where there is always more to do, we must make conscious decisions to control our work or our work will soon control us.

Similarly, a good bishopric or presidency usually enjoys each other's company and has an almost endless supply of subjects they could discuss. Consequently, without setting some kind of limit, weekly meetings can extend to several hours. Perhaps such lengthy meetings are necessary on special occasions, but multi-hour meetings on a weekly basis may cut into more important things each presidency or bishopric member could be doing—whether ministering individually to ward members or spending more time with their families. Consequently, some bishoprics and presidencies meet at a time when subsequent meetings or obligations impose a fixed ending time that will facilitate efficiency. Then when special needs arise and too many matters are left unresolved, they schedule an extra meeting.

Conscientious and dedicated gospel teachers are also capable of spending an almost infinite amount of time preparing their lessons for Sunday. Yet eventually, we must all ask ourselves whether we have reached the point of diminishing returns in our preparations. Surely there comes a time in every Gospel Doctrine teacher's lesson preparation where, instead of further researching the scripture passage at hand, the Lord would prefer we spend time applying what we've learned in our families, wards, and communities.

Too often when we overcommit ourselves, the obligation that suffers most is the one for which there is no report: our families.

A friend whose father taught religion for a living told me this painful story from his childhood. Eager to get to the father-and-son campout, he called his father at work repeatedly throughout the afternoon and evening to find out when his dad would be coming home. After a series of broken promises—undoubtedly caused by the engaging work of writing about or researching some doctrinal subject—the religion professor finally came home and took his son to the campout, where they pitched their tent in the dark.

Even as I write this book, I have to continually ask myself, my wife, my children, and the Lord whether I am striking the right balance in life. Should I work on another chapter or help with the dishes or play a game with my children? I don't know whether I always get it right, but I am confident that I strike a better balance when I at least ask whether I need to stop writing so that I can do something more important.

Finally, and perhaps most obviously, most Sprinters need to learn to say no more often. When worthy tasks and opportunities parade before us, many of us struggle to turn down the opportunity to help. This is especially true when people ask us directly to give another fireside, serve on another committee in the community, or prepare another casserole for a family in need. If we have time and means to help, we should, often at the expense of leisure activities. But once our plates become full, most Sprinters need to engage in zero-sum time management: no new optional commitments should be added until some existing obligations are completed.

Perhaps the primary reason to develop such discipline is that too often when we overcommit ourselves, the obligation that suffers most is the one for which there is no report: our families. Elder Neal A. Maxwell noted: "Even consecrated and devoted Brigham Young was once told by the Lord, 'Take especial care of your family' (D&C 126:3). Sometimes, it is the most conscientious who need this message the most!"[20] Our ability to say yes to doing the best things in life often requires us to say no to other good requests. "We have to forego some good things," Elder Dallin H. Oaks taught, "in order to choose others that are better or best because they develop faith in the Lord Jesus Christ and strengthen our families."[21]

Sharing the load. As an attorney, my primary objective was to get work done myself. When I became a vice-president at the company where I had been an attorney for several years, I apparently employed this same lawyerly approach to my new job. I worked closely with some experienced business consultants on a challenging project we were overseeing, and I had instructed them to tell me what I needed to hear, not what I wanted to hear. One day, one of the consulting partners took me up on my offer. He sat me down and provided me with a leadership lesson that would be invaluable not only during my short stint as an executive, but in my Church callings as well.

"Rob, as a lawyer, you spent most of your energy getting things done yourself," he explained, as nearly as I can recall. "You're still doing that here, but as an executive, you need to spend most of your energy helping others get things done." As he elaborated on this concept, the partner almost surely used the word *leverage,* because consultants always do. But in this context it made perfect sense. Instead of just doing things myself, I needed to leverage my abilities by helping the directors and managers who worked for me so that they and their teams could work more productively. If I succeeded, we would accomplish much more than if I tried to do everything myself.

With hindsight, I realize that I probably made the same mistake as a missionary that I did as a new executive. I was so busy trying to find new investigators myself (through techniques that were only marginally effective) that I didn't spend nearly enough time and energy trying to enlist and inspire members in the cause.

I recently helped a ward member and friend move and watched a good elders quorum president put this principle into action. He was plenty willing to work himself—he was the second one on the scene and one of the last to leave. But shortly after he arrived and saw that none of the others who had committed to come had shown up yet, he took a ten-minute break to make some calls on his cell phone. Those ten minutes of calls saved us several hours of labor, because soon several more brethren showed up to help. Watching him in action, it occurred to me that the best thing an elders quorum president can do is not so much to move stuff himself, but to inspire and invite the larger group of elders to move things—not just physically, but spiritually.

The bottom line is that we can simultaneously lighten our load and increase our effectiveness by sharing opportunities with others. As Elder Ballard explained:

> There is a difference between being responsible for getting the work done and doing the work yourself. For example, gone should be the days when the elders quorum president feels he needs to personally finish the home teaching visits that others have missed. . . . Counsel, advise, persuade, motivate—but don't do the work for them. Allow others to progress and grow, even if it means sometimes getting less-than-perfect results on the reports.[22]

When we adopt this approach, we may find that we have some initial investments to make as we train and inspire others to share the load. At first, it may even take longer to get some things done. And we may also have to adjust to the idea (as I did as an executive and as a Church leader) that others sometimes approach things in a different way than we would have. But when we do more in our callings and families to share responsibilities and opportunities to serve, we will find that the promise Jethro made to Moses applies to us. After encouraging his overworked son-in-law to appoint other judges to hear many of the matters Moses was handling himself, Jethro predicted, "so shall it be easier for thyself, and they shall bear the burden with thee" (Exodus 18:22).

The Savior Himself exemplified this wise leadership trait. Noted Elder Joseph B. Wirthlin: "We are all aware of leaders who have sought to be so omni-competent that they try to do everything themselves, which produces little growth in others. Jesus trusted his followers enough to share his work—even his very glory—with them so that they could grow."[23]

Being content with the best we can do. Some of the best counsel I ever received as a bishop was to master the art of selective neglect. Whenever I felt bogged down and frustrated by the fact that it

seemed mathematically impossible to do all the things I was supposed to do, I took comfort in remembering that it probably was
impossible. Somehow this was a liberating realization. Rather than
feeling resentful about the fact that I wasn't able to complete all the
things a bishop ought to do ideally, I was better able to focus my
efforts on accomplishing the things that were most important.

Elder Ballard acknowledged that none of us will ever complete
all that we'd like to do:

> I would like to let you in on a little secret. Some of you
> have already learned it. If you haven't, it's time you knew.
> No matter what your family needs
> are or your responsibilities in the
> Church, there is no such thing as
> "done." There will always be more
> we can do. There is always another
> family matter that needs attention,
> another lesson to prepare, another
> interview to conduct, another meet-
> ing to attend. We just need to be
> wise in protecting our health and in
> following the counsel that President
> Hinckley has given often to just do
> the best we can.
>
> The key, it seems to me, is to
> know and understand your own
> capabilities and limitations and
> then to pace yourself, allocating and
> prioritizing your time, your attention, and your resources
> to wisely help others, including your family, in their quest
> for eternal life.[24]

Perfectly decorated Young Women's activities, perfectly weeded yards, and perfectly worded talks may come at the expense of other tasks the Lord would have had us perform instead.

Coming to this realization can be especially challenging for
Sprinters and Rigid Planners who are perfectionists. While we need

to keep our aims high, we must realize that perfectly decorated Young Women's activities, perfectly weeded yards, and perfectly worded talks may come at the expense of other tasks the Lord would have had us perform instead.

I faced precisely this challenge in a secular setting several years ago when my company's manager of public policy quit at a critical time. At my boss's request, I temporarily took on the responsibilities of that position while continuing to fulfill my own already demanding legal duties. When it quickly became apparent that I was unable to produce *A* quality work for both jobs, I became frustrated. (I should note that my perfectionist tendencies are limited to a fairly narrow field of endeavors; my wife undoubtedly wishes I had higher standards for myself when it comes to tidiness in the home, among other things.) Eventually I decided that although it wasn't ideal, the best approach under the circumstances was to temporarily do more *B* quality work to enable me to get both jobs done. I let my boss know what I was doing, and he approved completely. Producing work that was a lower quality than I normally created ran contrary to my instincts and training, but it was the only way I could do all that needed to be done. Thus, just as many Saunterers may need to raise their standards to accomplish all that the Lord desires them to accomplish, a perfectionist Sprinter may need to be willing to polish his Mother's Day talk less so he can spend more time making breakfast for his wife.

Selectively saunter. Our lives often fall into certain rhythms, and these rhythms have their own inertia. Consequently, I sometimes find myself in perpetual hurry-up mode, even when the circumstances no longer require it. For example, when my travel at work and responsibilities as a bishop left little time for dinner, I got in the habit of eating my meals very quickly. One evening when I was eating in this mode, my wife politely asked, "Are you in a hurry, honey? Do you have a meeting tonight?" I did not, and she knew it, but I had forgotten. She was gently reminding me that I could afford to slow down and probably should.

On another occasion, my wife, Dianne, exercised what one friend of mine has called the "rhetorical priesthood" by reminding me to change rhythms as we began a vacation together as a couple. As I rushed toward the closing doors of an elevator in our hotel, Dianne again asked, "Are you in a hurry?" Realizing the foolishness of scurrying to get to the beach, I adopted a new mantra for the week: *saunter.* Any time we were tempted to adopt our usual harried pace, we repeated the mantra to ourselves and each other in soothing tones, only half jokingly, "Saunter, saunter, saunter."

As our collective responsibilities help us pack productivity into every minute of the day, some Sprinters may need to make conscious efforts in our lives to selectively saunter. For example, missionaries who walk faster will meet more people, which is good. But, once in a home, if they are unable to shift gears and slow down enough to fully focus on the needs of those they meet, their quickened pace will be to no avail. Similarly, the busy parents who scramble all day long to get things done at work, around the house, and in their callings will fail miserably as parents if their children feel like they are simply another task on a long list of things to do. Indeed, when it comes to the most important things in life, President Spencer W. Kimball taught that "we will move faster if we hurry less."[25]

In sum, while the balance between Sprinting and Sauntering may be difficult to strike, it would be a mistake not to prayerfully pursue it. As George Durrant put it: "Somewhere between the two extremes of being too busy and not doing anything is that glorious, yet elusive, condition called *balance.* It's by approaching the many aspects of our life with a sense of balance that we can be champions in life's great decathlon."[26]

Notes

1. Neal A. Maxwell, *Wherefore Ye Must Press Forward* (Salt Lake City: Deseret Book, 1977), 73.

2. David A. Bednar, "Steadfast and Immovable, Always Abounding in Good Works," *New Era,* Jan. 2008, 5.

3. Bednar, "Steadfast and Immovable," 5.

4. M. Russell Ballard, "O Be Wise," *Ensign,* Nov. 2006, 18.

5. Ezra Taft Benson, "A Mighty Change of Heart," Oct. 1989, 5.

6. Bednar, "Steadfast and Immovable," 5.

7. M. Russell Ballard, "Keeping Life's Demands in Balance," *Ensign,* May 1987, 13.

8. David A. Bednar, "The Tender Mercies of the Lord," May 2005, 101–2.

9. This dictionary is available online at www.cbtministries.org/resources/webster1828.htm.

10. Dallin H. Oaks, "Why Do We Serve?" *Ensign,* Nov. 1984, 14–15.

11. Dallin H. Oaks, "Sharing the Gospel," *Ensign,* Nov. 2001, 8.

12. Oaks, "Sharing the Gospel," 8.

13. *Teachings of Presidents of the Church: Wilford Woodruff* (Salt Lake City: The Church of Jesus Christ of Latter-day Saints, 2004), 176.

14. Boyd K. Packer, "Washed Clean," *Ensign,* May 1997, 9; see also Boyd K. Packer, "'The Standard of Truth Has Been Erected,'" *Ensign,* Nov. 2003, 24; Dallin H. Oaks, "Gospel Teaching," *Ensign,* Nov. 1999, 78; Boyd K. Packer, "Do Not Fear," *Ensign,* May 2004, 79; Boyd K. Packer, "Little Children," *Ensign,* Nov. 1986, 16.

15. Henry B. Eyring, "Education for Real Life," *CES Fireside for Young Adults,* Moscow, Idaho, May 6, 2001.

16. Eyring, "Education for Real Life."

17. Ballard, "O Be Wise," 18–19.

18. "Rise Up, O Men of God," *Hymns of The Church of Jesus Christ of Latter-day Saints* (Salt Lake City: The Church of Jesus Christ of Latter-day Saints, 1985), no. 324.

19. I am indebted to Dr. Stan Taylor, a mentor and friend, for this life tip.

20. Maxwell, "'Take Especial Care of Your Family,'" *Ensign,* May 1994, 90.

21. Dallin H. Oaks, "Good, Better, Best," *Ensign,* Nov. 2007, 107.

22. Ballard, "O Be Wise," 19.

23. Joseph B. Wirthlin, "Guided by His Exemplary Life," *Ensign*, Sept. 1995, 36.

24. Ballard, "O Be Wise," 19.

25. Spencer W. Kimball, "Let Us Move Forward and Upward," *Ensign*, May 1979, 83. I am indebted to my friend John Thomas for bringing this quote to my attention in his own masterful discourse on this subject, "Don't Be in a Hurry," BYU–Idaho devotional address, Nov. 6, 2007, www.byui.edu/Presentations/Transcripts/Devotionals/2007_11_06_Thomas.htm.

26. George D. Durrant, "Doing Genealogy: Finding That Glorious, Elusive Condition Called 'Balance,'" *Ensign*, Apr. 1985, 18; emphasis in original.

CHAPTER 5

UNDERACHIEVERS AND OVERACHIEVERS

I've often heard a story along the following lines[1] to demonstrate the need for dedication and sacrifice in achieving excellence.

After a concert, a woman gushed to the featured violinist, "I'd give my life to play the violin like that."

The violinist's reply was something of a pithy rebuke: "Madam, I have."

For me, this anecdote raises a fascinating question: Is it a boast or a confession to claim to have given our all or our lives to anything other than the gospel of Jesus Christ? How are we to balance our efforts to excel professionally, athletically, and artistically with the Lord's injunction that we place Him first in all that we do? At what point on the road to secular success, if any, does the Lord's pleasure in our faithful stewardship become disappointment in our obsession?

UNDERACHIEVERS

Preparing to Provide

At a minimum, it's clear that God expects us to be able to provide for our families responsibly. In a capitalistic society, the rules for doing that are brutally straightforward. If a company can hire and train anyone off the street to perform a job in a short period of time, the company doesn't have to pay workers much to do the job. If workers get frustrated and quit, the company can always hire someone else to replace them. On the other hand, the fewer people who have the necessary skills for a position, the more an employer is willing to pay laborers to fill the position. Consequently, most positions that provide an income sufficient to support an entire family require significant education or specialized training. This is especially true in our current economy, in which two-income families are becoming the norm. Obtaining a job that will support a family on a single income requires considerable education, training, or talent.

So now, more than ever, men and women who approach education and work lackadaisically threaten their ability to provide for their families. President Gordon B. Hinckley consistently counseled the youth of the Church: "It is so important that you young men and you young women get all of the education that you can. . . . Education is the key which will unlock the door of opportunity for you."[2]

"The world will largely pay you what it thinks you are worth."[3]

Women and Education

This counsel to prepare to provide is not limited to men. It is true, as the proclamation on the family indicates, that "by divine design, fathers . . . are responsible to provide the necessities of life and protection for their families" while "mothers are primarily responsible for the nurture of their children."[4] Unfortunately, some of our young women who are admirably committed to this ideal feel no need to pursue educational opportunities or prepare in earnest for careers. They assume that they will marry husbands who will provide for them while they nurture the children. But President Hinckley specifically encouraged the young women of the Church to "get all of the education that you possibly can. Life has become so complex and competitive."[5]

President Thomas S. Monson explained why such preparation

makes sense for a young woman, even if she plans to become a full-time mother: "We do live in turbulent times. Often the future is unknown; therefore, it behooves us to prepare for uncertainties. Statistics reveal that at some time, for a variety of reasons, you may find yourself in the role of financial provider. I urge you to pursue your education and learn marketable skills so that, should such a situation arise, you are prepared to provide."[6]

Pursuing Excellence

It is not enough merely to be able to provide for our families. The Lord and His servants have made it clear that we are to cultivate our talents and abilities in the pursuit of excellence. As president of Brigham Young University, Dallin H. Oaks wrote: "Strive for excellence, use the talents that the Lord has given you, meet and master the learning of men."[7] In a stirring address to BYU students and faculty, President Spencer W. Kimball voiced his hope and expectation that BYU would foster "brilliant stars in drama, literature, music, art, science, and all the scholarly graces."[8]

> *If our hearts become set on attaining praise and preeminence at all costs, we will find ample opportunities to sell our souls.*

In sum, whether we wish to develop musical, athletic, professional, or spiritual abilities, more than haphazard interest and effort is necessary. We must steadily strive for excellence.

OVERACHIEVERS

In light of such counsel to achieve, is it really possible to overachieve? Can we ever become too talented, too successful, or too excellent? The answer hinges on what such secular success costs us. The issue is not so much the destination as the price and perils of the journey.

Setting Our Hearts on the Things of the World

The Savior cautioned us that "where your treasure is, there will your heart be also" (Matthew 6:21). Joseph Smith reminded us that what prevents many who are called from being truly chosen is that "their hearts are set so much upon the things of the world, and [they] aspire to the honors of men" (D&C 121:35). If our hearts become set on attaining praise and preeminence at all costs, we will find ample opportunities to sell our souls to reach our worldly goals. Like Balaam, we may well find those willing to "promote [us] unto very great honour" and shower us with riches (see Numbers 22:17–18) if we will but compromise our principles. A promising politician whose heart is absolutely set on obtaining office may do whatever it takes to win—including misrepresenting his opponent's positions and changing his own opportunistically. A woman dead set on becoming an astronaut might choose to postpone or forego having children altogether if they would interfere with her stellar dream. An aspiring executive may choose to fudge numbers and cut other ethical corners to get a promotion.

Saints fixated on secular success at all costs will find the costs can be great, indeed. They may discard honesty, neglect family, violate the Sabbath, betray friends, and abandon the Word of Wisdom because such things inhibit their ability to climb to the top—"only to find," as Elder Boyd K. Packer warned aspiring artists in a 1976 devotional address, "that [their ladder] is leaning against the wrong wall."[9] They discover they have ended up like Balaam, who Elder Bruce R. McConkie notes "lost his soul in the end because he set his heart on the things of this world rather than the riches of eternity."[10]

Yet many good people do climb to the top of their chosen fields without making such sacrifices. How? For disciples who succeed temporally and spiritually, getting to the top can never be the ultimate goal. Grounded and settled followers of Christ who work hard and wisely are usually blessed with some degree of success—sometimes extraordinary success—but they would rather lose an election or a

EXTREMES

promotion or a competition than be untrue. When faced with a choice between sacrificing worldly honor and divine confidence, they will always choose the high road. They understand well the Savior's counsel, "For what shall it profit a man, if he shall gain the whole world, and lose his own soul? Or what shall a man give in exchange for his soul?" (Mark 8:36–37). Surely the Savior contemplated such willingness to lose worldly success as a key to salvation when He taught, "But whosoever shall be willing to lose his life for my sake, and the gospel, the same shall save it" (JST, Mark 8:38).

Saving Time for the Celestial

Is it okay to climb as high as we can as long as we are true to our principles? Surely—as long as we remember those principles obligate us to do many other even more important things than pursuing secular excellence. President Spencer W. Kimball wrote of a man who "was called to a position of service in the Church, but he felt that he couldn't accept because his investments required more attention and more of his time than he could spare for the Lord's work. He left the service of the Lord in search of Mammon, and he is a millionaire today." Sadly, noted President Kimball, "If we insist on spending all our time and resources building up for ourselves a worldly kingdom, that is exactly what we will inherit."[11]

Of course, the decision to take another step up the ladder of worldly success rarely requires us to forgo all spiritual activity. Instead, pursuit of secular success tends to encroach on celestial pursuits only incrementally. As C. S. Lewis has a devil's minion point out in an oft-quoted passage from *The Screwtape Letters,* "It does not matter how small the sins are, provided that their cumulative effect is to edge the man away from the Light and out into the Nothing. . . . Indeed, the safest road to Hell is the gradual one—the gentle slope, soft underfoot, without sudden turnings, without milestones, without signposts."[12] Certainly, Satan's subtle, gradual efforts to lead us astray can involve sins of omission and distraction as well as sins of commission.

Consequently, I find I need to step back from time to time to conduct a personal inventory to see how my secular pursuits are affecting my celestial aims. These words of President Kimball have weighed heavily on my mind at critical junctures in my professional life:

> It is hard to satisfy us. The more we have, the more we want.
>
> Why another farm, another herd of sheep, another bunch of cattle, another ranch? Why another hotel, another cafe, another store, another shop? Why another plant, another office, another service, another business? Why another of anything if one has that already which provides the necessities and reasonable luxuries? Why continue to expand and increase holdings, especially when those increased responsibilities draw one's interests away from proper family and spiritual commitments, and from those things to which the Lord would have us give precedence in our lives? Why must we always be expanding to the point where our interests are divided and our attentions and thoughts are upon the things of the world? Certainly when one's temporal possessions become great, it is very difficult for one to give proper attention to the spiritual things.[13]

STRIKING THE BALANCE

Climbing the Ladder

Like many members of the Church, I often revel in the secular accomplishments of our fellow members, as if their success somehow vindicates my faith. Growing up and seeing the success of such individuals heralded, I assumed that as long as we didn't lie or cheat our way to the top, the Lord wanted us to climb to the greatest heights of secular accomplishment we possibly could. I no longer believe that.

I got my first inkling that worldly success sometimes comes at a great cost just after I graduated from high school. My father taught journalism at a community college, and many of his students went on to have careers in print and broadcast journalism. At that point in my life I had some interest in pursuing a career in broadcast journalism, so I was delighted to get to talk with a veteran broadcast journalist who visited my father's class. Seeing my interest, this former student of my father's invited me to spend a couple of days with him watching him on the job in Portland, Oregon, where he was the weekend anchor for a local network affiliate.

I gladly took him up on his offer. After a day of riding with a reporter, meeting a gubernatorial candidate, and watching the evening news in person, my appetite was more than whetted. But in his home that evening, this good man (who was not a member of the Church) gave me some simple but profound advice. He urged me to think about the impact a career in broadcasting would have on my family. Although he had thought his marriage was just fine, he was shocked when his wife had recently left him. He pointed out that being an anchor wasn't particularly conducive to family life, since anchors were gone in the afternoons and evenings when families tended to be home. (Twenty-five years later, with the proliferation of morning shows, the situation is certainly different.)

What I learned was not that good Latter-day Saints should never become broadcast journalists—in fact, some have—but that the quest for unbridled secular success involves risks that need to be taken very seriously. That awareness has influenced each major career decision I have made. As in other areas, I am not sure that I'm always making the right decisions. But I am confident I make better decisions when I stop to ask what the Lord would have me do rather than pushing ahead to get all the secular success I can without reflecting on the costs.

One juncture stands out in my mind in particular. I was at law school and had already decided to forgo some post–law school opportunities because of the impact they would have on my family life. As sort of a consolation prize, I was seriously considering seeking a position during my third year that would have been both a significant honor and a significant time commitment. The honor could open doors for me throughout my career, I reasoned, and the impact would only be temporary. I dutifully fasted and prayed and received no particular answer—which I took as a green light to pursue my secular goal.

I make better decisions when I stop to ask what the Lord would have me do rather than pushing ahead to get all the secular success I can without reflecting on the costs.

Over the course of the next week, in what amounted to a prolonged audition of sorts, I had the opportunity to perform some of the duties I would have for the following academic year if I got the position. The work was rewarding, interesting, and demanding. I felt I was capable of handling the load, yet as I worked later each evening to finish these new duties and my usual studies, I began to have doubts. Would taking on so many additional responsibilities really be fair to my wife, our little girl, and the baby we would soon welcome into our family? What were my real motives for pursuing the position—improving my ability to provide for my family or simply obtaining the honors of men? My wife feared I was losing my soul, while some (even in the Church) would have thought I was losing my mind not to pursue this position.

I decided to fast and pray a second time. During my second fast, I shared my concerns with a classmate. Although he was not a Latter-day Saint, his advice was profound. He said, in essence, "You've been blessed to climb fairly high up the ladder of success without having to choose between the values you tell me are most important to you and climbing higher. But the time will eventually come when you have to make that decision—when you can't climb any higher without sacrificing your values. Maybe this is the rung." Inspired by his advice, I felt prompted to choose the course of less worldly honor and more rewarding time with my family—and I've never regretted it.

Our circumstances, capacities, and motives all differ, so none of us can ever say that what may be wrong for one person's secular pursuits cannot be right for others. In my own career as a student, for example, I spent far more time studying and working before I was married than afterwards. And if the position I had contemplated had been a research fellowship in which I could have helped discover a cure for cancer or Alzheimer's disease, my decision might well have been different. But whatever the particular circumstances, I have come to see the wisdom in asking my friend's question: Can I climb the next rung of the ladder of success without sacrificing my values?

Getting Up off the Couch

After letting this chapter sit for a while, an interesting irony dawned on me: some (like me) can simultaneously struggle with being Sprinters or Overachievers in some aspects of our lives and Saunterers or Underachievers in others. Earlier in our marriage, I confess that a combination of my wife's domestic diligence, my demanding career, and my time-consuming callings allowed me to get out of doing my share of dishes without feeling guilty. I often dined and dashed to my next obligation.

However, my unhelpful habits have not changed as my circumstances have. As I write this chapter, I am in a better position than at any time in my marriage to prepare Sunday dinners. And without a time-consuming calling occupying me most evenings, there is no reason I shouldn't be doing the dishes more often than my wife. Yet I am so accustomed to sprinting in other areas that I have become far too comfortable sauntering on the home front. So whether I'm taking a break from sprinting at work during the day or now engaged in some evening sprinting with hobbies such as writing books or making movies of the family, I realize that I've become domestically delinquent. In recent weeks I have struggled to repent in this area, setting a goal for the year to be a "full-service" husband and father. In the process, I have been struck by the fact that some of us may simultaneously struggle with overachieving in some aspects of our lives while underachieving in others. In fact, overachieving in one aspect of our lives may even lead directly to underachieving in other areas.

So where do we draw the line? We begin by placing first things first—giving top priority to our families and service to the Lord. And we work hard to be able to support our families well. Recognizing our talents and abilities as a gift from God, we treat them as stewardships—seeking both to magnify them and to use them as our Master directs rather than merely for our own gratification.

Notes

1. Some attribute this story to Fritz Kreisler, an internationally renowned violinist who died in 1962.

2. Gordon B. Hinckley, "Inspirational Thoughts," *Ensign,* June 1999, 4.

3. Gordon B. Hinckley, "Living Worthy of the Girl You Will Someday Marry," *Ensign,* May 1998, 50.

4. "The Family: A Proclamation to the World," *Ensign,* Nov. 1995, 102.

5. Gordon B. Hinckley, "Stay on the High Road," *Ensign,* May 2004, 113.

6. Thomas S. Monson, "If Ye Are Prepared Ye Shall Not Fear," *Ensign,* Nov. 2004, 116.

7. Dallin H. Oaks, "Strive for Excellence," *Ensign,* Dec. 1971, 109.

8. John W. Welch and Don E. Norton, eds., *Educating Zion* (Provo, Utah: BYU Studies, 1996), 77.

9. Boyd K. Packer, "The Arts and the Spirit of the Lord," *Ensign,* Aug. 1976, 61.

10. Bruce R. McConkie, "The Story of a Prophet's Madness," *New Era,* Apr. 1972, 7; citations omitted.

11. Spencer W. Kimball, "The False Gods We Worship," *Ensign,* June 1976, 5, 6.

12. C. S. Lewis, *The Screwtape Letters* (1961), 56; as quoted in James E. Faust, "The Forces That Will Save Us," *Ensign,* Jan. 2007, 7.

13. Spencer W. Kimball, *The Teachings of Spencer W. Kimball,* ed. Edward L. Kimball (Salt Lake City: Bookcraft, 1982), 354–55.

CHAPTER 6

SELF-RIGHTEOUS SAINTS AND ANYTHING-GOES RELATIVISTS

I served my mission in northern Germany in 1983 and 1984—a generation after that nation found itself at the center of one of the worst man-made catastrophes in the history of the world. The men and women born after World War II were appropriately repulsed by the horrors wrought by the Nazis, whose misplaced confidence and Aryan arrogance knew no bounds. Determined not to repeat such sins, these younger Germans became much more open-minded, reflective, and cautious about embracing any kind of dogma. They also became much more tolerant of diverse political and religious viewpoints, cherishing freedoms long venerated in the United States. But by the early 1980s, the mind-set of some Germans had swung beyond tolerance to complete moral relativism. When we asked investigators if they believed Joseph Smith's story, a common response went something like this: "If that works for you, great. All roads lead to Rome."

Of course, the mistake of believing that all religions and philosophies must be equally valid absolutely pales when compared to the sin of slaughtering millions of Jews. Still, the Germans' experience in the twentieth century illustrates how society and individuals can veer between extremes of dangerously misplaced dogmatism and tolerance gone awry. This chapter explores the hazards of both extremes for those striving to be Saints.

SELF-RIGHTEOUS SAINTS

When I was a counselor in a bishopric in a student ward at BYU, a student from outside the United States expressed a desire to speak in sacrament meeting. "I would like to give a talk on how self-righteous those Utah Mormons are," he announced confidently, with no hint of intentional irony.

I reflected for a moment on just how to respond to such a suggestion. Finally, I wondered aloud, "That would be interesting, but how would you do it without sounding self-righteous yourself?" The paradox may have been lost on him, but I learned something: when we pride ourselves on not being self-righteous and criticize others who are (in our eyes), we are committing the very sin we've been decrying. So there is almost no other way for me to begin this chapter than to acknowledge that I write from the position of one who struggles to combat the sin of self-righteousness, not one who has conquered it.

In fact, for all those who strive to keep their standards high in a world that generally doesn't, looking down on others who are less committed is a natural temptation. Richard L. Anderson wisely noted: "Any religious group that values purity and morality must deal with the problem of clannishness."[1] After all, the Savior taught that many people walk the broad path that leads to destruction, while relatively few enter into the narrow way that leads to eternal life (see Matthew 7:13–14). Is it self-righteous for those who strive to walk in God's path to acknowledge they are more righteous than someone who lives without God in this world? What exactly does it mean to be self-righteous?

We can start by noting what should be obvious but perhaps is not: simply because someone is more righteous than I am does not make her self-righteous. I have a friend who is one of the most unassuming, consistently Christlike people I know. At college she had some roommates who must have felt guilty about some of their conduct in comparison to hers, even though she never said or did anything to disapprove of their behavior. Consequently, she was stunned and hurt one day when one of them announced out of the blue, "The problem with you is that you're so self-righteous!" Even as we take the sin of self-righteousness seriously, we must realize that the urge to call others self-righteous sometimes has as much to do with our own guilt as it does with others' sanctimony.

What *does* it mean, then, to be self-righteous? When we suffer from self-righteousness, symptoms often include the following:

- an inflated sense of our own righteousness
- an unduly harsh view of others' unrighteousness
- taking satisfaction—often swelling to smugness—in being more righteous than others

Focusing on each of the elements, in turn, may help us combat self-righteousness.

Avoid Creating an Inflated Sense of Our Own Righteousness

Richard L. Anderson has written that self-righteousness "is a form of egotism that breeds intolerance and impatience. Lack of empathy is its major symptom. Since self-righteousness is an unhealthy inner pride, the cure for it is honest humility."[2]

When discussing this subject with my students, I sometimes provide them with a diverse list of commandments and invite them to candidly assess which commandments they keep the best and the worst. I then ask them to compare how they view others who struggle with the commandment they are the worst at keeping themselves. Personally, I tend to be quite understanding and tolerant of those who fall short in the same areas I do. Conversely, I tend to take a harsher view of those who battle sins I may have overcome (or think I have). By comparing my strengths to others' weaknesses, I create an unrealistically generous view of my own relative righteousness. (We'll discuss the bigger problem with thinking in relative terms later in this chapter.) On the other hand, when I focus on my own weaknesses, I tend to become much less judgmental of others' faults. Aleksandr Solzhenitsyn helps me remember the need for such introspection: "If only there were evil people somewhere insidiously committing evil deeds, and it were necessary only to separate them from the rest of us and destroy them. But the line dividing good and evil cuts through the heart of every human being."[3] Remembering the battles I'm still fighting against evil helps me be less judgmental of others who are waging battles of their own.

Acknowledging our own imperfections can help deflate exaggerated views of righteousness, but what if we are blissfully unaware of our shortcomings? When drawing mental pictures of ourselves in which we look better than we really are, we often base our image disproportionately on how well we keep the most measurable commandments, such as not drinking coffee. (I once asked an adorable little nephew to tell me which commandments were most important. He thought for a moment and then said confidently, "Don't kill. . . . Don't drink coffee. . . .") It's easy to focus on commandments like the Word of Wisdom while forgetting less measurable but even more important commandments such as the two the Savior identifies as the greatest: loving God and loving others (see Matthew 22:36–40).

Keeping the Word of Wisdom is certainly important, but if I am not careful, I find myself using outwardly observable commandments like it and Church attendance as the principal criteria for judging the righteousness of myself and others. We may even find ourselves believing, as some have told me, that any behavior that is truly important can be quantified. Sadly, such a mind-set allows us to think we've done all that is required of us when we achieve 100 percent home teaching. Focusing on the quantifiable, we may feel that we are perfectly obedient in the category of home or visiting teaching, even though we have not yet come close to loving our assigned families as we love ourselves and as Christ loves them.

SELF-RIGHTEOUS SAINTS AND RELATIVISTS

The Pharisees shared that kind of mechanical preference for commandments whose observance was an objective rather than subjective matter. They carefully complied with the letter of the law in paying tithing right down to the herbs in their garden, even as they overlooked what the Savior called the "weightier matters of the law"—judgment, mercy, and faith. "These ought ye to have done," confirmed Jesus of their precise obedience in minor matters, but He reprimanded them as He admonished them "not to leave the other undone." Doing so was the virtual equivalent of removing nasty little bugs from one's drink while not bothering to sift out an animal that is exponentially larger: "Ye blind guides, which strain at a gnat, and swallow a camel" (Matthew 23:23–24).

This kind of skewed perspective led one Christian who traveled abroad to gush over the wonderful qualities he saw in the dynamic leader of a foreign country he had visited. This leader neither smoked nor drank, and he opposed pornography. "It was a great relief to be in a country where salacious sex literature cannot be sold," observed this American delegate to the Baptist World Alliance Congress in 1934, "where putrid motion pictures and gangster films cannot be shown."[4] Unfortunately for him and the rest of the world, his assessment of Adolf Hitler proved to be wildly off the mark.

We may also judge ourselves too generously when placing too much weight on the wrong things. Elder Jeffrey R. Holland warned: "Perhaps sometimes we come to Christ too obliquely, focusing on structure or methods or elements of Church administration. Those are important and, like the tithes of mint and anise and cummin Christ spoke of (see Matt. 23:23), should be observed—but not without attention to the weightier matters of the kingdom."[5] As President James E. Faust reminded us, the gospel is about more than just avoiding evil. It's also about doing good, "most importantly, [doing] the things of greatest worth. We are to focus on the inward things of the heart, which we know and value intuitively but often neglect. . . . This higher gospel requires that we look inward to our own souls, for we cannot deceive the Lord."[6]

Those who engage in such introspective exercises aren't terribly tempted to trumpet their own perceived righteousness, as did the Zoramites, or to go "about to establish their own righteousness" (Romans 10:3). Instead, like Alma, they are moved to pray, "O Lord, forgive my unworthiness" (Alma 38:14). Ironically, it is those who freely admit their own unworthiness—like Alma, the brother of Jared, and the penitent publican—who are justified in the eyes of heaven, rather than the Zoramites and Pharisees who pray, "God, I thank thee, that I am not as other men are" (Luke 18:11–14). Moreover, because they are not blinded by the need to justify themselves, publicans and prophets are more likely to "see as they are seen, and know as they are known, having received of his fulness and of his grace" (D&C 76:94)—a characteristic of all celestial citizens.

> *The sanctimonious corollary to seeing only the best in ourselves is seeing only the worst in others.*

Such an accurate image of ourselves leads not to self-loathing but simultaneously to humility and self-confidence. Moses, who was "very meek, above all the men which were upon the face of the earth" (Numbers 12:3), realized after one of his encounters with God that relatively speaking, "man is nothing, which thing I never had supposed" (Moses 1:10). Yet when Satan himself appeared on the scene to tempt Moses, the prophet declared with confidence, "Who art thou? For behold, I am a son of God, in the similitude of his Only Begotten" (Moses 1:13). Those who see themselves accurately approach God's throne and live life like the brother of Jared—in humility and in faith (see Ether 3:2).

Seeing the Best in Others

The sanctimonious corollary to seeing only the best in ourselves is seeing only the worst in others. It's easy enough to do; indeed, it's our natural instinct to do so. "However, true religion is not looking primarily for weaknesses, faults, and errors," taught President Faust. "It is the spirit of strengthening and overlooking faults even as we would wish our own faults to be overlooked. When we focus our entire attention on what may be wrong rather than what is right, we miss the sublime beauty and essence of the sweet gospel of the Master."[7]

I made this mistake personally as a young man when I noticed racist tendencies in a loved one. Having been raised watching Sesame Street and living in multiethnic areas, I understood that racism was terribly wrong. Unfortunately, I didn't stop to consider the vastly different circumstances under which this loved one had been raised. Worse yet, I fear I let my awareness of this particular sin obscure my view of much of the extraordinary goodness in this relative. Years later I read this humble plea from Moroni, and it pricked me like a voice from the dust: "Condemn me not because of mine imperfection . . . ; but rather give thanks unto God that he hath made manifest unto you our imperfections, that ye may learn to be more wise than we have been" (Mormon 9:31).

Whether it is racism, profanity, alcoholism, or any other sin, we err when we condemn others wholesale because of individual sins. I think of a student I taught in institute and at BYU–Idaho. A relatively recent convert, he still struggled with occasional swearing, but he had made extraordinary progress in his life. Yet his roommates, who had come from active Latter-day Saint families, were so troubled by his profane lapses that they treated him (he felt, anyway) as if he were a heathen. "If only they realized how far I've come," he confided.

Joseph Smith was able to see past such flaws and into the goodness of a man's heart. "I love that man better who swears a stream as long as my arm yet deals justice to his neighbors and mercifully deals his substance to the poor, than the long, smooth-faced hypocrite."[8] On another occasion he taught: "Don't be limited in your views with regard to your neighbor's virtue, but beware of self-righteousness, and be limited in the estimate of your own virtues, and not think yourselves more righteous than others; you must enlarge your souls towards each other, if you would do like Jesus, and carry your fellow-creatures to Abraham's bosom."[9]

How do we manage to see the best in others when their flaws are so easy to notice? Elder Stephen L Richards offered this profound insight into how such Christian vision is possible. Speaking of the gift of discernment, he taught: "The highest type of discernment is that which perceives in others and uncovers for them their better natures, the good inherent within them. . . . I never ordain a bishop or set apart a president of a stake without invoking upon him this divine blessing, that he may read the lives and hearts of his people and call forth the best within them."[10]

The ability to uncover and call forth the good inherent within others is a spiritual gift indeed. Surely this gift to love as Christ loves is available to those who "pray unto the Father with all the energy of heart, that ye may be filled with this love, which he hath bestowed upon all who are true followers of his son, Jesus Christ" (Moroni 7:48).

Stop Using the Curve

What if we manage to see ourselves and others absolutely clearly? Is it then wrong for someone who truly is more righteous than others in obedience to a particular commandment to be aware of that fact? The Savior Himself taught that "except your righteousness shall exceed the righteousness of the scribes and Pharisees, ye shall in no case enter into the kingdom of heaven" (Matthew 5:20). If the Savior can make the comparison, can't we?

The problem for those who are truly more righteous than others—and the Savior's teachings makes it clear that some are—is not necessarily in being aware of the gap in righteousness but in focusing on it and taking satisfaction in it. Unlike the Pharisees, who not only mistakenly "trusted in themselves that they were righteous" but also "despised others" (Luke 18:9), the truly righteous are not pleased when they look across from the strait and narrow path to see the masses partying on the road that leads to destruction. To the contrary, like Lehi, real Saints are deeply troubled over the potential fate of those who stray. Nor does the disobedience of others somehow bolster their own hopes for salvation; they realize, in the words of Elder Jeffrey R. Holland, that "the race is against sin, *not* against each other."[11]

President Ezra Taft Benson reminded us about the problem with measuring ourselves in comparison to others by quoting C. S. Lewis: "Pride gets no pleasure out of having something, only out of having more of it than the next man. . . . It is the comparison that makes you proud: the pleasure of being above the rest. Once the element of competition has gone, pride has gone."[12] The Zoramites made the mistake not only of vastly overestimating their own righteousness, but in rejoicing over what they assumed was their superior spiritual position. "Thou hast elected us that we shall be saved, whilst all around us are elected to be cast by thy wrath down to hell," they prayed, apparently with straight faces, with this extraordinary kicker: "for the which holiness, O God, we thank thee" (Alma 31:17). For the Zoramites, apparently, there was nothing quite like the prospect of everyone else going to hell to make them feel good about themselves. By contrast, God's prophets pray with all their hearts in behalf of those who truly are in spiritual danger (see, for example, 1 Nephi 1:5).

ANYTHING-GOES RELATIVISTS

Sadly, some who have been exposed to self-righteous Church members are so determined not to repeat sins of spiritual smugness that they swing to the opposite extreme. Rather than judge others too harshly, they adopt a standard that virtually eliminates judgment altogether, for others and for themselves. We live in "a society in which, instead of a rush to judgment," noted Elder Neal A. Maxwell, "there is almost a rush to mercy, because people are so anxious to be nonjudgmental."[13] Rather than make the mistake of being overly confident in erroneously held religious views, they make the mistake of questioning the faith of anyone who confidently holds religious views of any kind. The result is often a rather dogmatic insistence that people should not be too dogmatic, with judgment being reserved only for those who dare judge any conduct as inappropriate. In effect, such individuals "call evil good, and good evil" (Isaiah 5:20).

It's hard to go wrong if you believe everything you do is right.

The Lord must have had such revisionist theology in mind when, in His preface to the Doctrine and Covenants, He expressly condemned those in our day who walk in their own ways and according to the rules of a god of their own creation, typically "in the likeness of the world" (D&C 1:16). Elder Maxwell called such a life philosophy "everyman ethical relativism—and we are swamped by it in our time."[14]

Terrance Olson defined relativism as "the false idea that all moral stands are equally valuable, and it is prejudicial to assume one way is better than some other way. . . . The result is that morality becomes relative to one's personal, possibly unique, understanding."[15] Such an accepting, nonjudgmental approach to life definitely avoids the excesses of self-righteousness, but it also leaves us rudderless as we try to navigate the tempestuous seas of popular opinion.

Of course, the short-term appeal of Anything-Goes Relativism is obvious. Aldous Huxley once candidly acknowledged the carnal conflict of interest that plagues many of those tempted to walk without God in this world:

> I had motives for not wanting the world to have a meaning; and consequently assumed that it had none, and was able without any difficulty to find satisfying reasons for this assumption. . . .
>
> The philosopher who finds no meaning in the world

is not concerned exclusively with a problem in pure meta-physics. He is also concerned to prove that there is no valid reason why he personally should not do as he wants to do. . . .

For myself, as no doubt for most of my friends, the philosophy of meaninglessness was essentially an instru-ment of liberation from a certain system of morality. We objected to the morality because it interfered with our sexual freedom.[16]

Those who wish to serve "the creature more than the Creator" (Romans 1:25) will always have an incentive to doubt God and His commandments.

Others try to have it both ways by embracing a God who requires no sacrifices. As a missionary I once spoke with some adher-ents of a small religious movement led by a sort of New Age sage. If I understood their German correctly, these disciples' master taught them that the only sin was in trying to change themselves.

The Lamanites' religion at the time of Ammon included a simi-larly accommodating approach. "Notwithstanding they believed in a Great Spirit, they supposed that whatsoever they did was right" (Alma 18:5). Korihor preached an even more assertive and atheistic refrain on the same theme, arguing that "whatsoever a man did was no crime" (Alma 30:17). It's hard to go wrong if you believe every-thing you do is right.

While members of the Church are not likely to fall for such extreme forms of relativism, we may be more susceptible to subtler shades of the philosophy. Chauncey Riddle described some of these milder flavors, beginning with the argument that we should enjoy "the Church social organization without getting uptight about the-ology or religious commandments. Another kind of relativism says that the commandments are great but open to broad private inter-pretation. A third acknowledges that there are commandments, but allows indulgence in sin since 'nobody's perfect.'"[17]

I sensed a current of such relativism in an English class when I was in college, where I learned that the cardinal sin of literature was "didacticism," which amounted to a preachy oversimplification of the world that made it look black and white. According to my professor, good literature showed that people were not always what they seemed and life was more complicated than moralists believe. While I'm no fan of two-dimensional characters or simplistic thinking myself, I could not help but notice that many of the authors the professor preferred seemed to have distinct agendas of their own. They took great pains to show that the world was mostly full of shades of gray, with few things, if any, that were clearly right or wrong. The critics and my professor didn't seem to have much problem with literary pontificating of this sort, as long as the message was suitably relativist.

A few in the Church follow this literary trend. Pointing out changes in Church policy over the years, they call into question current policies that trouble them. Bristling at absolute statements about the conflict between good and evil, they delight in discovering exceptions to what appear to be straightforward commandments. Others comb through Church history looking for prophetic idiosyncrasies and institutional quirks, apparently in hopes of reducing the Church and its leaders to little more than a man-made organization led by well-meaning but flawed individuals. Such members often end up viewing the Church's teachings not as divine directives but as cultural traditions with varying degrees of usefulness.

Bishop Glenn L. Pace warned powerfully against engaging in such intellectual gymnastics:

> While it would seem the search for and discovery of truth should be the goal of all Latter-day Saints, it appears some get more satisfaction from trying to discover new uncertainties. I have friends who have literally spent their lives, thus far, trying to nail down every single intellectual loose end rather than accepting the witness of the Spirit

and getting on with it. In so doing, they are depriving themselves of a gold mine of beautiful truths which cannot be tapped by the mind alone. . . .

Inappropriate intellectualism sometimes leads one to testify that he knows the *gospel* is true but believes the *Brethren* are just a little out of touch. . . . A prophet doesn't take a poll to see which way the wind of public opinion is blowing. He reveals the will of the Lord to us.[18]

STRIKING THE BALANCE

While both relativism and self-righteousness are dangerous extremes, for those diligently striving to obey God's commandments, slipping toward sanctimony is often the greater temptation. In fact, although he never devoted a full talk to the subject, President Gordon B. Hinckley frequently addressed the dangers of self-righteousness. His comments in the April 1999 general conference are typical: "We can all be a little kinder, a little more generous, a little more thoughtful of one another. We can be a little more tolerant and friendly to those not of our faith, going out of our way to show our respect for them. We cannot afford to be arrogant or self-righteous. It is our obligation to reach out in helpfulness, not only to our own but to all others as well. Their interest in and respect for this Church will increase as we do so."[19]

One of President Hinckley's concerns in warning against spiritual arrogance seems to be that whether we are sharing the gospel or trying to help straying members return, we will be more effective if we are not smug. In noting how ancient Israel sometimes rested on its genetic laurels, S. Michael Wilcox observed that "a self-righteous attitude of superiority will also prevent Abraham's modern seed from fulfilling our covenant responsibility. We are to radiate to the world a spirit of love in order to bring others to the truths of the gospel.

Sometimes, if we are not careful, our neighbors and friends who are not of the Church may think we are aloof or feel superior."[20]

While the self-righteousness of the Pharisees undoubtedly hindered any efforts they made to lead others unto God, the humility and empathy of the Savior paved the way for the return of publicans and prodigals. When summarizing His mortal ministry, the One who will ultimately be our Judge carefully separated the roles of saving and judging: "I came not to judge the world, but to save the world" (John 12:47). Similarly, Christ explained that His Father "sent not his Son into the world to condemn the world; but that the world through him might be saved" (John 3:17). For Jesus, final judgment would come later, so as not to interfere with His primary mission of saving.

We, too, are to set aside final judgment so that it does not undermine our efforts to help save others. By and large, our task is simplified because we can cast the burden of judging at the Savior's feet, leaving that terrible task to the One who is uniquely qualified to perform it.

Although I know this principle is true, I sometimes struggle to implement it. One way to change how we think of others, suggested Elder Dallin H. Oaks, is to remember that "whenever possible we should refrain from judging people until we have an adequate knowledge of the facts."[21] My wife and I were taught this principle vividly one Sunday afternoon early in our marriage when we had dressed our only daughter at the time in a beautiful, brand-new dress. Danielle looked adorable in the outfit and behaved sweetly most of the day. However, on a few occasions for no apparent reason whatsoever, our otherwise well-behaved daughter began to scream. Not yet old enough to talk, Danielle had a well-developed set of lungs that would later help her earn a vocal scholarship to BYU–Idaho.

Her screams wore on our nerves, and I became frustrated with her, reasoning that she was perfectly capable of not screaming, as demonstrated by the fact that most of the day she hadn't screamed at all. Finally, as we changed Danielle out of her dress at the end of the day, we discovered the reason for her annoying behavior. In unpacking the new dress, we had somehow overlooked a couple of straight pins, tucked away on the inside. Every time we picked her up or gave her a hug, we had been unwittingly driving the pins into her body. The very conduct that seemed like it should have been creating joy for our daughter was creating pain instead.

Elder Marvin J. Ashton taught, "If we could look into each other's hearts and understand the unique challenges each of us face, I think we would treat each other much more gently, with more love, patience, tolerance, and care."[22] When I see faults or annoying behavior in others, I now try to remember the pins in Danielle's dress, reminding myself that everyone has hidden challenges. Because I do not know or cannot understand such hidden challenges, I am much better off judging others mercifully or refraining from judging them at all.

In cutting others such slack, I need not condone behavior that God condemns. Instead, I simply remember that I will be judged with the same degree of mercy I extend to others. As Joseph Smith famously taught: "The nearer we get to our Heavenly Father, the more we are disposed to look with compassion on perishing souls . . . to take them upon our shoulders, and cast their sins behind our backs. . . . There should be no license for sin, but mercy should go hand in hand with reproof."[23]

Notes

1. Richard Lloyd Anderson, "Parables of Mercy," *Ensign,* Feb. 1987, 21.

2. Anderson, "Parables of Mercy," 23.

3. Aleksandr I. Solzhenitsyn, *The Gulag Archipelago* (New York: Perennial Classics, 2002), 75. I am indebted to my friend Rosemary Reeve for bringing this quote to my attention.

4. Walter Wink, *Naming the Powers* (Philadelphia: Fortress, 1984), 116; as quoted in Philip Yancey, *What's So Amazing About Grace?* (Grand Rapids, Michigan: Zondervan, 1997), 201.

5. Jeffrey R. Holland, "Come unto Me," *Ensign,* Apr. 1998, 16.

6. James E. Faust, "The Weightier Matters of the Law: Judgment, Mercy, and Faith," *Ensign,* Nov. 1997, 53, 59.

7. Faust, "The Weightier Matters of the Law," 54.

8. Joseph Smith, *History of The Church of Jesus Christ of Latter-day Saints,* 7 vols. (Salt Lake City: The Church of Jesus Christ of Latter-day Saints, 1932–1951), 5:401.

9. Joseph Smith, *Teachings of the Prophet Joseph Smith,* sel. Joseph Fielding Smith (Salt Lake City: Deseret Book, 1979), 228.

10. Stephen L Richards, in Conference Report, Apr. 1950, 162–63.

11. Jeffrey R. Holland, "The Other Prodigal," *Ensign,* May 2002, 64; emphasis in original.

12. C. S. Lewis, *Mere Christianity* (New York: MacMillan, 1952), 109–10; as quoted in Ezra Taft Benson, "Beware of Pride," *Ensign,* May 1989, 4.

13. Neal A. Maxwell, "Jesus, the Perfect Mentor," *Ensign,* Feb. 2001, 12.

14. Neal A. Maxwell, "The Richness of the Restoration," *Ensign,* Mar. 1998, 9.

15. Terrance D. Olson, "Truths of Moral Purity," *Ensign,* Oct. 1998, 45.

16. Aldous Huxley, *Ends and Means* (New York: Harper, 1937), 312–16; as quoted in David P. Johnson, "Some Thoughts on Intelligent Design and Its Relationship to Evolutionary Theory," *Perspective,* 6:2 (Autumn 2006), 102.

17. Chauncey C. Riddle, "Korihor: The Arguments of Apostasy," *Ensign,* Sept. 1977, 20.

18. Glenn L. Pace, "Follow the Prophet," *Ensign,* May 1989, 26.

19. Gordon B. Hinckley, "Thanks to the Lord for His Blessings," *Ensign,* May 1999, 88. Other talks in which he repeated this message include "An Ensign to the Nations, a Light to the World," *Ensign,* Nov. 2003, 82; "Personal Worthiness to Exercise the Priesthood," *Ensign,* May 2002, 52; "Living in the Fulness of Times," *Ensign,* Nov. 2001, 4.

20. S. Michael Wilcox, "The Abrahamic Covenant," *Ensign,* Jan. 1998, 48.

21. Dallin H. Oaks, "'Judge Not' and Judging," *Ensign,* Aug. 1999, 13.

22. Marvin J. Ashton, "The Tongue Can Be a Sharp Sword," *Ensign,* May 1992, 20.

23. *History of the Church,* 5:24.

CHAPTER 7

FOREVER FRIVOLOUS OR JOYLESSLY SOLEMN

"To every thing there is a season," wrote the Preacher. "A time to weep, and a time to laugh; a time to mourn, and a time to dance" (Ecclesiastes 3:1, 4). Unfortunately, some seem stuck in a season of somberness, while others are perpetually frivolous. In fact, some are so sober that they practically squeeze the joy out of life, while others are so light-minded that their attitude threatens to chase the Spirit out of their lives.

FOREVER FRIVOLOUS

In describing his teenage demeanor, Joseph Smith characterized himself both as "guilty of levity" and as having a "native cheery temperament" (Joseph Smith—History 1:28). The reference to levity gets a footnote to that same term in the Topical Guide, where we find a list of references cautioning us against taking serious things too lightly. On the other hand, the reference to having a cheery temperament gets a footnote to *cheerfulness* in the Topical Guide, where we find several scriptures extolling the benefits of having a merry heart. Similarly, the Lord commands us to live "with cheerful hearts and countenances," but "not with much laughter, for this is sin, but with a glad heart and a cheerful countenance" (D&C 59:15). So where is the line between cheerfulness and light-mindedness? Just when does good fun spill over into inappropriate levity? And what is the harm in too much laughter?

Failing to Take the Sacred Seriously

We can start by acknowledging that there are times, places, and subjects that require our reverence. The Lord declared, "Remember that that which cometh from above is sacred, and must be spoken with care, and by constraint of the Spirit" (D&C 63:64). "Sacred matters deserve sacred consideration," noted President Gordon B. Hinckley.[1] At a minimum, this includes temple worship, sacrament meeting in general, and partaking of the sacrament in particular. Everything that occurs in the temples, taught President Hinckley, "is eternal in its consequences. We there deal with matters of immortality, with things of eternity, with things of man and his relationship to his Divine Parent and his Redeemer. Hands must be clean and hearts must be pure and thoughts concerned with the solemnities of eternity when in these sacred premises."[2] President Ezra Taft Benson explained that we cannot reflect on the solemnities of eternity when our "minds are preoccupied with the cares of the world."[3] Whether in the temple, the chapel, or our homes studying the scriptures, engaging in "serious reflection" (Joseph Smith—History 1:8) requires us to take a step back from the world and "have done with lesser things."[4]

Sometimes members of the Church (including myself) enjoy fellowship, friendliness, and laughter so much that we have a hard time establishing reverence even in these sacred settings. "It is in our meetings that the godly traits of good cheer and solemnity meet on a collision course," acknowledged Elder Spencer J. Condie.[5] I am certainly not suggesting that we should never laugh in sacrament meeting, general conference, or the lobby of the temple. But in such settings laughter is more subdued and less frequent, and it certainly is never our principal aim as speakers or our greatest expectation as worshipers.

Robert Millet shared a disappointing story that underscores the dangers of slipping into an entertainment mind-set in sacred settings:

> Several years ago, a young man who addressed our ward in sacrament meeting began by saying, in essence, "Brothers and sisters, it's great to be in your ward today. I am told that the best way to get a congregation with you is to liven them up with a few jokes." He related several humorous stories, including some inappropriate for the occasion. The congregation roared—or at least some of them did. Others wondered what was going on. After fifteen or twenty minutes, the young man looked at his watch and said, "Well, I'd better close now. I say all these things in the name of Jesus Christ, amen."
>
> His address was amusing and entertaining, something that might have been fun under other circumstances. But we were in a sacrament meeting, a sacred worship service. There was something haunting about his closing words, "In the name of Jesus Christ." I had, of course, heard those very words thousands of times over the years. That day, however, I thought of all the times I had delivered talks or offered prayers in the name of Jesus Christ, but had done so without much reflection upon whose name I had taken.[6]

While visiting Kirtland with a group of colleagues from BYU–Idaho, I had the wonderful opportunity to participate in an Amish worship service. As an early spring snow fell outside, we gathered together with about fifty to sixty fellow Christians in a simple, clean room above a stable. With the exception of a few elderly worshipers who sat in chairs, men, women, and children sat on plain, white benches, with the males on one side of the room facing the females on the other. For three hours we sang and listened as two or three leaders took turns expounding (in a mixture of German and English) on the assigned New Testament text for the day. It was a single, continuous meeting. Afterwards as we ate a light meal we socialized for two hours, but not while we worshipped. During those three hours, an extraordinary level of reverence prevailed.

I am certainly not advocating that we adopt the Amish model; reverently fellowshipping with fellow Church members is an important part of our Sunday services. However, when I returned to my home ward the next Sunday, I was taken aback by just how much noisier and how much less reverent the setting was. It helped me better understand why President Boyd K. Packer has pled with us to improve the reverence in our sacrament meetings:

> When we meet to learn the doctrines of the gospel, it should be in a spirit of reverence. . . . Inspiration comes more easily in peaceful settings. . . .
>
> The world grows increasingly noisy. . . . This trend to more noise, more excitement, more contention, less restraint, less dignity, less formality is not coincidental nor innocent nor harmless. . . .
>
> Irreverence suits the purposes of the adversary by obstructing the delicate channels of revelation in both mind and spirit.
>
> Our sacrament and other meetings need renewed attention to assure that they are truly worship services in which members may be spiritually nourished and have their testimonies replenished and in which investigators may feel the inspiration essential to spiritual conversion.
>
> Our meetinghouses are designed so that we may enjoy socials, dancing, drama, even sports. All of these are important. But . . . [w]hen we return for Sunday meetings, the music, dress, and conduct should be appropriate for worship. Foyers are built into our chapels to allow for

the greeting and chatter that are typical of people who love one another. However, when we step into the chapel, we *must!*—each of us *must*—watch ourselves lest we be guilty of intruding when someone is struggling to feel delicate spiritual communications.

. . . Leaders should teach that reverence invites revelation.[7]

President Packer's comment about not intruding when someone is trying to receive revelation resonates with me as a teacher—and pricks me as a worshiper. On many occasions with youth, I have watched how one or two students who simply won't settle down can disrupt the Spirit for the entire class. To combat this when facing a recurring reverence problem, I've occasionally pulled out a *Magic Eye* book and had one of the talkative students look at a picture until he can see the three-dimensional image. Just as it finally comes into focus, I bump the book and the student abruptly loses the image he'd worked so hard to bring into focus. I then ask the students how learning by the Spirit can be like trying to see the three-dimensional image. Among the many parallels that can be drawn is the fact that without realizing it, our behavior may sometimes bump someone else's book as it were—or, in the words of Elder Boyd K. Packer, intrude "when someone is struggling to feel delicate spiritual communications." As an adult, I wonder how many times I've played precisely that role myself as I've conversed with a friend or made smart remarks aimed at getting a laugh when the teacher might have been trying to steer us toward more profound subjects.

Fixated on Fun

A bit of spice can make a good meal great, but too much spice can ruin even the best dinner. In the same way, a dose of well-advised humor can defuse tense situations or bring a lesson to life. President James E. Faust even blessed newborn children with a sense of humor "with the hope that it will help guard them against being too rigid, that they will have balance in their lives, and that situations and problems and difficulties will not be overdrawn."[8]

But if we drench our lives in humor and frivolity, we may miss out on the subtle joys of spiritual moments that require finely tuned hearts. As Elder Glenn L. Pace observed: "Once one has felt the joy of the gospel, there is no going back into a frivolous world. Try as we might, travel where we may, there is an emptiness all the laughter the world has to offer cannot fill. That emptiness can be filled only by placing ourselves in tune with eternal truths and living according to the prescribed laws of God."[9]

> *If we drench our lives in humor and frivolity, we may miss out on the subtle joys of spiritual moments that require finely tuned hearts.*

Seeing the humor in life is not a problem for me; keeping my humor in check is. When I was hired by the Church Educational System, I quickly discovered that I was not alone. Before attending my first daylong in-service meeting with seminary teachers, a colleague warned me that while this was a group of great people, they were a handful as students. "Almost every one of these guys was the class clown," my friend explained. "So when we get together, it's a whole class of class clowns."

He was right. This was a remarkable group of dedicated men who knew their scriptures and cared deeply about the doctrine and their students—an extraordinary peer group. Yet almost to a man these brethren could also be very, very funny. It was one of the most entertaining groups with whom I had interacted. I quickly slipped into the culture of such CES meetings, making a stab at getting an occasional laugh myself.

Yet when we had a longer retreat intended to provide spiritual rejuvenation, I couldn't help but be a bit disappointed. In the corporate world, I had attended several retreats where high-paid consultants had tried to teach us important principles about how to understand and communicate with each other better. These intensive training sessions were often quite productive, but more than once I had found myself thinking how much more rewarding it would be to have a retreat with fellow Latter-day Saints, where we could explore such issues in a gospel framework. With the CES retreats, I thought I might finally get to realize my wish.

The CES retreats were unquestionably more spiritual (and incomparably more economical) in nature than the corporate retreats. Yet they were less spiritually rewarding than I had hoped— and than they could have been. Based on all the evidence, my impression was that these men all taught their seminary and institute students with the Spirit and an appropriate degree of seriousness about sacred things. In Washington and Alaska, though, most of them worked alone and looked forward to area meetings as opportunities to enjoy each other's company. Frankly, making a comment or playing a prank that would make others laugh was probably a higher priority for many of us than was becoming spiritually rejuvenated.

Before one training meeting, our area director observed this phenomenon and gave the group a gentle rebuke. The quality of that meeting improved significantly. Similarly, one of my colleagues in the Religious Education Department at BYU–Idaho had the courage to make a heartfelt plea to the department before some of us traveled to Kirtland, Ohio. Knowing our group's proclivity for humor, he asked that we might create an environment for the Spirit to teach us as we visited the sacred sites where Joseph had received so many revelations. I needed the reminder

Over time, a fixation on frivolous things can become like a plaque that hardens our spiritual arteries.

as much as any of my colleagues, but because of one professor's courageous request, that week in Kirtland proved to be the kind of spiritual retreat of which I had dreamed.

Was any of the humor in my department or CES area meetings inherently inappropriate? No. But it came with an opportunity cost, sometimes robbing us of spiritual experiences we might have had, if we had only been more "spiritually minded" (Romans 8:6). And over time, a fixation on frivolous things can become like a plaque that hardens our spiritual arteries. "If prolonged," wrote C. S. Lewis, "the habit of flippancy builds up around a man the finest armour plating against [God] that I know. . . . It is a thousand miles away from joy; it deadens, instead of sharpening, the intellect."[10]

Late one evening as I struggled to fall asleep, I decided to remove myself to the couch where I could read and watch television. In fact, I'm embarrassed to admit, I did both simultaneously, reading a conference *Ensign* while watching a late-night comedy show. I was reading a talk by President James E. Faust, who quoted a stanza of a William Wordsworth poem that cut me to the core under the circumstances:

> *The world is too much with us; late and soon,*
> *Getting and spending, we lay waste our powers: . . .*
> *We have given our hearts away, a sordid boon! . . .*
> *For this, for everything, we are out of tune.*[11]

How foolish I was to think I could be spiritually in tune while simultaneously keeping the world with me so late. Wordsworth highlights a peculiar problem for our generation, with radio, television, and personal digital players that allow us to be entertained from the moment we get up until the moment we fall asleep—leaving no time for us to "be still, and know that" God is God (Psalm 46:10).

On another occasion I fared a bit better. I was driving through my ward taking care of some business I had as bishop on a Saturday, and I was tempted to turn the radio on and listen to the Mariners' game. Listening to a baseball game on a Saturday was certainly no sin, but on this particular day something prompted me to drive in silence. As I returned from the northern end of my ward, the name of a much less-active ward member came into my mind. I was near his home and had not successfully contacted him in several years—he often worked long hours at the business he owned—so I changed my plans and stopped by this brother's house. To my surprise, he was home. Nothing dramatic came of the visit, but I was still touched when he observed, "It's funny that you should stop by today. This is the first day in about a month that I haven't worked late. It's the only day you could have caught me at home all month."

God knew this man by name, and He knew that his bishop was within a few hundred yards of his house. Could I have recognized the prompting if I'd been listening to the Mariners' game? I strongly doubt it. I wonder how many times I have missed such promptings because I did not create enough space for the Spirit to get through to me.

For many of us, then, finding the right balance between a merry heart and a light mind involves shifting what I call the sacred-to-silly or sacred-to-secular ratio in our lives. I still have a television in my home and rock music in my CD collection. But as I focus more on sacred things, I find myself naturally choosing a soundtrack for my life that is more sacred, or at least not so blaringly secular. Even though a song or show or type of humor may not be objectionable per se, I find that I am happier and more useful to the Lord when I increase the amount of time I spend immersed in activities that are conducive to the Spirit. Similarly, I find that I value and want to create more activities for youth that help them feel the Spirit rather than merely have fun. President Gordon B. Hinckley framed the issue this way: "Nor can you afford to idle away your time in long hours watching the frivolous and damaging programming of which much of television is comprised. There are better things for you to do."[12]

Crossing the Line

Even if the sacred-to-secular ratio is appropriate, the movies, television shows, jokes, and comments that make true Saints laugh are never the kind that leave them with a vile aftertaste. Brigham Young noted that we are fooling ourselves if we are hoping for inspiration and indulging ourselves in the baser things of life. If we expect God will inspire us "while [we] are aiming after the vain and frivolous things of the world; indulging in all the vanity, nonsense, and foolery which surrounds [us]; drinking in all the filthy abominations which should be spurned from every community on the earth—so long as [we] continue this course, rest assured—he will not come near [us]."[13]

Sadly, we can no longer assume that programming is reasonably wholesome, simply because it is on broadcast television, or that a movie will not be unobjectionable simply because it is not R-rated. More than once, I have made the mistake of leaving a television show on or staying in a movie theater longer than I should have, only to be reprimanded by the Spirit for my poor choice. Once humor reaches a certain level of coarseness, even modest doses of such lewd levity can drive out the Spirit.

Elder David A. Bednar encouraged us to learn from such mistakes:

> We should also endeavor to discern when we "withdraw [ourselves] from the Spirit of the Lord, that it may have no place in [us] to guide [us] in wisdom's paths that [we] may be blessed, prospered, and preserved" (Mosiah 2:36). Precisely because the promised blessing is *that we may always have His Spirit to be with us,* we should attend to and learn from the choices and influences that separate us from the Holy Spirit.
>
> The standard is clear. If something we think, see, hear, or do distances us from the Holy Ghost, then we should stop thinking, seeing, hearing, or doing that thing. If that which is intended to entertain, for example, alienates us from the Holy Spirit, then certainly that type of entertainment is not for us. Because the Spirit cannot abide that which is vulgar, crude, or immodest, then clearly such

things are not for us. Because we estrange the Spirit of the Lord when we engage in activities we know we should shun, then such things definitely are not for us.[14]

Finally, I must add one more thought under the heading of crossing the line with humor. We can go too far not only with humor that is crude, but also with humor that hurts others. If the dominant mode of humor in our day is being coarse, a close second is making fun of others. Sometimes such humor is mean-spirited (often when the target of the humor is not present), but especially among men in our society, good-hearted ribbing has become a common mode of interaction, even a sign of friendship. When I worked at a law firm, in fact, I remember feeling almost honored when a partner started teasing me about my politics. Soon I was drawn into the dance of parrying and thrusting with verbal jousts, a dance that never seemed to stop at our law firm. I became part of the club.

Only when I left the firm did I realize that the constant barrage of sarcasm we directed at each other wore thin after a while. The kernel of truth that was often behind the teasing could sting more than the teased target ever let on. I was reminded of all this recently when I directed some humor toward a friend in the law-firm spirit of things. However, a combination of factors—including my ill-advised attempt at humor—led this friend to leave work that day with a heavy heart. His reaction has caused me to make a more conscious consideration of how my humor might hurt others. While I still firmly believe that humor can be an invaluable tool in building rapport and defusing tense situations, I wonder how many times I may have unknowingly crossed the line and sent someone home feeling beaten down rather than lifted up by my attempts at humor.

OVERLY SOMBER SAINTS

For some, the dangers of excessive laughter and light-mindedness are obvious, but it's not so clear what harm could possibly come from being overly solemn in our approach to life. Let me outline three possible downsides to being perpetually grave in our gospel outlook.

Failing to Be of Good Cheer

First, some may mistakenly assume that since it pleases God for us to fast and make other sacrifices, it will please Him even more if we forgo anything enjoyable in life and adopt an attitude of monastic soberness. In its most extreme form, this leads to a philosophy known as asceticism, which moved one fifth-century monk to think he was being spiritually valiant when he sat atop a fifty-foot pillar for thirty-six years.[15] Ascetic beliefs have inspired multitudes of others to mutilate themselves in hopes of pleasing God.

> Saints who live under a self-imposed ban on happiness do so not only unnecessarily, but in violation of God's counsel and commands.

While such extreme practices have no appeal for Latter-day Saints, we may find ourselves looking beyond the mark in subtler ways. For example, Erma Bombeck wrote of a churchgoing mother whose toddler was attracting the attention of other parishioners with his silent but adorable smile. Glaring at her young son, the mother declared, "Stop that grinning! You're in church!" She then smacked the child, who began to cry, and declared, "That's better."[16]

Smiling is not only acceptable in the Lord's Church, it's commanded.

Elder Jeffrey R. Holland noted that "we should honor the Savior's declaration to 'be of good cheer.' (Indeed, it seems to me we may be more guilty of breaking that commandment than almost any other!)"[17] Even in our worship services, where a spirit of reverence should prevail, successful teaching will lead Saints to "rejoice together" (D&C 50:22). Thus, Saints who live under a self-imposed ban on happiness do so not only unnecessarily, but in violation of

God's counsel and commands. After all, He created us for the very purpose that we "might have joy" (2 Nephi 2:25).

Missing Out on Joy

Second, when we mistake solemnity alone for spirituality, not only may we be breaking the commandments, but we are probably missing out on the joy of real spirituality. Frankly, if we are always somber, there's a fair chance we're not really getting the gospel of Jesus Christ, which means "good news," after all. Those who feast on the fruit of the gospel discover that it is "desirable to make one happy" (1 Nephi 8:10). The gospel, then, is happy fruit, and those who truly live it have a hard time suppressing smiles. Even in the midst of afflictions, living the gospel leads to "joy and consolation" in the lives of Saints (see Helaman 3:34–35).

Undermining the Cause

Third, if we are not careful, we may send the same message to our children and friends that the overly earnest mother in Erma Bombeck's story sent to her child: Church is not a place to be happy but a place to be stern. That's not much of a light to set on a hill. When Enos finally paused to reflect on life and his father's teachings, one of the catalysts for his conversion was "the joy of the saints" which sank "deep into [his] heart" (Enos 1:3). Although his father's sermons were often quite serious, the joy of the gospel must have permeated Jacob's life, and it was this joy that led Enos to hunger for something better. What a shame it would be if our approach to living the gospel led our children or friends to conclude that the gospel of Jesus Christ sapped Church members of joy rather than filled them with it.

Sometimes those who take their callings and responsibilities most seriously are more likely to be "cumbered," like Martha—never quite at peace until our task is accomplished (Luke 10:40). Ironically, if our sense of responsibility bogs our spirits down with anxiety, the joy of the gospel may be masked from those we seek to serve, undermining our very efforts to help them.

Elder F. Enzio Busche related just one such story about himself as a young branch president. He presided over a branch with an unacceptably low activity rate, so he dedicated many hours each week to his calling—sometimes "every free minute outside [his] life in the business world"—conscientiously visiting branch members and inviting them to come to church. Week after week, families committed to come but failed to appear at church. Young President Busche could not help but be disappointed.

Finally, one week the missionaries arrived with a family of investigators. The family sat close enough to the front that Elder Busche was able to hear the young boy in the family comment as he pointed to President Busche, "Mom, what is the man with that mean face doing up there?" This stinging but innocent remark from the child prompted Elder Busche to reexamine how he approached his calling and was a pivotal point in his branch's growth. "I had obviously forgotten that the most important element—wanting to convert a soul—has nothing to do with programs, organizations, and industrious busyness. We can do nothing unless we are under the influence of the Spirit, therefore radiating joy, light, and love in our countenance." From then on, he served with greater love and joy, working just as hard but probably appearing less "cumbered." Not surprisingly, as he lightened up in his approach, many less active members began returning to Church, and the branch experienced significant growth.[18]

Indeed, as we come to serve more out of a genuine love for those we serve and less out of a sense of duty, we become both more joyful and more effective in our service. "Our joy now and forever," concluded Elder John H. Groberg, "is inextricably tied to our capacity to love."[19]

Why Live without Joy?

What would lead true followers of Christ to become unduly somber in their approach to the gospel? First, we may sometimes foolishly feel that we must accomplish everything on our own—a belief that could suck the joy out of any life. On the other hand, as we turn to the Lord for help in our lives, our burdens are lightened and our joy is increased. Perhaps nowhere is this concept articulated more clearly than in the hymn "How Gentle God's Commands":

> *How gentle God's commands!*
> *How kind his precepts are!*
> *Come, cast your burdens on the Lord*
> *And trust his constant care. . . .*
>
> *Why should this anxious load*
> *Press down your weary mind?*
> *Haste to your Heav'nly Father's throne*
> *And sweet refreshment find.*
>
> *His goodness stands approved,*
> *Unchanged from day to day;*
> *I'll drop my burden at his feet*
> *And bear a song away.*[20]

Insisting on going it alone spiritually not only makes us grouchy, but it also sets at naught the Savior's atoning sacrifice and His invitations to harness its enabling power. "Come unto me, all ye that labour and are heavy laden, and I will give ye rest. Take my yoke upon you . . . and ye shall find rest unto your souls. For my yoke is easy, and my burden is light" (Matthew 11:28–30). When we become yoked with Christ, "relying wholly upon the merits of him who is mighty to save" (2 Nephi 31:19), we effectively cast our burdens at His feet, relieving ourselves of the anxiety that stems from the belief that we must do it all on our own. Truly, those who come unto Christ "bear a song away."

STRIKING THE BALANCE

In striving to find the right balance of solemnity and cheerfulness, we have perhaps no better model than Joseph Smith (other than the Savior Himself). If he listed naturally toward one extreme in this regard, by his own admission it would be too much levity (see Joseph Smith—History 1:28). Yet unlike typical teenagers of his day or ours, he engaged in "serious reflection" that unlocked the windows of heaven (Joseph Smith—History 1:8). The revelations contained in the Doctrine and Covenants stand as a witness that Joseph managed to disentangle himself from the "vanities of the world" and "let the solemnities of eternity rest upon" his mind (D&C 20:5; 43:34).

Still, Joseph clearly saw pondering and meditating on the mysteries of God as an entirely different matter than the ostentatious piety displayed by many preachers in his day. Alexander Baugh suggested that one reason "the Prophet was so sportive was that he hoped to dispel many of the sanctimonious attitudes of many religionists who believed activities such as athletics were not consistent with Christianity."[21] For example, on one occasion a visiting clergyman addressed Joseph with a flowery greeting: "Is it possible that I now flash my optics upon a Prophet, upon a man who has conversed with my Savior?" Perhaps demonstrating his feelings toward the "super-abundant stock of sanctimoniousness," Joseph replied simply, "Yes. I don't know but you do; would not you like to wrestle with me?"[22] Joseph's jovial disposition drove off more than one potential member who could not fathom such a cheerful man being a prophet.

What is most remarkable about Joseph's joyful approach to life is that he maintained such an outlook through an almost endless stream of afflictions. In doing so, he not only enjoyed greater happiness himself, but he constantly helped to lift the spirits of others with his good humor. Perhaps my favorite story underscoring Joseph's ability to do this occurred in the fall of 1838, a bleak time for the Church. Joseph was marching with a group of men to help protect the Saints in Adam-ondi-Ahman. Although it was only mid-October, four to five inches of snow fell one night, catching the tentless travelers off guard and delivering a blow to their morale. For many, such an act of God could have been the straw that broke the camel's back.

Not for Joseph. "The Prophet, seeing our forlorn condition," wrote Edward Stevenson, who was eighteen years old at the time, "called on us to form into two parties—Lyman Wight at the head of one line and he (Joseph) heading the other line—to have a sham battle. The weapons were snowballs. We set to with a will full of glee and fun."[23]

Leonard Arrington summed up Joseph's temperament this way: "The Prophet recognized as unhealthy the mind that lacked balance, perspective, and humor. . . . The Prophet was also concerned about extremes—becoming so concerned about the danger of over-exuberance that we swing the pendulum back and focus too heavily on repressing wrong desires."[24] Indeed, Joseph's example teaches us all that there is a time for prayerful pondering and a time for snowball fights.

Notes

1. Gordon B. Hinckley, "Keeping the Temple Holy," *Ensign,* May 1990, 52.

2. Hinckley, "Keeping the Temple Holy," 51.

3. Ezra Taft Benson, "Seek the Spirit of the Lord," *Ensign,* Apr. 1988, 2.

4. "Rise Up, O Men of God," *Hymns of The Church of Jesus Christ of Latter-day Saints* (Salt Lake City: The Church of Jesus Christ of Latter-day Saints, 1985), no. 324.

5. Spencer J. Condie, *In Perfect Balance* (Salt Lake City: Deseret Book, 1993), 176.

6. Robert L. Millet, "Honoring His Holy Name," *Ensign,* Mar. 1994, 10.

7. Boyd K. Packer, "Reverence Invites Revelation," *Ensign,* Nov. 1991, 21–22.

8. James E. Faust, "The Need for Balance in Our Lives," *Ensign,* March 2000, 4.

9. Glenn L. Pace, "Crying with the Saints," *Ensign,* Sept. 1988, 73.

10. C. S. Lewis, *The Screwtape Letters* (New York: HarperCollins, 2001), 61.

11. William Wordsworth, "The World," in *The Oxford Book of English Verse,* ed. Sir Arthur Quiller-Couch (1939), 626; as quoted in James E. Faust, "'Search Me, O God, and Know My Heart,'" *Ensign,* May 1998, 18.

12. Gordon B. Hinckley, "'A Chosen Generation,'" *Ensign,* May 1992, 71.

13. Brigham Young, in *Journal of Discourses,* 26 vols. (London: Latter-day Saints' Book Depot, 1854–86), 1:120.

14. David A. Bednar, "That We May Always Have His Spirit to Be with Us," *Ensign,* May 2006, 30.

15. Daniel K. Judd, "Hedonism, Asceticism, and the Great Plan of Happiness," in *The Fulness of the Gospel: Foundation Teachings from the Book of Mormon,* The 32nd Annual Sidney B. Sperry Symposium (Salt Lake City: Deseret Book and the BYU Religious Studies Center, 2003), 200.

16. Erma Bombeck, *At Wit's End* (N. p.: Thorndike Large Print Edition, 1984), 63; quoted in Philip Yancey, *What's So Amazing About Grace?* (Grand Rapids, Michigan: Zondervan, 1997), 32.

17. Jeffrey R. Holland, "The Tongue of Angels," *Ensign,* May 2007, 18.

18. F. Enzio Busche, "Lessons from the Lamb of God," *The Religious Educator,* vol. 9, no. 2 (2008), 2–3.

19. John H. Groberg, "The Power of God's Love," *Ensign,* Nov. 2004, 10.

20. "How Gentle God's Commands," *Hymns,* no. 125.

21. Alexander L. Baugh, "Joseph Smith's Athletic Nature," in Susan Easton Black and Charles D. Tate, Jr., eds., *Joseph Smith: The Prophet, The Man* (Provo, Utah: The Religious Studies Center, BYU, 1993), 145.

22. Jedediah M. Grant, in *Journal of Discourses,* 3:67.

23. Hyrum L. Andrus and Helen Mae Andrus, *They Knew the Prophet* (Salt Lake City: Bookcraft, 1974), 86.

24. Leonard Arrington, "Joseph Smith and the Lighter View," *New Era,* Aug. 1976, 9–10.

CHAPTER 8

MISPLACED SELF-RELIANCE AND CHEAP GRACE

Perhaps no pair of doctrines better illustrates Satan's ability to distort pure truths into countervailing extremes than divine grace and individual obedience. Both are essential to our salvation, yet neither is sufficient alone. Emphasizing either doctrine to the exclusion of the other can lead to spiritually fatal misunderstandings—which is precisely what the adversary has persuaded many to do. Yet so often as we focus on the foolishness of those who exalt one principle while ignoring the other, we are blind to our own tendency to over-compensate and swing to the other end of the doctrinal spectrum.

MISPLACED SELF-RELIANCE

More than once I have been in a Sunday School or priesthood class whose assigned topic was "Faith in Jesus Christ," only to have the actual focus of the class become the importance of our own good works. Clearly, there is peril in buying into what one writer has called, in contrast to the good news of the gospel of Jesus Christ, "the bad news of an insidious easy-believism that makes no moral demands on the lives of sinners."[1] Latter-day Saints are quick to recognize such dangers, as we should be.

Yet even as Church leaders repeatedly emphasize the importance of exercising faith in Christ and the critical nature of the Savior's grace in our lives, some of the students who arrive in my classes at BYU–Idaho are still a bit slow to recognize the problem with believing that our works alone will save us. As Robert L. Millet puts it, "Sometimes in our efforts to emphasize the importance of good works—of receiving the ordinances of salvation, of living by every word of God, of standing as witnesses of Christ at all times, and of involving ourselves in the acts of Christian service that always characterize the disciples of Jesus in every age—we are wont to overlook the simple yet profound reality that the plan of salvation, the gospel of Jesus Christ, is truly a gospel of grace."[2]

What's the Harm in Simply Working As If Everything Depends on Us?

In some of my conversations with evangelical Christians, it seems as if one of their concerns is that members of the Church of Jesus Christ believe we have to do more than is actually required for salvation. It's as if they're saying, in essence, "Only the first chapter of math was assigned as homework, but you're trying to do all five chapters!" In other words, they might say, we've needlessly mistaken the extra credit assignment for required work. Consequently, I'm tempted to ask what the problem is, as long as we're doing the one chapter which they think is required. If they believe that the only thing truly necessary for salvation is professing a belief in Jesus Christ,[3] what could be the harm in declaring just such a belief *and* striving to follow His teachings? What's wrong with trying to get through additional chapters, even if they prove not to be required in the end? To answer my own rhetorical questions, let me suggest three possible dangers in downplaying the critical role of faith and grace and unduly inflating the importance of our own good works.

First, to change the metaphor slightly, imagine a child who

misunderstands the teacher's instructions and believes she must complete her math homework all on her own, without any help from her parents. (Incidentally, with this analogy I'm not suggesting that it's learning alone that leads to salvation. I simply use learning schoolwork as a surrogate for whatever activity, conviction, and transformation are required for salvation.) She might put forth a valiant effort and even make some progress, but let's assume for the sake of argument—a critical assumption here—that neither this little girl nor any other student is capable of completing the homework without assistance. If she tries to do so, eventually she will fail and, in her frustration, give up altogether.

In *Digging Deeper,* I wrote about a student who felt that the idea of turning to God for help felt like cheating on the test of life, since we were sent here to be proved.[4] Elder Gene R. Cook surely had such individuals in mind when he wondered aloud, "How many of us, at times, try to resolve life's challenges ourselves, without seeking the intervention of the Lord in our lives? We try to carry the burden alone."[5]

For many people, surely the result of such a mistaken belief is depression and despair. As a counselor in a stake presidency, Robert L. Millet once counseled with a woman who had made a three-page list of all the things she'd been asked to do in the last six months. "I just can't do it all," she told President Millet. "I can't be the perfect mother, the perfect wife, the perfect Church leader, the perfect citizen. I'm tired. In fact, I'm worn out. I tell you, I just can't do it all! . . . Why can't I solve this problem?"[6] Like my student, this woman hadn't yet learned that it is hardly cheating on the test of life to turn to the Lord for help. On the contrary, one of the first questions we must ask in this test is whether we can solve this problem alone. Until we realize that we cannot, we will never seek and obtain the divine assistance we all require.

Elder Bruce C. Hafen noted precisely this phenomenon on a broader scale: "I sense that an increasing number of deeply committed Church members are weighed down beyond the breaking point with discouragement about their personal lives. When we habitually understate the meaning of the Atonement, we take more serious risks than simply leaving one another without comforting reassurances—for some may simply drop out of the race, worn out and beaten down with the harsh and untrue belief that they are just not celestial material."[7] The first danger of mistakenly believing that we must earn our spot in heaven by our own good works alone, then, is that we will eventually become overwhelmed by the realization that this is an impossible task, since, as John taught, if "we say that we have not sinned," God's "word is not in us" (1 John 1:10). Once we realize it's impossible to complete the task we mistakenly believe we have to do all on our own, we simply give up.

Second, while some are overwhelmed when they believe they must save themselves through their own good works, others are blissfully and offensively clueless. Imagine an overly confident little boy who understands that he may ask his parents for help with his math homework but stubbornly refuses to seek it. He completes the chapter on his own and proceeds to boast to his classmates about the fact that he is so smart that he was able to finish the homework all by himself. Only when the teacher returns his corrected paper will he realize that he failed—and that he made a huge mistake by not turning to his parents for help.

This is essentially the lesson Paul taught all those who confidently believed that they could gain salvation independently through sheer obedience to the law of Moses.

> As it is written, There is none righteous, no, not one;
> . . . [Nobody can finish this homework on his own—not anybody.]
> They are all gone out of the way, they are together become unprofitable; there is none that doeth good, no, not one. . . .
> Therefore by the deeds of the law there shall no flesh be justified in his sight. . . .

For all have sinned, and come short of the glory of God; [If we had to take the score we get by doing the homework alone, we would all flunk the class.]

Being justified freely by his grace through the redemption that is in Christ Jesus: . . . [Christ has made it possible for all of us to pass life's test, with the help of his grace.]

Where is boasting then? It is excluded. By what law? of works? Nay: but by the law of faith. (Romans 3:10–27) [So what's the basis for our bragging that we passed? Because we completed the home-work through our own hard work? No, we should boast that we finally had the good sense to turn to Christ for help and that He was able and willing to help us.]

Just as many Jews in Paul's time mis-takenly believed they could warrant salva-tion by rigid compliance to God's law, King Noah's wicked priests erroneously claimed that salvation came by the law of Moses. After first deriding their failure to

Those who arrive at the pearly gates and demand the kingdom they truly deserve by virtue of their own good works are in for a very rude surprise.

live the law by which they hoped to be saved, Abinadi articulated a doctrine that applies to any who believe that our obedience to God's law in any dispensation can save us: "And moreover, I say unto you, that salvation doth not come by the law alone; and were it not for the atonement, which God himself shall make for the sins and iniq-uities of his people, that they must unavoidably perish, notwith-standing the law of Moses" (Mosiah 13:28). In other words, like the little boy who submits the difficult math he did all by himself, those who arrive at the pearly gates and demand the kingdom they truly deserve by virtue of their own good works are in for a very rude surprise.

To make the next point, I must tweak the hypothetical one more time. What if the boy's parents actually helped him whenever he got stuck—but he was so cocky that he insisted he'd known all along what they had told him? If such a boy turned in his homework and did get an A, he would be ungrateful, indeed, if he bragged that he had completed the task all on his own. And his parents might be less willing to help him with future assignments. After reminding his people of a few of the ways in which God assists and blesses us, King Benjamin addressed the spiritual equivalent of such thinking with the piercing question, "therefore, of what have ye to boast?" (Mosiah 2:24).

In sum, those who believe they must save themselves through their own works alone *should* be incredibly depressed by the thought. If they aren't, they are probably making one of two mistakes: either they are failing the test of life and not realizing it, or they are passing with the help of God and not recognizing that their success is divinely enabled. And it is difficult to imagine that anyone who fails to acknowledge God's hand in all things—including his own spiritual success—could ever really be passing the test (see D&C 59:21). Just as a parent might be reluctant to continue assisting a child who repeatedly and naively insisted he "already knew that" each time the parent tried to help, if we fail to acknowledge God's hand in our blessings, it seems unlikely that further divine assistance will be forthcoming.

This leads to a third danger in mistakenly believing we've got to save ourselves. The problem isn't just that we offend God by failing to acknowledge His help. Indeed, if we believe we must obtain our salvation all on our own, we will ultimately fail to measure up because we have developed neither the capacity nor the inclination to seek the Savior's redeeming aid.

It is faith in Christ that enables us not only to be forgiven but to be transformed. Thus, John wrote of how the Savior gives those who receive Him "the power to become the sons" (and daughters) of God in the richest sense (John 1:12). On the other hand, those who are intent on transforming themselves all on their own will fail to harness the enabling power of the Atonement. Indeed, while Paul challenged us to "work out [our] own salvation with fear and trembling[,]" he immediately acknowledged that "it is God which worketh in you both to will and to do of his good pleasure" (Philippians 2:12–13). As the Bible Dictionary puts it, "It is likewise through the grace of the Lord that individuals, through faith in the atonement of Jesus Christ and repentance of their sins, *receive strength and assistance to do good works that they otherwise would not be able to maintain if left to their own means.*

This grace is an enabling power that allows men and women to lay hold on eternal life and exaltation after they have expended their own best efforts."[8]

"Thus," added Elder David A. Bednar, "the enabling and strengthening aspect of the Atonement helps us to see and to do and to become good in ways that we could never recognize or accomplish with our limited mortal capacity."[9] In King Benjamin's famous verse about putting off the natural man and becoming Saints, we often overlook a crucial prepositional phrase that lets us know how such a metamorphosis is possible: "through the atonement of Christ the Lord" (Mosiah 3:19). One of the great dangers of seeking to qualify for heaven based solely on our own good works is that we will fail to harness the grace of God necessary to transform us into souls who can abide His presence.

Exercising faith in Christ is not something we should do apart from bringing forth good works. Exercising faith in Christ actually enables us to bring forth good works.

In sum, "grace versus works is a false dichotomy."[10] Exercising faith in Christ is not something we should do *apart* from bringing forth good works. Exercising faith in Christ actually *enables* us to bring forth good works—to do more good and become more holy than we could ever hope to without the help of the Savior's grace. Faith and works, then, are not separate, noninteracting elements in the equation for salvation. Instead, they are synergistic. Faith in Christ serves as the catalyst that allows us to serve God more explosively than we ever could fueled solely by our own drive and determination; obedience allows us to experience God's mercy more fully, which leads to greater faith in Him and His plan.

Exercising Real Faith

So how do we exert the kind of faith in Christ that allows us to tap into this divine enabling power? Certainly, such faith requires more than a hollow recitation of professed belief in Jesus as our personal Savior. But saving, transforming faith is also far more than saying we believe in Jesus and then working hard on our own to keep the commandments. We may be tempted to diagram the equation this way:

Strong Belief in Christ + Works ➤ Salvation

But the faith described in the scriptures is more than just conviction combined with works. Between conviction and action lies something critical that is more metaphysical than physical. (The relationship between faith and works is also far too synergistic to fit into such a linear equation.)

Perhaps no passage demonstrates this more clearly than Enos's dialogue with the Lord about his own salvation. "Lord, how is it done?" an amazed Enos asked after receiving a remission of his sins. The Lord's answer makes no mention of Enos's good works to date or even his commitment to perform more good works in the future, although good works would undoubtedly follow his change of heart. Instead, the Lord explained simply: "Because of thy faith in Christ." Enos's faith was manifest not in traditional good works but in wrestling before God, hungering in his soul, and crying to the Lord in mighty prayer (see Enos 1:2–8).

Consider three other examples in which followers of Christ exercised faith in ways that transcended mere belief but still involved hearts and minds more than hands and feet. Alma the Younger was "harrowed up by the memory of [his] many sins" until he not only remembered Christ but "cried within [his] heart: O Jesus, thou Son of God, have mercy on me" (Alma 36:17–18). His plea for mercy was both the pivotal point in his life and the fulcrum of the Christ-centered chiasm we call Alma 36. Despite being physically incapable of any outward action at all, Alma had gone from being racked with inexpressible horror for his sins to being consumed with joy and light as a result of his faith in Christ (see Alma 36:14, 20).

The people of King Benjamin also experienced "a mighty change" in which they were not only "filled with joy, having received a remission of their sins, and having peace of conscience," but also had "no more disposition to do evil, but to do good continually." Why? "Because of the exceeding faith which they had in Jesus Christ who should come"—a faith expressed in their cry, "O have mercy, and apply the atoning blood of Christ that we may receive forgiveness of our sins, and our hearts may be purified; for we believe in Jesus Christ" (Mosiah 4:1–3; 5:2). Although Alma was a rebel who became good and the people of King Benjamin were temple-attending folks who became better through the Atonement of Christ, faith in the Savior was the catalyst for the change in both cases.

When Lucifer confronted Moses, the prophet twice rebuked and dismissed the tempter, but to no apparent avail. Just as Moses began to fear exceedingly, he finally called upon God, received strength, and commanded Satan for the third time to depart. Finally, filled with strength, Moses rebuked Satan for the fourth time, but now he issued his command in "the name of the Only Begotten" (see Moses 1:12–22). Only when he invoked the name of the Savior was Moses finally able to conquer the adversary, perhaps illustrating in part what Nephi meant when he said that we are to rely "wholly upon the merits of him who is mighty to save" (2 Nephi 31:19).

These scriptural examples remind us that true faith in the Lord

Jesus Christ certainly means more than mere belief, but it also means more than dashing off to comply with commandments. Those who exercised faith in these stories exerted great mental and spiritual effort and fastened their hopes on the Savior. They lived, spiritually speaking, because they looked to him (see Alma 33:19–23; 37:47).

So what is the danger of professing a belief in Christ *and* working as if salvation were otherwise up to us alone? In our rush to do good works, we may fail to exercise the real faith in Jesus Christ necessary to save our souls. "To push ourselves beyond the mark is, in a strange sort of way, a statement that we fear we must do the job ourselves if we expect it to get done," observed Brother Millet.[11] Only when we abandon the notion that we must save ourselves all on our own do we really come to exercise the kind of faith Peter contemplated when he wrote of "faith unto salvation" (1 Peter 1:5). Or as Mormon put it, "men also were saved by faith in [Christ's] name; and by faith, they become the sons of God" (Moroni 7:26). In sum, without true, gut-wrenching, humble, wholehearted faith, there is no forgiveness, no transformation, and no salvation—no matter how we might work alone to change and save ourselves. We must, in the words of President Stephen L Richards, "forsake the philosophy of self-sufficiency, which is the philosophy of the world, and adopt the philosophy of faith, which is the philosophy of Christ. Substitute faith for self-assurance."[12]

CHEAP GRACE

Writing about the opposite extreme in this theological pair is challenging—not because there is little to say about it, but because so much has been said so well already. Historically, Latter-day Saints have been highly attuned to the dangers of believing we can be saved by what German theologian Dietrich Bonhoeffer described as "cheap grace" or "grace without discipleship."[13] Still, as we become increasingly sensitive to the problems described in the first half of this chapter, it's important to avoid overcorrection. Jude warned against those who managed to transform something as sublime as grace into thing as perverse as licentiousness—or an "excuse for immoral (Jude 1:4).[14] Surely, no Latter-day Saint would be guilty of doing th intentionally, but just as parents who lavish praise on one child without mentioning the other may create doubt about their feelings for the second child, an imbalanced emphasis on grace may inadvertently create hazardous misperceptions.

A Dangerously Incomplete Picture

I recently read a book about grace I rather enjoyed (and from which I have quoted favorably in this book). However, as the non-LDS writer continually underscored the merciful nature of God, I found myself concerned that he almost never mentioned repentance or obedience. Toward the end of the book the author finally included a chapter in which he freely acknowledged, "To this point, I freely admit, I have painted a one-sided picture of grace. I have portrayed God as a lovesick father eager to forgive. . . . Depicting grace in such sweeping terms makes people nervous, and I concede that I have skated to the very edge of danger." My hope and expectation at this point was that the author would now describe the dangers of leaving repentance and obedience out of our discussion of Christ's gospel. Instead, he defended the way he had skated to the edge of danger with this explanation: "I have done so because I believe the New Testament does too."[15]

I would be more sympathetic to this defense if the New Testament consisted only of those few passages on which Protestants rely for the notion that we are saved by grace alone. But to suggest the Bible presents a message solely about faith, grace, and mercy, one must overlook not only James's sharp reminder that works matter (James 1–2), but also the entire Old Testament, the bulk of the Savior's teachings as recorded in the four Gospels, and, it turns out, most of what Paul had to say, since his epistles are replete with warnings to his readers—all of them already believers in Christ—that God will n set aside the lusts of the flesh and to fol-

of Paul's epistles to draw scriptures for
grace) and obedience (and accountabil-
see how much longer my list for the lesson on
here are a few of my favorite Pauline passages:
will "render to every man according to his deeds: . . . unto
m that are contentious, and do not obey the truth, but obey
unrighteousness, indignation and wrath, tribulation and anguish"
(Romans 2:6, 8–9).

"Know ye not, that to whom ye yield yourselves servants to obey,
his servants ye are to whom ye obey; whether of sin unto death, or
of obedience unto righteousness?" (Romans 6:16).

"For if ye live after the flesh, ye shall die: but if ye through the Spirit
do mortify the deeds of the body, ye shall live. For as many as are led
by the Spirit of God, they are the sons of God" (Romans 8:13–14).

"If any man defile the temple of God, him shall God destroy; for
the temple of God is holy, which temple ye are. Let no man deceive
himself" (1 Corinthians 3:17–18).

"Know ye not that the unrighteous shall not inherit the kingdom
of God? Be not deceived" (1 Corinthians 6:9).

"For we must all appear before the judgment seat of Christ; that
every one may receive the things done in his body, according to that
he hath done, whether it be good or bad" (2 Corinthians 5:10).

"Be not deceived; God is not mocked: for whatsoever a man
soweth, that shall he also reap" (Galatians 6:7).

"For this ye know, that no whoremonger, nor unclean person, nor
covetous man, who is an idolater, hath any inheritance in the kingdom
of Christ and of God. . . . For ye were sometimes darkness, but now
are ye light in the Lord: walk as children of light" (Ephesians 5:5, 8).

"Work out your own salvation with fear and trembling" (Philippians 2:12).

"Mortify therefore your members which are upon the earth; for-
nication, uncleanness, inordinate affection, evil concupiscence, and

covetousness, which is idolatry: for which things' sake the wrath of God cometh on the children of disobedience" (Colossians 3:5–6).

In two of Paul's most straightforward passages, he explicitly tells his readers not to be deceived on this point, perhaps seeking to disavow the very misunderstandings that have arisen about the roles of faith and grace. If we believe there is no connection between our behavior and our eternal station, we are deceived indeed.

Evangelical pastor John F. MacArthur Jr. has written eloquently about the perils of consistently omitting such aspects of Christ's gospel. "Repentance was a recurring motif in all [Jesus'] sermons," he wrote. Yet somehow it "is not fashionable in the twentieth century to preach a gospel that demands repentance. As early as 1937, Dr. H. A. Ironside noted that . . . 'professed preachers of grace . . . decry the necessity of repentance lest it seem to invalidate the freedom of grace.'"[17] Pastor MacArthur told of being asked to preview a training video from an international evangelical organization. The film explicitly urged young evangelists "*not* to tell unsaved young people they must obey Christ, give him their hearts, surrender their lives, repent of their sins, submit to his lordship, or follow him. Telling the unsaved they must do those things confuses the gospel message, the film said."[18]

The result of all this, according to MacArthur, is that the "gospel our age has popularized is a sugar-coated placebo designed more to soothe sinners than to convert them."[19] The fact is that our failure to repent and obey can keep us out of heaven.

I can imagine some of my evangelical acquaintances saying, "Wait a minute—are you really trying to suggest that God will deny some of us admittance to heaven because we finished with a few too many sins?" Yet with the parable of the ten virgins, Jesus made precisely the point that many—half, to be exact—of those expecting admittance to the wedding will be rejected because they failed to prepare (see Matthew 25:1–12). The unprepared virgins in that parable are turned away with language that echoes what Jesus said in the Sermon on the Mount to some who insist, "Lord, Lord, have we not prophesied in thy name? and in thy name have cast out devils? And in thy name done many wonderful works? And then will I profess unto them, I never knew you: depart from me, ye that work iniquity" (Matthew 7:22–23).

On what basis will the Savior issue such a seemingly harsh rebuke to those who wish to enter His kingdom? He makes no secret about the admission criteria: "Not every one that saith unto me, Lord, Lord, shall enter into the kingdom of heaven; but he that doeth the will of my Father which is in heaven" (Matthew 7:21).

Yes, Heavenly Father is extraordinarily merciful to those who repent and exercise faith in His Son, Jesus Christ, and such faith is also a prerequisite to entrance into God's kingdom. At times during His earthly ministry, the Savior emphasized God's mercy, as He did with the parable of the prodigal and the parable of the laborers. Yet just as those parables give hope to those who stray or come to Christ late in life, the parable of the ten virgins gives pause to those who procrastinate repenting and obeying.

Taken as a whole, the teachings of the Savior and His Apostles reveal both God's mercy and His judgment, the need for both faith-induced grace and wholehearted obedience. But if we paint a picture of God highlighting only His mercy, with little or no emphasis on repentance and commandments, we render a portrayal of God that is incomplete and dangerously misleading. While perhaps comforting now, such incomplete representations about God's plan could be the source of great disappointment one day for those who find themselves wishing they had focused on all God's instructions and warnings rather than a few selected passages.

With impressive candor, Pastor MacArthur criticized that segment of evangelicalism—and we should be clear that it is only one segment—that has painted just such an incomplete picture. In the estimation of MacArthur, the impact on Christianity of those who teach that the Bible "promises salvation to anyone who simply believes the facts about Christ and claims eternal life" has been "catastrophic. . . . Contemporary Christians have been conditioned to believe that because they recited a prayer, signed on a dotted line, walked an aisle, or had some other experience, they are saved and should never question their salvation. . . . I fear that multitudes who now fill church pews in the mainstream of the evangelical movement will be among those turned away because they did not do the will of the Father."[20]

Missing Out on Blessings in Mortality

Misapprehending the importance of obedience is problematic not only at Judgment Day, but today as well. Here's how.

Two questions I frequently hear from students make me wince. First, after missing a class, a student will often ask innocently, "Did I miss anything important?"

"No," I'm often tempted to reply sarcastically. "I was thinking of covering some really important stuff in class that day, but I just didn't get around to it. Now that I think of it, we simply squandered the hour. In fact, it was a complete waste for those students who did come. You didn't miss a thing."

The second question is more understandable but still disappointing, especially when combined with the usual reaction of students who ask it. "Is this going to be on the final?" Sadly, if the answer is no, the student who asked often drops his pencil and closes his mind. For such students, the goal is apparently only to get the desired grade, not to gain knowledge.

To be sure, understanding what is truly necessary for our salvation is critical. Yet I can't help but wonder how the Savior feels when some of His professed followers obsess over that question, asking essentially, "Is this required for salvation? Will good works be on the final?" Such an approach is risky not only because we might underestimate what is required for salvation, but because we may then ignore or neglect teachings and commandments we deem mere surplus—suggested living that is merely optional. What a shame it would be to gloss over the Savior's challenging and liberating imperatives in the Sermon on the Mount, for example, because we decide compliance with those commandments is not necessary for our salvation. (Perhaps recognizing the tension between their minimalist beliefs about what is required for salvation and the Savior's towering charge for His followers to become perfect like God, some Christians actually view the Sermon on the Mount as nonbinding in our day.[21])

When we strive to read the scriptures as a "workable whole," faith and works cease to be antagonists on the theological battlefield and become, instead, essential allies in our war on sin.

True disciples understand that commandments and counsel are intended to bless their lives, not weigh them down. Thus, they look forward to being "crowned with blessings from above, yea, and with commandments not a few" (D&C 59:4). They are less concerned with whether a particular course of action is necessary for their salvation than they are with whether knowing it is something the Lord would have them do. Eager to serve the Lord they love and to receive the fullness of joy He promises those who abide in Him (see John 15:4–12), they seek to obey His commands wholeheartedly rather than looking for the most efficient, least labor-intensive route to heaven.

Striking the Balance

Judges faced with the task of interpreting a statute are governed by a simple yet powerful rule: if possible, they must interpret the statute in a way that gives meaning to all parts of the law as well as other statutes enacted by the legislature. The idea is that the legislature "always intends its enactments to be construed together as a workable whole."[22] In other words, judges shouldn't interpret ambiguous sentences in a statute in a way that doesn't agree with the intent of the statute when read as a whole. The same could be said of the teachings of the Savior and His Apostles: the doctrines of faith and obedience were never intended to be construed in isolation.

Indeed, when we read the New Testament as a whole, it's hard to avoid reaching two conclusions. First, the gospel is replete with directives for us to do and become things that seem impossible. Second, with Jesus—whose name, after all, means *God is help*—all things are possible. Reading the scriptures as a "workable whole," we see both that Jesus commands us to become perfect like His Father (Matthew 5:48) and that such a transformation will only occur when we "come unto Christ, and [become] perfected in him, and deny [ourselves] of all ungodliness" so that "by his grace [we] may be perfect in Christ" (Moroni 10:32). In fact, when we strive to read the scriptures as a "workable whole," faith and works cease to be antagonists on the theological battlefield and become, instead, essential allies in our war on sin. To borrow C. S. Lewis's metaphor, good works and faith are like two blades in a pair of scissors—and asking which is more important is a rather futile exercise.[23]

Understanding that God truly does expect our obedience to His commandments—and that such a task exceeds our limited abilities—can lead us to exercise the faith necessary to harness the Savior's redeeming, transforming, enabling grace. In turn, exercising genuine faith leads to grace-aided obedience that transcends anything even the most zealous Saints could have done on their own. "Men and women who turn their lives over to God," taught President Ezra Taft Benson, "will discover that he can make a lot more out of their lives than they can."[24]

While men and women are nothing alone, with Paul, Saints of God can emphatically declare, "I can do all things through Christ which strengtheneth me" (Philippians 4:13).

Notes

1. John F. MacArthur Jr., *The Gospel According to Jesus* (Grand Rapids, Michigan: Zondervan, 1994), 27–28. While I do not agree with everything

MacArthur writes, his popular book clearly demonstrates both a diversity of opinion among Christian evangelicals and an awareness by some of the dangers of watering down Christ's gospel.

2. Robert L. Millet, *Grace Works* (Salt Lake City: Deseret Book, 2003), 14.

3. Although some Christians outside the Church do believe this, it vastly oversimplifies the kind of genuine, life-changing faith many other non-LDS Christians believe is necessary to produce salvation. See, for example, MacArthur, *The Gospel According to Jesus,* 27–29.

4. Robert Eaton, *Digging Deeper,* (Deseret Book: Salt Lake, 2006), 40.

5. Gene R. Cook, "Receiving Divine Assistance through the Grace of the Lord," *Ensign,* May 1993, 79.

6. Millet, *Grace Works,* 85–87.

7. Bruce C. Hafen, *The Broken Heart: Applying the Atonement to Life's Experiences* (Salt Lake City: Deseret Book, 1989), 5–6.

8. LDS Bible Dictionary, "Grace," 697; emphasis added.

9. David A. Bednar, "In the Strength of the Lord," *Ensign,* Nov. 2004, 77.

10. Millet, *Grace Works,* vi.

11. Millet, *Grace Works,* 132.

12. Stephen L Richards, *Where Is Wisdom* (Salt Lake City: Deseret Book, 1955), 49; quoted in Millet, *Grace Works,* 142.

13. Dietrich Bonhoeffer, *The Cost of Discipleship* (New York: MacMillan, 1959), 47; quoted in Hugh W. Nibley, "The Atonement of Jesus Christ, Part 3," *Ensign,* Sept. 1990, 24.

14. Weymouth New Testament.

15. Philip D. Yancey, *What's So Amazing About Grace* (Grand Rapids, Michigan: Zondervan, 1997), 178.

16. So often in responding to arguments about grace, we respond with James. Personally, however, I prefer to use Paul so as not to leave the misimpression that Paul thought obedience didn't matter. Since both Paul and James were inspired, James was presumably not correcting Paul; at most, he was correcting those who might have misunderstood Paul by focusing on selected passages of Paul's writings.

17. H. A. Ironside, *Except Ye Repent* (Grand Rapids: Zondervan, 1937), 11; quoted in MacArthur, *The Gospel According to Jesus,* 185–86.

18. MacArthur, *The Gospel According to Jesus,* 185–86.

19. MacArthur, *The Gospel According to Jesus,* 141.

20. MacArthur, *The Gospel According to Jesus,* 28–29.

21. MacArthur, *The Gospel According to Jesus,* 32–33.

22. See, for example, *Oregon v. Stamper,* 197 Or App 413, 106 P 3d 172, *rev den,* 339 Or 230 (2005).

23. C. S. Lewis, *Mere Christianity* (New York: Touchstone, 1996), 131–32; quoted in Millet, *Grace Works,* 125.

24. Ezra Taft Benson, *Teachings of Ezra Taft Benson* (Salt Lake City: Bookcraft, 1988), 361; quoted in Millet, *Grace Works,* 67.

CHAPTER 9

PERMISSIVE PARENTS AND OVERCONTROLLERS

In the recent (and wholly unnecessary) remake of the film *Yours, Mine and Ours,* a Coast Guard admiral courts an old high-school girlfriend who has become something of a flower child as an adult. Both are widowed and have a gaggle of children—and a definite opinion about how to run a home and raise a family. The admiral barks orders to his children, directing their lives with the help of elaborate chore charts, military discipline, and unquestioned order. Loving chaos reigns in the mother's home, where a pig running through the kitchen epitomizes the mother's tolerance, patience, and, frankly, lack of judgment.

These parents are Hollywood caricatures, of course, but they highlight two extreme approaches to parenting—our "most important calling in time and eternity," according to President Ezra Taft Benson.[1] Many of us feel drawn to one extreme or the other, and some of us may feel torn between the two. As Patricia Holland once acknowledged, parents often find themselves wondering just how strict or easygoing they should be: "Should I spank them or should I reason with them? Should I control them or should I just ignore them?"[2] If we are too lenient, our children may not develop the discipline or wisdom to choose to stay on the strait and narrow; if we are too controlling, they may not develop the capacity or the will to choose the right on their own. And while overcorrecting is a danger with each of the attributes discussed in this book, it's a particular danger in this context. As we are adamant about avoiding flaws we may have perceived in how our parents raised us, we often inadvertently overcompensate, creating a whole different set of problems for our children.[3]

PERMISSIVE PARENTS

Those who are overly lenient in their parenting might well defend their tendencies with arguments like these: "My children have enough challenges in their lives—they don't need me to make any more for them. The best thing I can do for them is to be their friend and their fan. Besides, they have their agency. Who am I to try to force them to live a certain way? It wouldn't work, even if I did." Although well intentioned, such an approach ultimately robs our children of disciplined direction they genuinely need—even if they won't realize that until they are adults themselves.

Guides Needed

When I served as a teachers quorum adviser, for part of their high adventure activity the young men in our ward rafted down the Hoback, a popular whitewater stretch of the Snake River in Wyoming. Because I'd had some rafting experience, I was asked to be the guide on one of the rafts, assisted by a counselor in the bishopric who had less experience. While I worked hard on this particular outing to create some spiritual opportunities for the boys, my goal on the float trip was to build rapport with the young men by having fun on the river. We wore life jackets and followed appropriate safety precautions as we shot the rapids, but we also swam, splashed, and played.

We actually floated the same stretch twice, and on our second run our raft was in hot pursuit of another group of boys in hopes of playing king of the raft with them. We paddled hard, but we were unable to catch up to them until we reached the departing point, where a bit of an eddy created some backwater next to the concrete ramp used for exiting the river. (With hindsight, the water here flowed much more quickly than I had imagined.) When the boys in the other raft least expected it, I leaped onto their raft in hopes of throwing a young man or two into the water. They repelled my attack, and I soon found myself alone in the water. Richard Whiting, our Young Men's president, pointed out an escaping paddle that had gotten knocked loose in the fray, which I quickly volunteered to retrieve. I managed to fetch the paddle and shove it back to Richard without much trouble, but as I swam back toward the raft, I was surprised that I was unable to make much headway. I'd gotten caught in the current of the river, so I finally signaled to Richard, who threw me a lifeline and pulled me to safety.

In the meantime, both my raft and his had also gotten caught in the current, floating downriver from the designated point for getting out. As we looked downriver, we saw another set of rapids crashing around an island of jagged rock, with the water to the right forming a narrow, churning alley of rapids. Under the direction of the guides in the boats, the boys in both rafts paddled furiously for the shore. Richard's raft reached safety first, and he threw a line to my former raft, which was drifting perilously close to shooting the unwelcome rapids. Fortunately for the young men in the boat I'd abandoned, Richard is a former football player. Looking something like I imagined Captain Moroni would have looked had he been with us, Richard held the line tightly as he stood firm against the current, gradually hauling the young men to safety.

I apologized profusely to the boys in both rafts, but it was evident from many of their comments that some of them had been unnerved by the whole episode, as had I. As I retired to my tent that night, I poured out my heart in prayer, thanking Heavenly Father for watching over us and guiding us to safety, despite my thoughtlessness.

I also pled for . . . was forgiveness the right word? In jumping out of my raft, my intentions had actually been good; in a bizarre way, a youth leader's willingness to engage in horseplay during the week can often help build rapport that improves his ability to teach them on Sundays. Clearly I had made a mistake, but it was one of the head rather than the heart.

Yet as I communed with Heavenly Father and apologized for putting those young men at risk, I was simultaneously comforted and chastened. The thought occurred to me that in telling folks I was sorry, I had left out someone to whom I owed the biggest apology: David Magleby, the bishopric counselor who had helped guide our raft. Together we were charged—and I was given primary responsibility—for getting the boys safely through the river. By jumping onto the other raft just as we were ready to get out, I had not only jeopardized the safety of the young men, but I had left the other guide all alone with the difficult task of getting the young men to safety. (I subsequently apologized to David for leaving him in the lurch.)

No amount of rapport building could compensate for my failure to bring them safely to their destination. My main job was to be a guide, not just a friend.

The next morning, as I continued to mull over the previous day's events and to plead with the Lord for forgiveness for my poor judgment, I came to see a powerful object lesson regarding my responsibilities as a father and youth leader. Certainly, there is definitely a time and season for levity and even horseplay. Yet my foremost responsibility in this situation was to bring the young men to their destination unharmed. No amount of rapport building could compensate for my failure to bring them safely to their destination. My main job was to be a guide, not just a friend.

Similarly, while appropriate fun and humor can help us be better parents and leaders, we cannot let our efforts to have fun with those we love blind us to our paramount responsibility: to help them return safely to Heavenly Father. Sometimes, a parent or youth leader may want to be the fun one, leaving the guiding duties to the other parent or leaders by default. However, just as I put my guiding partner in an unfair position by abandoning our raft, we put our spouses or fellow leaders in a difficult spot when we expect them to handle the heavy lifting all alone.

This is particularly true for fathers, who are "expected by God and His prophets not only to provide for their families but also to protect them," taught Elder M. Russell Ballard. "Dangers of all sorts abound in the world in which we live. Physical protection against natural or man-made hazards is important. Moral dangers are also all around us, confronting our children from their early years. Fathers play a vital role in protecting children against such snares."[4]

In a world where distractions abound for parents as well as children, prophets have reminded us emphatically that "parents have a sacred duty to rear their children in love and righteousness, to provide for their physical and spiritual needs, to teach them to love and serve one another, to observe the commandments of God and to be law-abiding citizens wherever they live. Husbands and wives—mothers and fathers—will be held accountable before God for the discharge of these obligations."[5] Our children will have plenty of eligible candidates to play the role of friend, but only we can play the role of parent—complete with the sacred duties that role entails.

Vegetables or Ice Cream

As parents and leaders, we often see dangers our children and youth do not perceive. Yes, they have agency, but for us to easily accede to reckless requests is irresponsible, if we perceive risks they do not. For instance, no prudent parent would allow a three-year-old to eat nothing but brownies and ice cream all day long, no matter how earnestly the child begged to do so or how popular it would make us in the short term. "It can be . . . destructive when parents are too permissive and overindulge their children, allowing children to do as they please," explained Elder Ballard. "Parents need to set limits in accordance with the importance of the matter involved and the child's disposition and maturity."[6]

Most of us can resist such outlandish requests from a toddler, but holding firm becomes more difficult as children grow older and their requests more tempting. It's surprising just how much upward pressure children and youth can exert on their parents and leaders. In the short term, parents will be better liked if they let children watch any movie they want; Primary teachers will be more popular if they play more games; and professors' scores on student evaluations may go up if they assign less work. But as I tell students in my Missionary Preparation classes, I'm much more concerned about what they think of me in two years than in two months. Once on their missions, former students regularly thank me for making them do work about which some of them grumbled at the time.

For our youth to be valiant in a world of declining moral standards requires our youth to stand up to others and, occasionally, parents to stand up to their youth.

The time may come—indeed, it invariably comes—when we must allow our children to decide for themselves how they will live, even if they choose poorly. But shouldn't that time be preceded by years of teaching and vetoing and warning? It's one thing when a parent is no longer able to persuade an 18-year-old to attend Church, but quite another when a 12-year-old says she doesn't feel like going to Mutual, a 13-year-old wants to buy a bikini, or a 15-year-old wants to date. As Elder Jeffrey R. Holland taught in urging parents to review *For the Strength of Youth* with their children, "Second only to your love, they need your limits."[7]

Some parents may also feel pressure to be more permissive so that their children can fit in. For our youth to be valiant in a world of declining moral standards requires our youth to stand up to others and, occasionally, parents to stand up to their youth. "Some parents seem to be almost pathologically concerned about their children's popularity and social acceptance and go along with many things that are really against their better judgment, such as expensive fads, immodest clothes, late hours, dating before age sixteen, R-rated movies, and so on," warned Elder Joe J. Christensen. "For children and parents, standing up for what is right may be lonely at times. There may be evenings alone, parties missed, and movies which go unseen. It may not always be fun. But parenting is not a popularity contest."[8]

In the final analysis, Dr. William J. Doherty describes many parents in this generation as "devoted, caring, and sensitive—and afraid of displeasing their children. They are parents who set too few limits, because they are afraid to upset their children too much."[9] Our intentions may be good, but by trying to spare our children and ourselves the costs of discipline now, we simply defer and probably increase the price they will eventually have to pay to learn important life lessons. "If parents do not discipline their children, then the public will discipline them in a way the parents do not like," taught President James E. Faust.[10]

The research of BYU professors Brent Top and Bruce Chadwick confirms this:

> Youth who grow up in homes without specific rules or expectations often fail to learn to positively control their own behavior. They tend to act impulsively and are highly susceptible to peer influences, both of which contribute to delinquency. It was interesting to note that few youth complained about the strictness of their parents or number of family rules. On the contrary, several youth wrote they wished their parents would have been *more* strict and had given them *more* guidance through these difficult years."[11]

Just as children often thank their parents years later for encouraging them to press ahead with piano lessons rather than quit, children who have learned discipline, obedience, and the ability to work are usually grateful as adults, despite whatever resistance they may have offered in their youth.

It's worth noting that what children need is not necessarily a slew of complicated, arbitrary rules, but simply rules and guidance in key areas. Research by William Dyer and Phillip Kunz suggests that the most successful LDS families have rules but only a few, and those are quite specific. However, what rules they do have are accompanied by high expectations.[12]

Like any young movie star whose life is spiraling out of control, what straying children often need is a wise, firm parent, not a better lawyer to keep them out of jail or a better publicist to put the best spin on their irresponsible behavior.

The Love of Mother Bears

Rooting for our children is certainly a virtue, and failing to help them see their potential would be a shame. A few parents move beyond offering positive encouragement to their children to the point where their love blinds them to any of their children's flaws. Slavish devotion to our children can make it difficult for us to provide loving, needed course correction, since we may fail to see how they are sailing off course. Some parents overlook warning signs provided by concerned friends or others, and they may even develop something of a bunker mentality as they rally behind their child to defend her against all those who now conspire against her. Moreover, when mother bear parents (who can be fathers too) finally realize that their children have gone astray, their primary goal is often to excuse their children rather than to reform them. They may blame their son's friends for his poor decisions or find fault with a principal or bishop for doling out punishment they deem too severe.

I remember one woman who was concerned that the bishop might be alienating her son by not allowing him to go to the temple to perform baptisms for the dead, shortly after the young man had participated in some significant vandalism. I was grateful for the bishop's wisdom. What kind of message would he have sent the boy if he'd allowed him to enter the house of the Lord so soon after committing such an act? When our love for our children leads us to shield them from the consequences of their misconduct, how well are we really serving them? Like any young movie star whose life is spiraling out of control, what straying children often need is a wise, firm parent, not a better lawyer to keep them out of jail or a better publicist to put the best spin on their irresponsible behavior.

Another manifestation of the mother bear problem occurs when we want our children to succeed so desperately that we are unwilling to let them fail. We might buy them clothes or cars or provide so generously for their education that they never have to have a job—until they've finished their schooling and have to provide for their families. But those who are spared the need to work until adulthood may discover they are at a great disadvantage when it comes to succeeding in the workplace. At an executive retreat I once attended, we were all asked to describe our first and our worst jobs. I was pleasantly surprised that almost to a person, each executive in the room had begun working at a relatively young age and had undertaken tasks that ranged from menial to repugnant. Yet by refusing to spare these future business leaders the pains of hard work, their parents had given them a valuable foundation for their careers.

OVERCONTROLLERS

Recognizing the problems outlined in the first half of this chapter, many swing to the opposite extreme. Determined not to let their children sink into the lake of moral decadence that has become so large in our day, they build fences and even walls to prevent their children from stumbling in—only to discover their children still find a way to sneak through the barriers and immerse themselves in trouble. Eager to make sure their children make no wrong turns, they may try to program every single step of their journey—only to find their children eagerly taking detours as soon as they can break free from parental control. Adamant about producing obedience in their children, they may make disciplinary mountains out of behavioral molehills—only to find themselves engaged in power struggles with their children that they cannot win. Focused on rallying the troops to righteousness, such parents might shout at their children to be quiet for family prayer (I plead guilty)—only to discover that they have chased away the Spirit with the tone of their invitation.

In its extreme form, this kind of parenting may even border on exercising unrighteous dominion. Elder H. Burke Peterson offered this inventory for parents who naturally list toward a more dominant form of parenting. His questions were targeted toward fathers but are almost equally applicable to mothers:

"Do I criticize family members more than I compliment them?"

"Do I insist that family members obey me because I am the father or husband and hold the priesthood?"

"Do I seek happiness more at work or somewhere other than in my home?"

"Do my children seem reluctant to talk to me about some of their feelings and concerns?"

"Do I attempt to guarantee my place of authority by physical discipline or punishment?"

"Do I find myself setting and enforcing numerous rules to control family members?"

"Do family members appear to be fearful of me?"

"Do I feel threatened by the notion of sharing with other family members the power and responsibility for decision making in the family?

"Is my wife highly dependent on me and unable to make decisions for herself?

"Does my wife complain that she has insufficient funds to manage the household because I control all the money?

"Do I insist on being the main source of inspiration for each individual family member rather than teaching each child to listen to the Spirit?

"Do I often feel angry and critical toward family members?"[13]

For those sometimes drawn to this overcontrolling extreme, I offer nine principles to consider.

1. Nothing works quite like love. Heavy-handed parenting can be not only improper but ineffective. President Gordon B. Hinckley once noted that discipline "with severity, discipline with cruelty, inevitably leads not to correction, but rather to resentment and bitterness. It cures nothing. It only aggravates the problem. It is self-defeating." On the other hand, observed President Hinckley, "there is no discipline in all the world like the discipline of love. It has a magic all its own. . . . Remember that it is love, more than any other thing, that will bring them back. Punishment is not likely to do it. Reprimands without love will not accomplish it."[14]

The Spirit may certainly inspire us to warn our children in bold terms at times, but if such warnings are not undergirded by genuine love, they will likely fall on deaf ears. What precipitated Enos's epiphany in the woods was not so much Jacob's stern warnings, but "the words which [he] had often heard [his] father speak concerning eternal life, and the joy of the saints, [which] sunk deep into [his] heart" (Enos 1:3).

Even as adults in the workplace or our Church callings, most of us respond much better to love than coercion. Joseph Smith noted this principle when he said: "Nothing is so much calculated to lead people to forsake sin as to take them by the hand, and watch over them with tenderness. When persons manifest the least kindness and love to me, O what power it has over my mind, while the opposite course has a tendency to harrow up all the harsh feelings and depress the human mind."[15]

2. The best solutions cannot be imposed. I once had a young home

160

teaching companion who, like many young men, struggled to decide whether to go on a mission. For me and most active members of the Church, recognizing that he ought to go on a mission was relatively simple. But we sometimes mistakenly think that's the end of the analysis rather than the midpoint. This may be especially true for parents who have ruled by edict with apparent success in their children's younger years. If their children are on the verge of making a bad decision—such as not going on a mission or not marrying well—their instinct may be to simply announce to their children that they must make a better choice.

Sadly, such parents have overlooked a critical step that must follow the realization that our children are sailing off course: rather than try to push them back on course, we must find a way to persuade them to choose the right course. M. Catherine Thomas observed: "We learn that no child of any age can be forced to accept solutions he doesn't want. A child may even prefer the trouble to the solution. Parents can pray for readiness in a child but must wait for that spiritual readiness to come to the child. As we learn divine patience, we come to understand our Savior's love more and more."[16]

Patricia Holland candidly told of a battle she had with her daughter, Mary, that will be familiar to almost every parent whose children have taken piano lessons. Although her daughter was musically gifted, Sister Holland felt that the girl would not develop her talents without constant supervision. However, the friction between mother and daughter soon began to strain their relationship. After seeking direction from the Lord in private prayer, this wise mother felt inspired to take an entirely different tack. She gave her daughter an apron—with the strings clearly cut—and this note tucked inside: "Dear Mary, I'm sorry for the conflict I have caused by acting like a federal marshall at the piano. I must have looked foolish there—just you and me and my six-shooters. Forgive me. You are becoming a young woman in your own right. I have only worried that you would not feel as fully confident and fulfilled as a woman if you left your talent unfinished. I love you. Mom."

Mary's reaction was as impressive as her mother's humility. "Mother, I know you want what is best for me, and I have known that all my life. But if I'm ever going to play the piano well, *I'm* the one who has to do the practicing, not you!" According to Sister Holland, Mary then "threw her arms around me and with tears in her eyes she said, 'I've been wondering how to teach you that—and somehow you figured it out on your own.' Now, by her own choice, she has gone on to even more disciplined musical development."[17]

3. Explanations instill obedience more than directives. Wise parents' aims are never simply to get children to comply with God's commandments and their rules. Instead, they seek to cultivate in their children a desire to keep the commandments and follow meaningful rules. When we keep foremost in our minds that our children must ultimately choose without any compulsion from us whether to repent, serve missions, marry faithfully, forgive others, keep the Word of Wisdom, and live the law of chastity, we will bombard them not so much with rules to prevent them from making bad choices as with teachings to inspire them to make good ones. Just as employees who understand the reason for a company policy are more likely to adhere to it, children who understand why they should behave in a certain way are more likely to obey.

> When we keep foremost in our minds that our children must ultimately make their own decisions, we will bombard them not so much with rules to prevent them from making bad choices as with teachings to inspire them to make good ones.

Elder Robert D. Hales told of being on the receiving end of such inspired instruction as a child. His father was a busy commercial artist in New York City. One Saturday, he was working at home to meet an important deadline. Contrary to their father's instructions, Robert and his sister gleefully chased each other around the dining room table directly over the studio where their father was working. "He had told us to please stop at least twice, but to no avail. This time he came bounding up the steps and collared me. He sat me down and taught a great lesson. He did not yell or strike me even though he was very annoyed. He explained the creative process, the spiritual process, if you will, and the need for quiet pondering and getting close to the Spirit for his creativity to function. Because he took time to explain and help me understand, I learned a lesson that has been put to use almost on a daily basis in my life."[18]

4. Act in council rather than unilaterally. Occasionally, my children strike a nerve with me, and my natural-man reflex is to react quickly and sternly. In such situations, I have always behaved more wisely by counseling with my wife before pronouncing punishments or new rules. (On rarer occasions, she may even benefit from my tempering influence if she is the one whose buttons have been pushed.) And our best results have always come when we have been able to involve our children in setting the rules or prescribing punishments. It is difficult for children to protest rules or consequences they helped establish.

Not only are rules set unilaterally less effective, but Elder Peterson went so far as to say that when "a father demands compliance with rules he has arbitrarily set," he is exercising unrighteous dominion. "This is contrary to the spirit of gospel leadership. Indeed, a man can add a rich dimension to his leadership when he considers rules with his wife and children who, together with him, can set them in place."[19]

5. Allow choice within proper frameworks. The day will come—often sooner than we think—when our children will make choices on their own. We may be able to control some decisions almost right up until they leave the home, but we cannot control others even when they live in our homes. But if our children are allowed little independence and opportunity to exercise agency before leaving home, they will almost certainly use their agency poorly when they are finally free to act for themselves.

Wise parents introduce choice incrementally to their children. When I was about six or seven years old, a friend asked if I could play soccer with him on Sunday. I knew the family rule against sports on Sundays, but decided to ask my dad anyway. "It's up to you," he said, or something along those lines.

If our children are allowed little independence and opportunity to exercise agency before leaving home, they will almost certainly use their agency poorly when they are finally free to act for themselves.

"Really?" I tested, stunned at this turn of events. He assured me that the choice was mine, although I knew where my parents stood.

I gleefully played soccer with my friend, puzzled by my good fortune. As I recall, there was no real deliberation involved in the matter: allowed to play, I immediately jumped at the chance.

That's the last time I remember being given a choice in such a matter for several years. But another opportunity arose when I was about eleven and had signed up to play organized football in pads for the first time. After three weeks of challenging conditioning that left my young body quite sore, my best friend and I were named starting running backs for the exhibition game, which was held on a Saturday. It was something of a little boy's dream come true, but the dream was short-lived. Our games were announced on a week-by-week basis rather than released to us as part of a printed schedule for the season, so I was taken aback when the coach announced that the next game would be on a Sunday.

"What am I going to do?" I recall asking my mother when I returned home from the game.

"I don't know," she replied. "What are you going to do?"

I had wanted her to make the decision for me, but she declined.

This time, I did deliberate about whether or not to play on Sunday. I don't know how much soul searching I actually did, but something caused me to tell the coach I would not be playing in the game the next week. In fact, I went to practices every weekday all season long and played in only those two or three games that fell on Saturdays. Because I made the decision and the sacrifice on my own, I developed a strong conviction about the importance of keeping the Sabbath day holy at a young age. I also developed a sense of spiritual independence—a sense of ownership, if you will—feeling like I was going to have to take responsibility for important decisions in my life.

With hindsight, I was obviously unprepared at age seven to deal with that much choice. But by giving me another chance a few years later to make such a decision, my parents helped prepare me to make far more important decisions on my own. Just what kinds of decisions we should allow children at what age will vary from child to child. But as we gradually give our children more choices as they handle their agency responsibly, we prepare them well for that season of life when we can and should no longer control their decisions.

6. *Choose our battles carefully.* When I was an assistant to my mission president, President Richard Klein, he taught me a valuable lesson about choosing battles. He had done such a masterful job of instilling obedience in his missionaries that most of the obedience problems we encountered as mission leaders were relatively minor. One day on exchanges with a companionship, we encountered a missionary who was reading a newspaper from back home. Most missionaries would have at least tried to hide the newspaper or might have apologized if caught in the act, but this elder was rather brazen. He continued to read the paper and showed no inclination to stop when I confronted him about this clear violation of mission rules.

At a loss for what to do next, I told him that he'd be having an interview with the mission president about this matter. It seemed to me it was going to take someone with much more authority than I had to resolve the problem. But when I told President Klein what I'd done, he was visibly frustrated. I cannot remember his exact words, but the gist of his message to me was that he wanted to be able to choose his own battles—and this was not one he would have chosen. He was already aware that he was dealing with an elder who had a rebellious streak, but I had just escalated matters and thus put my mission president in a difficult spot.

At a time in life when I was being taught the importance of total obedience, it was all too easy for me to want to make a federal case out of any blatant disobedience. But as I watched my mission president work with missionaries who struggled, I learned that he had a goal in mind that was larger than mere compliance with each mission rule. While he certainly would not have tolerated any serious misconduct such as sexual sin, he patiently tried to work through minor offenses with missionaries in a way that allowed them to complete their missions with dignity. He understood that as long as these missionaries remained in full fellowship in the gospel, there was plenty of opportunity for them to continue to grow and improve bit by bit. But if he sent them home or otherwise alienated them, he knew that he could push them away from the Church altogether, where subsequent spiritual improvement would become dramatically more difficult.

Perhaps President Klein's approach influenced me years later when I counseled with an irate father. This father was a forceful parent who was passionate about his rules, and his teenage son had violated one of them by playing his electric guitar at a time or a place in the house that the father had expressly forbidden. This latest bit of defiance was apparently the culminating act in a series of minor rebellions, and the furious father said he'd had enough: his son had repeatedly violated the rules of the home, so he would no longer be allowed to live there. As I listened to his frustrations, we counseled together, and I tried to walk him through the possible consequences of such a stern punishment. Ultimately, the father agreed that he would rather not permanently alienate his son by expelling him for playing a guitar.

This parent's reaction may have been a bit extreme, but most of us feel torn at times about how to handle blatant defiance of our rules. As one writer observed: "When the adolescent rebels or deviates from the expected behavior in some way, parents usually try to increase their control in an effort to bring them back in line. But such control tends to cause further deviation rather than improving the situation. By arbitrarily imposing more control, parents may innocently cause—or at least encourage—the very behavior they don't want. And the result is a power struggle over who is going to control whom."[20]

There will be times when we need to place a foot down firmly, but we may have a limited number of battles we can fight with our children before we lose the war. That makes choosing those battles carefully a critical exercise. We can sometimes avoid squandering our conflicts on relatively minor matters simply by stepping back and taking a deep breath before acting.

I remember one evening when my daughter Rebecca, who was about three at the time, was being particularly difficult. I was getting so annoyed with her that I found myself almost wanting to have an excuse to discipline her. As I asked her unsuccessfully to *please* go to her bedroom and get in bed for what seemed like the third time, I was on the verge of losing my temper when I felt prompted to pause and pray for guidance. (Please do not think I'm a better parent than I am; this is far too rare an occurrence.) I managed to step back emotionally and offer a feeble prayer, which was apparently just enough for the Spirit to whisper a bit of inspiration to my ill-tempered soul: *Make a game out of it; turn out the lights.* This simple idea allowed me to rise above the power struggle into which I'd gotten sucked with this three-year-old. "Oh, oh!" I exclaimed in a completely different tone, which caused Rebecca to stop in her tracks. "The lights are going out, and I'm going to beat you to the bedroom!" I had barely flicked off the lights when my daughter, who was now darling once again, had dashed into her bedroom.

7. Correct out of love rather than anger. My encounter with

Rebecca illustrates the wisdom of the time-tested maxim that parents should punish only out of love and never out of anger. As Joy Evans declared: "Discipline is given in love by a parent in control for the benefit of the child. Abuse is given in anger as a release for the parent."[21]

When disciplining, time is rarely of the essence; we can often wait a few moments or even hours to cool down and consider our options before dealing with the matter. One writer advised: "Wait until the anger dissipates. . . . It is surprising how many potentially explosive situations can be controlled simply by waiting until the emotion is gone. You are in control. You have many creative ideas about the problem. Now you can approach with calmness, communicate freely, and, if necessary, discipline—with love."[22]

Some parents may mistakenly rely on the scriptural direction to "reprove betimes with sharpness" to justify harshly reprimanding their children. "Perhaps we should consider what it means to reprove with sharpness," suggested Elder Peterson. "Reproving with sharpness means reproving with clarity, with loving firmness, with serious intent. It does not mean reproving with sarcasm, or with bitterness, or with clenched teeth and raised voice. One who reproves as the Lord has directed deals in principles, not personalities. He does not attack character or demean an individual."[23]

8. Allow for failure. Some parents are so intent on making sure that their children succeed that they do much of the work their children should have done. We commonly joke that mothers should be awarded the Eagle instead of their sons, and some parental prodding is certainly in order. But at what point does parents' desire for their son to get his Eagle actually backfire? What lesson does a young man learn if he can obtain such an award without putting forth much effort? Might he actually learn a more valuable lesson if, after persistent nagging from his parents and continued procrastination on his part, he did not receive the award at all?

I vividly remember counseling with a talented student who was failing my class. She acknowledged that she had not really learned how to discipline herself to get her assignments done on her own because her mother had carried her through her last two years of high school so that she could graduate. Her mother's efforts had been extraordinary and well meaning, but as this young woman realized, she had leaned so heavily on her parent for help that she had not yet learned to stand on her own. Elder Neal A. Maxwell said: "Those who do too much *for* their children will soon find they can do nothing *with* their children. So many children have been so much *done for* they are almost *done in*."[24]

9. Leave doors and options open. Unfortunately, our conflicts with our children may occasionally reach the boiling point, culminating in them leaving home. Having never personally experienced that terrible situation, I can only imagine how difficult it must be for parents to exercise restraint and love under those circumstances. But Elder Hales wisely counseled temperance in what otherwise could become a fiery farewell: "We must never, out of anger, lock the door of our home or our heart to our children."[25] He pointed out that one of the keys to the return of the prodigal son was that "the son knew that upon his return he would be loved and welcomed home by his father."[26] Elder Hales's insight leads me to wonder what the parting words of the prodigal's father might have been. For the son to have had such confidence upon his return, surely they must have been uttered out of love rather than anger. "Like the prodigal son," concluded Elder Hales, "our children need to know that when they come to themselves they can turn to us for love and counsel."[27]

STRIKING THE BALANCE

I recall sharing some thoughts about how my parents had raised my brother and sisters and me during a priesthood meeting when I was home from college. After the lesson, a longtime ward member who was quite reserved with his advice pulled me aside and pointed out, in a very kind way, that our family was, frankly, not normal. What had worked in our home would not necessarily work in other homes, he cautioned—and he was right. And I freely concede that I am in the same situation with my own children. They are the ones, for instance, who insist that I wear my seatbelt! I can claim little or no credit for their good behavior, nor can I safely extrapolate from my experience with them about what will work with other children.

President Faust noted that "one of the most difficult parental challenges is to appropriately discipline children. Child rearing is so individualistic. Every child is different and unique. What works with one may not work with another. I do not know who is wise enough to say what discipline is too harsh or what is too lenient except the parents of the children themselves, who love them most. It is a matter of prayerful discernment for the parents. Certainly the overarching and undergirding principle is that the discipline of children must be motivated more by love than by punishment."[28]

While our disciplinary decisions must be based on children's individual needs and motivated by love, I have also found some metaphors used by my family sciences colleague Steve Dennis to be useful in striving to strike the appropriate balance. In teaching about different types of parenting styles, Professor Dennis uses a marshmallow, a jawbreaker, and a tennis ball to represent the extremes and the ideal. Marshmallow parents are soft but tend to melt under pressure. Jawbreaker parents have structure but are overly rigid and authoritarian. Tennis ball parents strike the perfect balance, being soft and flexible enough to bounce but strong enough to be durable.

Notes

1. Ezra Taft Benson, "To the Fathers in Israel," *Ensign*, Nov. 1987, 51.

2. Patricia T. Holland, "Parenting: Everything to Do with the Heart," *Ensign*, June 1985, 12.

3. For the record, I should note that I was blessed with model parents in this regard. My aim has been to mimic them in striking the best balance of discipline and love.

4. M. Russell Ballard, "The Sacred Responsibilities of Parenthood," *Ensign,* Mar. 2006, 30.

5. "The Family: A Proclamation to the World," *Ensign,* Nov. 1995, 102.

6. Ballard, "The Sacred Responsibilities of Parenthood," 32.

7. Jeffrey R. Holland, "To Young Women," *Ensign,* Nov. 2005, 29.

8. Joe J. Christensen, "Rearing Children in a Polluted Environment," *Ensign,* Nov. 1993, 11.

9. William J. Doherty, *Take Back Your Kids: Confident Parenting in Turbulent Times* (Notre Dame, Indiana: Sorin Books, 2000), 14

10. James E. Faust, "A Thousand Threads of Love," *Ensign,* Oct. 2005, 5.

11. Brent L. Top and Bruce A. Chadwick, "Helping Teens Stay Strong," *Ensign,* Mar. 1999, 33; emphasis in original.

12. William G. Dyer and Phillip R. Kunz, *Effective Mormon Families: How They See Themselves* (Salt Lake City: Deseret Book, 1986), 42.

13. H. Burke Peterson, "Unrighteous Dominion," *Ensign,* July 1989, 10–11.

14. Gordon B. Hinckley, "The Environment of Our Homes," *Ensign,* June 1985, 4, 6.

15. Joseph Smith, *Teachings of the Prophet Joseph Smith,* sel. Joseph Fielding Smith (Salt Lake City: Deseret Book, 1976), 240.

16. M. Catherine Thomas, "A Parent's Love and Fear," *Ensign,* July 1993, 24.

17. Holland, "Parenting: Everything to Do with the Heart," 14; emphasis in original.

18. Robert D. Hales, "How Will Our Children Remember Us?" *Ensign,* Nov. 1993, 9.

19. Peterson, "Unrighteous Dominion," 8.

20. C. Richard Chidester, "The Fine Art of Raising Teenagers," *Ensign,* July 1981, 39–40.

21. Joy Evans, "Help for Parents in Times of Stress: Preventing Abuse," *Ensign,* Apr. 1984, 60.

22. Arlyn L. Jesperson, "Learning to Lead Our Family—'Without Compulsory Means,'" *Ensign,* Apr. 1983, 54.

23. Peterson, "Unrighteous Dominion," 10.

24. Neal A. Maxwell, "The Man of Christ," *Ensign,* May 1975, 101; emphasis in original.

25. Robert D. Hales, "Strengthening Families: Our Sacred Duty," *Ensign,* May 1999, 33.

26. Robert D. Hales, "'Some Have Compassion, Making a Difference,'" *Ensign,* May 1987, 77.

27. Hales, "Strengthening Families: Our Sacred Duty," *Ensign*, May 1999, 33.

28. Faust, "A Thousand Threads of Love," 4–5.

CHAPTER 10

IDOLIZERS AND
DETRACTORS

Many good Christians believe that the Bible is the inerrant word of God, meaning it contains no mistakes of translation, doctrine, or fact. At the other extreme, many scholars who call themselves Christians have concluded that the Bible is merely inspired fable or even the fanciful concoction of overzealous disciples. When it comes to this particular pair of extremes, Latter-day Saints have built-in doctrinal guidance reminding us that we believe "the Bible to be the word of God as far as it is translated correctly" (Articles of Faith 1:8).

Yet we face a similar dilemma when it comes to how we view our Church leaders, from bishops to prophets. A few view our prophets as virtually infallible and idolize Church leaders in ways that become problematic when their perceptions of perfection prove to be unfounded. Others are fixated on finding flaws in prophetic character and statements, eager not just to cut back on the scope of teachings we consider to be prophetic but to cut down the overall standing of prophets.

Ironically, those who assume the scriptures or God's leaders must be perfect in every way sometimes swing to the opposite extreme after discovering they were mistaken. For them, it's all or nothing with God's word and His leaders. Having concluded that those documents and individuals were not all they once hoped them to be, they then dismiss them as nothing at all.

Rather than discuss each extreme separately in this chapter, I discuss both extremes together as they apply in various contexts, beginning with how we view God's word.

GOD'S WORD

The Bible

One of the leading New Testament scholars in the world today, Bart Ehrman, began his religious odyssey by becoming a born-again Christian as a teenager. He obtained his bachelor's degree at Moody Bible Institute, a theologically conservative Bible college where he was taught that the Bible is the inerrant word of God—perfect in every way. He then pursued graduate studies in theology at Princeton Theological Seminary, where his view of the Bible was first seriously challenged. Grappling with a difficult New Testament passage in which Mark seems to make a factual error, Ehrman wrote a paper defending Mark's assertion with rather tortured logic. His professor, who was a believer, wrote one line of feedback that began to shatter the young scholar's theological worldview: "Maybe Mark just made a mistake."[1]

Ehrman proceeded with his studies and soon discovered that almost all modern Bible translations (including the King James) are based on later Greek copies of the New Testament than the oldest Greek copies that are now available. His belief that the Bible was inerrant simply could not withstand the discovery of literally thousands of variations that crept into the text through the centuries. In *Misquoting Jesus* the scholar documents how this could have occurred and provides examples that must be disturbing to others who believe their translation of the Bible contains no deviations from the original text. In fact, he makes a compelling argument that the greatest changes were likely to have occurred with the earliest generations of Christian scribes, who were probably untrained volunteers doing the best they could with limited education. Because our oldest copies of the entire set of New Testament books dates only to roughly 200 A.D., Ehrman notes we have no idea just how many more errors were introduced by lay scribes before that date.[2] (From an LDS perspective, we would not be surprised to find even greater errors of omission and commission introduced during this period of apostasy.)

So far, so good. For Latter-day Saints equipped with the eighth article of faith, reading about such errors actually bolsters rather than undermines our faith. But for someone who began with a belief in the inerrancy of the Bible, such discoveries can be deeply unsettling. In fact, once he acknowledged the possibility of error in the Bible, Ehrman admits, "the floodgates opened." Indeed, once an earnest born-again Christian who believed in the infallibility of the Bible, Ehrman became a theologian who admits, "The Bible began to appear to me as a very human book. Just as human scribes had copied, and changed, the texts of scripture, so too had human authors originally *written* the texts of scripture. This was a human book from beginning to end."[3]

Why would someone who had believed so fervently in the Bible come to take it so lightly? Ehrman explains his about-face this way: "If [God] really wanted people to have his actual words, surely he would have miraculously preserved those words, just as he had miraculously inspired them in the first place. Given the circumstance that he didn't preserve the words, the conclusion seemed inescapable to me that he hadn't gone to the trouble of inspiring them."[4] (Ehrman's view, of course, fails to take into account God's extraordinary commitment to agency—a commitment that has led Heavenly Father to allow prophets to be stoned, kings to apostatize, and Israel to be scattered in unbelief.) Built on a faulty premise, Ehrman's conviction of the Bible's inspired nature crumbled when he discovered the flaw in his original thinking.

Interestingly enough, then, while Latter-day Saints have been much maligned for believing in the Bible only as far as it is translated correctly, this very caveat actually guards against the kind of pendulum swing Ehrman made. When pastors and theologians insist the Bible is mistake-free, what are their followers to believe when they come across contradictions between the Gospels, let alone evidence of thousands of scribal errors?

The Book of Mormon

Publication errors. With a divinely commissioned translator and a limited number of scribes, the Book of Mormon would seem to be free of the issues we have just discussed with the Bible. Indeed, the eighth article of faith contains no caveat about translation for the Book of Mormon; we simply believe it to be the word of God. From this, some might assume that the Book of Mormon must be free of all errors of any kind—and that any mistake it contained would prove the book untrue altogether. Indeed, some Christians who believe the Bible to be the inerrant word of God have made essentially this attack on the Book of Mormon, pointing out a number of changes between the first edition and later editions. Because the book has been changed, they argue, the book must not contain the word of God.

How is it possible that errors could have crept into the Book of Mormon with such a brief, divinely overseen translation process? After all, didn't the Lord declare to Oliver Cowdery, David Whitmer, and Martin Harris that the book was "translated by the gift and power of God"?[5] Interestingly, this divine confirmation occurred in June 1829, nine months before the publication of the Book of Mormon. It's clear, then, that the Lord's statement is about the translation itself; it is not a declaration that there were no errors in the first edition that would be published in March 1830. In March of 1830, the Lord did declare that the Book of Mormon contained "the truth and the word of God" (D&C 19:26), but He made no claim of infallibility for the first edition produced by Grandin Press.

When Joseph completed his translation and the book was ready for publication, his scribes had produced a single English manuscript.

To avoid having to give the printer the original, Joseph Smith directed Oliver Cowdery to create a copy to be used by the printer.[6] It was no great shock, then, when a review of the original manuscript resulted in the discovery of "minor errors. Some were simple errors of spelling, grammar, or style; others were apparently printing errors."[7] Consequently, the 1981 edition of the Book of Mormon indicates that it includes changes that were made to "bring the material into conformity with prepublication manuscripts and early editions edited by the Prophet Joseph Smith." According to Elder Boyd K. Packer, none of these changes "altered the doctrine. Each change, however small in detail, was carefully and prayerfully considered and approved by the Council of the First Presidency and the Quorum of the Twelve Apostles in a meeting in the temple."[8] In short, whatever minor imperfections may have crept into the record certainly did not detract from its overall doctrinal message.

Royal Skousen, an English professor at BYU, is conducting meticulous research documenting other instances in which other minor mistakes may have crept in during the publication process. In many cases, the mistakes are almost faith-promoting because the original is more consistent with a Hebraic literary style. Indeed, Skousen's research leads him to conclude that "the original manuscript provides firm evidence in support of what Joseph Smith, Oliver Cowdery, and all witnesses have testified: that Joseph Smith was not the author of the Book of Mormon, but instead he received its English translation by revelation from the Lord through the use of the Urim and Thummim and the seer stone."[9]

The intent of Skousen's research (and of many New Testament scholars who engage in what is called textual criticism)[10] is not to attack the text or undermine faith but to discover what the original text most likely said. For those who believe anything that is of God must be flawless, such an exercise seems heretical. Like Ehrman, they think that if God were behind a work of scripture, He would not have allowed any mistakes to creep in. The last prophet to write in the Book of Mormon humbly took a much wiser view. Moroni acknowledged that reliance on reformed Egyptian rather than Hebrew may have led to some imperfections in the record. But he added this caution for those tempted to dismiss the work in its entirety because of any flaws they discovered: "Condemn me not because of mine imperfection, neither my father, because of his imperfection, neither them who have written before him; but rather give thanks unto God that he hath made manifest unto you our imperfections, that ye may learn to be more wise than we have been" (Mormon 9:31).

Seeking a middle ground that does not exist. I often ask my students why the Lord didn't let the Book of Mormon come forth in a way that would have been less polarizing. If the Lord had allowed it to emerge like the Dead Sea Scrolls—discovered by a shepherd and translated by a team of international scholars—surely it would be a perennial best-seller. The same might be true if Joseph Smith had simply said, "Here's a story I made up. I hope it might be of worth to some of you. I felt inspired as I wrote it."

Either method of producing the book would be much less objectionable and divisive to the general public than the book's actual origin. But Terryl Givens, a widely respected scholar who is LDS, observed incisively that Joseph's account of how he produced the book leaves no room for creative attempts at finding a theologically neutral explanation of the book's origin. "With Joseph Smith serving as translator rather than author, a comfortable middle ground— that the record is a human product perhaps meriting some divine approbation—is well-nigh impossible."[11] Of the events that Joseph claimed happened, President Gordon B. Hinckley similarly declared: "They either happened or they did not. There can be no gray area, no middle ground."[12] We certainly welcome the work of many scholars outside the Church who are taking Joseph Smith and the substance of the Book of Mormon more seriously, even though they continue to reject the story of its origin. But in the end, no amount of increased respect for the content of the book can ever truly bridge the gap between those who disagree about its origin.

Surely the Lord intended it to be so. My follow-up question to my students is, "What benefits would be lost if the Book of Mormon had come forth in one of those more conventional ways?" They quickly note that investigators of the Restoration would be robbed of the ultimate proving ground for testing Joseph Smith's claims. With the Book of Mormon, the Lord not only provided us with the restoration of plain and precious truths, but he did so in a way that forces the issue of whether Joseph was a prophet or not. We can enjoy the fictional works of J.R.R. Tolkien, Paulo Coelho, and others without believing they are prophets because they never claimed their works were delivered to them by an angel. Precisely because Joseph's story about the book's origin is so concrete and fantastic, the method by which God delivered the book provides us with a claim that serves as the ultimate litmus test for all of Joseph's claims about the Restoration. If we learn through the Spirit that his story about the Book of Mormon's origin is true, we know all his claims are true. Conversely, if he lied about how he got the Book of Mormon, it is inconceivable that he told the truth about seeing Heavenly Father, the Savior, or any other heavenly messengers.

In the end, no amount of increased respect for the content of the book can ever truly bridge the gap between those who disagree about its origin.

Thus, no matter how earnestly a few may strive to stake out a middle ground in hopes of bridging the gap between the book's detractors and defenders, any bridge they try to construct collapses under the weight of logic. If any explanation other than the one Joseph himself gave is accurate, then Joseph was a fraud and the book is a work of fiction. The book might be considered brilliant or inspiring, and Joseph's lies could be considered well-intentioned or delusional, but the fact would remain that Joseph was a liar. But if the book is what Joseph claims it is, one cannot escape the conclusion that Joseph was a prophet who communed with heaven.

Confusing ends and means. Whether we are speaking of the Bible, the Book of Mormon, or any other volume of scripture, one other subtle but serious danger is worth noting: becoming so enamored with the study of scriptural trivia that we miss the messianic forest through the trees. The Savior chastised Jewish leaders who had become master scriptorians but were unable to recognize the Master of whom the scriptures taught: "Search the scriptures; for in them *ye think* ye have eternal life: and they are they which testify of me" (John 5:39; emphasis added). In other words, if we believe that the scriptures or our knowledge of them will save us, we are making a tragic mistake. The scriptures are invaluable because they point us to the Savior, who alone can give us eternal life.

Perhaps in our own scripture study a few of us become so zealous in mastering every bit of historic, geographic, cultural, or even textual detail that we are in danger of looking beyond the mark. Richard L. Anderson—a great gospel scholar who managed to become extremely knowledgeable without losing sight of the true purpose of the scriptures—observed that "it is an occupational hazard to be so technically proficient that only technicalities are of interest."[13] Often such individuals are among those Paul identified as "ever learning, and never able to come to the knowledge of the truth" (2 Timothy 3:7). So, while many members of the Church need to take their study of the scriptures more seriously, a few of us may need to guard against becoming so excited about ancillary aspects of the scriptures that we overlook the purpose for which they were written: "But these are written, that ye might believe that Jesus is the Christ, the Son of God; and that believing ye might have life through his name" (John 20:31).

GOD'S LEADERS

The Dangers of Idolizing

Dashed expectations. While it's usually safer to think too much of someone rather than too little, there is some danger in placing Church leaders on pedestals of perfection. To begin with, whether we're talking about missionaries, seminary teachers, Young Women's presidents, bishops, mission presidents, General Authorities, or even prophets, if we expect flawlessness of our leaders, our expectations will inevitably be dashed. Some members are able to adjust their thinking when they begin to perceive shortcomings in leaders, recognizing that the Church and its doctrines remain true even though our leaders are imperfect. But others seem to have such idealized conceptions of what a leader should be that their belief in the Church of Jesus Christ is rocked to the core when they discover blemishes in individual Church leaders. Like Bart Ehrman's view of the Bible, they conclude that if the leaders aren't perfect, then the Church can't be of God.

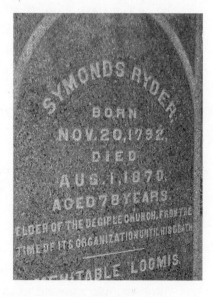

This is almost exactly what happened in the well-known case of Symonds Ryder. Converted by a miracle, he apparently thought the world of the Prophet—until his name was misspelled in a revelation Joseph dictated for him. That misspelling not only rocked the foundation of Symonds's shaky testimony, but it was the beginning of a wild swing of the pendulum. Sadly, Symonds went from being a supporter of Joseph to a leader of the mob that tarred and feathered the young prophet in Hiram, Ohio. (Ironically, Ryder's tombstone misspells the name of the church to which he belonged.)

In short, if we expect our leaders to be perfect spellers, perfect communicators, or perfect human beings, we are bound to be disappointed. Having set unrealistically high expectations for them, we are poorly situated for their inevitable falls.

Difficulty shifting gears. A second danger of becoming inordinately attached to certain Church leaders or placing them on pedestals occurs when they pass on, move, or are released. When we have grown to love a particular missionary, bishop, mission president, or even prophet more than the doctrines they have taught and the Savior of whom they testify, we may have great difficulty adjusting to their replacement.

One colleague told me about how a ward member approached him a month after he'd been released as bishop in hopes that my friend would counsel with him on a matter that was clearly the exclusive purview of the new bishop. My friend said he'd be happy to talk with the man as a friend but that only the new bishop who held the keys could give him the help he really needed. "But you and I both know that the bishop swears," pointed out the disappointed ward member, and it was true (or at least had been). The new bishop lived in their neighborhood, and both my friend and the man in his ward had heard him swearing on more than one occasion while working on his car. Because this ward member's expectation was that a bishop should never swear, he was unwilling to go to the new bishop for counsel. My friend wisely reminded this ward member that while the office, mantle, and keys of the bishop were perfect, bishops were not, and that despite his imperfections, the new bishop alone had the keys to help this man. As Elder Spencer J. Condie observed, "callings in the Church are for the 'perfecting of the saints,' not necessarily for perfect Saints."[14]

My friend resisted the temptation to be flattered by the request of the ward member and to undermine the new bishop in any way. Similarly, wise stewards in any position of influence in the Church avoid doing anything to stand between the Savior and those for whom they have stewardship. I distinctly remember being pricked and inspired by the words of a fellow institute director at one training meeting several years ago. A humble, Christ-centered man, this teacher said, "I cringe when students mention me in the closing prayer." *I* cringed when he said that, because I had to admit I felt touched if students mentioned me in a closing prayer. This wise brother went on to explain that he felt like he had failed in his mission if students remembered him instead of the Savior and His doctrines. Whether teaching, ministering, or leading in the Church, we might wisely follow the counsel of John the Baptist about the Savior: "He must increase, but I must decrease" (John 3:30). Wise disciple-leaders always point others to Christ rather than themselves.

Following only favorites. After writing this chapter, I realized that I was guilty of a slight variation of this theme. By placing some friends or leaders on the platform I reserve for extraordinary people from whom I believe I have much to learn, I fear that I subconsciously limit my willingness to learn to a circle of people that is far too small. One problem with thinking some people can do no wrong is thinking other leaders or teachers who don't completely measure up to our high hopes can do no right. I have caught myself subconsciously paying less attention to some individuals than I should simply because I'd noticed what I perceived to be some minor imperfections in them. Sometimes I'll even catch myself mentally tuning out someone whose teaching or speaking style doesn't work particularly well for me, even though the substance of what they're saying is sound.

One problem with thinking some people can do no wrong is thinking other leaders or teachers who don't completely measure up to our high hopes can do no right.

By contrast, Nephi was able and willing to learn from prophets whose styles were quite different from his. He made no qualms about indicating that he preferred to write in a plainer and more straightforward style than Isaiah. "I shall prophesy according to the plainness which hath been with me from the time that I came out from Jerusalem with my father; for behold, my soul delighteth in plainness" (2 Nephi 25:4). Yet even while he chose not to mimic Isaiah's style, Nephi relished the earlier prophet's teachings: "Yea, and my soul delighteth in the words of Isaiah" (2 Nephi 25:5). Nephi's example powerfully reminds us not to let stylistic differences blind us to substantive merit.

Intimidating examples. One final danger of placing our leaders on pedestals is that by focusing solely on the finished product, we are intimidated rather than inspired by their examples. In reading some biographies, I come away with great respect for the man or woman described in the book—as well as a firm conviction that I can never become as good as they are. On the other hand, when I read *A Disciple's Life,* the biography of Elder Neal A. Maxwell, I came away with hope because the author (Elder Bruce C. Hafen) showed us not only the finished product but the work in progress. While the seasoned Elder Maxwell was a paragon of patience and compassion, young Neal Maxwell showed flashes of impatience and required spousal tutoring to become such a compassionate disciple of Christ. I was inspired by what Elder Maxwell became; and because I was allowed to see the process I found myself thinking, "Maybe I can become more patient too."

In the foreword to *A Disciple's Life,* Elder Hafen made it clear that Elder Maxwell approved this approach. In one of his most public acts of charity, Elder Maxwell allowed his biographer to show us the journey rather than merely the destination of the apostle's discipleship: "'It isn't that we're searching for weakness as much as we are for growth,' Elder Maxwell said, having earlier written: 'We must be careful . . . not to canonize [our role] models as we have some pioneers and past Church leaders—not to dry all the human sweat off them, not to put ceaseless smiles on their faces, when they really struggled and experienced agony. Real people who believe and prevail are ultimately more faith-promoting and impressive than saccharine saints with tinsel traits.'"[15]

I have always appreciated those Church leaders, both local and general, who allow me to see some of their growth in a similar fashion. While they are always careful to avoid airing dirty laundry inappropriately, when they share self-deprecating examples that allow me to see they are still struggling and progressing, I am inspired rather than simply intimidated by their righteousness.

The Dangers of Detracting

Our Natural Strength in Seeing Weaknesses

For most of us, finding fault with others comes quite naturally. At an executive retreat I once attended, we were asked to share our reactions to a design for an unconventional wheelbarrow that was more vertical than horizontal. Our list of concerns flowed freely: it would be unstable, it would be difficult to roll, and it would be highly impractical. We quickly agreed that such a design was imprudent and unworkable—only to learn that such wheelbarrows existed and were used very successfully in construction sites for very specific purposes, such as dumping heavy loads in tight spots.[16]

While we're good at finding faults in others generally, we're even better at finding faults in those who are correcting us or telling us something we don't want to hear.

Most of us are naturally more prone to see flaws than strengths. And while we're good at finding faults in others generally, we're even better at finding faults in those who are correcting us or telling us something we don't want to hear. I'm embarrassed to admit that when one senior companion (who had only been out a few months longer than I had) corrected my German in a way I found condescending, my instinctive reaction was to try to point out flaws in *his* German rather than to thank him for helping me with mine. When the Lord's leaders correct natural men and women, we may be tempted to look for ways to pull them down, even as we lift up those who tell us what we want to hear (see Helaman 13:26–28).

For some writers, such natural tendencies are compounded by one of the most pervasive intellectual trends of our day: humanizing our heroes by revealing their flaws and pulling them down a notch or two so that they're more like the rest of us. In academia we love to expose faults of those long lauded for their accomplishments, and in popular entertainment we relish complex characters who manage to perform great feats despite dark secrets and conflicting motives. President Stephen L Richards described this academic sport this way: "If a man of history has secured over the years a high place in the esteem of his countrymen and fellow men and has become imbedded in their affections, it has seemingly become a pleasing pastime for researchers and scholars to delve into the past of such a man, discover, if may be, some of his weaknesses and then write a book exposing hitherto unpublished alleged factual findings, all of which tends to rob the historic character of the idealistic esteem and veneration in which he may have been held through the years."[17]

Mistaking Symmetry for Objectivity

Whatever our reasons for finding fault in others, this troublesome practice is particularly dangerous when applied to Church leaders. For starters, those who claim to be creating what they might call a more balanced view of prophets past and present are often creating a less accurate view. This is because they have fallen prey to the fallacy of equating symmetry with objectivity.

Let me explain what I mean by that phrase with two examples. A reporter writing a story about a company may think she is writing an unbiased article by quoting from an equal number of disgruntled and content employees. But her article is accurate only if the workers are evenly split on how they feel about working for the company. If only a small number of employees are unhappy, the article is actually misleading because it creates the misimpression that just as many employees hate the company as love the company. The same would be true of a sportscaster's year-end highlight reel that showed the league's best quarterback throwing an equal number of interceptions and touchdowns, when he actually threw three times as many touchdowns as interceptions. Symmetry should not be confused with objectivity.

Similarly, in the name of objectivity some may try to create portraits of Church leaders past or present that focus as much on flaws as on strengths. Such depictions would be accurate if their subjects were merely mediocre men, the kind of complex characters we often find in modern literature whose foibles threaten to overwhelm their virtues. But suggesting that Joseph Smith had as many weaknesses as strengths is like suggesting that Steve Young had as many bad games as good ones.

Truth As a Defense

Of course, Joseph Smith and our current Church leaders do have weaknesses. Is it wrong, then, to share critical information or insights about them, as long as we're accurate? Many raise truth as a defense for making negative comments about Church leaders and others, but Elder Dallin H. Oaks taught that "the fact that something is true is not always a justification for communicating it."[18]

Suggesting that Joseph Smith had as many weaknesses as strengths is like suggesting that Steve Young had as many bad games as good ones.

Why not? Do we need to protect the feelings of sensitive Church leaders? Elder Oaks observed that most Church leaders "are durable people. They made their way successfully in a world of unrestrained criticism before they received their current callings. They have no personal need for protection; they seek no personal immunities from criticism—constructive or destructive." So why limit our criticism of them? "The counsel against speaking evil of Church leaders is not so much for the benefit of the leaders," concluded Elder Oaks, "as it is for the spiritual well-being of members who are prone to murmur and find fault."[19] Quoting Elder George F. Richards, Elder Oaks added, "'When we say anything bad about the leaders of the Church, whether true or false, we tend to impair their influence and their usefulness and are thus working against the Lord and his cause.'"[20] This counsel applies with equal force to finding fault with one's spouse or parents.[21]

Distractions That Lead to Dismissiveness

When we focus on faults (and sometimes magnify them), we are often blinded to the wisdom in the inspired counsel of imperfect leaders. That's why those who immerse themselves in the search for chinks in prophetic armor are often the quickest to dismiss the teachings of current prophets. Perhaps that is why President David O. McKay referred to speaking against Church authorities as "one of the most poisonous things that can be introduced into the home of a Latter-day Saint."[22]

The Jewish leaders of the Savior's day expected religious leaders to be men of letters. Jesus and His Apostles weren't, for the most part—a perceived flaw that blinded the Jewish aristocracy to the Savior's true identity.

As I write this chapter, I serve on a high council with a stake president who had limited opportunities for an education but presides over a stake that includes many college professors. He is self-conscious about this disparity in training, although he doesn't need to be, because he is one of the most natively intelligent people I know: he has memorized more scriptures, I suspect, than the entire BYU–Idaho religion faculty combined. Yet his humility only makes him a more powerful leader. I do not know that I have ever worked directly with a priesthood leader more filled with the spirit of prophecy. Those who would discount or dismiss his counsel because he lacks academic credentials would be making a terrible mistake.

Temporal success escaped Joseph Smith[23] almost as surely and naturally as it flowed to Brigham Young—a fact that would have tried the faith of lesser men. But Brigham concluded, "Though I admitted in my feelings and knew all the time that Joseph was a human being and subject to err, still it was none of my business to look after his faults. . . . He was called of God; God dictated him, and if He had a mind to leave him to himself and let him commit an error, that was no business of mine. . . . He was God's servant, and not mine."[24]

While some Saints look for flaws in leaders to justify their own refusal to follow their counsel, others draw inspiration from the fact that God is able to use ordinary men and women to give us extraordinary counsel. Elder Lorenzo Snow took heart in the fact that Joseph was not perfect in just such a way: "I thanked God that He would put upon a man who had those imperfections the power and authority He placed upon him . . . for I knew that I myself had weakness, and I thought there was a chance for me."[25]

STRIKING THE BALANCE

In conclusion, allow me to add one thought about each extreme in this pair.

First, we are presumptuous—and not particularly helpful to God's cause—when we claim things for His scriptures and His leaders that they have not claimed for themselves. Imagine Mark's disappointment, for example, when people dismiss his Gospel because they expected it to be perfect—something Mark never professed his book to be. Those who thought they were doing him and other biblical authors a favor by insisting their works are without error actually do them a disservice, placing them on a pedestal from which they will fall if readers discover any errors in their work.

The same holds true for God's leaders. Modern prophets and apostles have never claimed to be infallible, either in character or their teachings. "I told them that a prophet was a prophet only when he was acting as such," declared Joseph Smith.[26] Moreover, President J. Reuben Clark Jr. taught that "only the President of the Church, the Presiding High Priest, is sustained as Prophet, Seer, and Revelator for the Church, and he alone has the right to receive revelations for the Church, either new or amendatory, or to give authoritative interpretations of scriptures that shall be binding on the Church, or change in any way the existing doctrines of the Church."[27]

But hasn't the Lord said that what the elders of the Church speak by the power of the Holy Ghost becomes scripture? (See D&C 68:4.)

189

Elder Harold B. Lee noted that some caution must be used in the way we interpret this particular statement from the Lord: "It is not to be thought that every word spoken by the General Authorities is inspired, or that they are moved upon by the Holy Ghost in everything they speak and write. Now you keep that in mind. I don't care what his position is, if he writes something or speaks something that goes beyond anything that you can find in the standard Church works, unless that one be the prophet, seer, and revelator—please note that one exception—you may immediately say, Well, that is his own idea."[28] Elder Ezra Taft Benson added that "doctrinal interpretation is the province of the First Presidency. The Lord has given that stewardship to them by revelation. No teacher has the right to interpret doctrine for the members of the Church."[29]

Not surprisingly, then, we can find a number of statements of individual Church leaders that do not represent the official views of the Church.[30] If we elevate every word uttered by Church leaders to scriptural status, then we are overlooking what they have taught us themselves.

Of course, some are unsettled by the notion that God could call men as apostles and prophets who might offer personal opinions that later prove to be off the mark or who still have room for spiritual growth. "How can that man be called of God if he taught *that?*" some might wonder. "How could *he* be an apostle if he *did* that?" (The same people might be shaken in their testimony of the Savior by the fact that He called Judas to be His Apostle.) Those who ask such questions hold a belief quite similar to Bart Ehrman's notion that if the Bible had been inspired, then God would have shielded it from the mistakes and malice of men through the centuries, preserving it in its pristine form. For Ehrman, anything less was evidence that God could not have been behind the book, just as some conclude that signs of imperfection in Church leaders demonstrate that they could not have been called of God. Stephen Robinson pointed out how those who seek to discredit LDS leaders by finding some flaw in their statements "would impose *their* inerrantist view on the

Latter-day Saints and their prophets. But the Latter-day Saints have no such inerrantist views, neither of the scriptures nor of the prophets. The scriptures *are* the word of God, but only as far as they are translated correctly; and prophets sometimes speak for the Lord, and sometimes they express their own opinions."[31]

For Latter-day Saints, shortcomings in the Bible and God's leaders are completely consistent with our view of a loving Heavenly Father who has always used imperfect mortals to further His work. While some would think that perfection is a prerequisite for a man to see Heavenly Father and the Savior in the flesh, Joseph Smith never pretended to be perfect. After seeing them, he freely admitted that he "was guilty of levity, and sometimes associated with jovial company, etc., not consistent with that character which ought to be maintained by one who was called of God" as he had been (Joseph Smith—

Like Abraham, Moses, and Peter, on a personal level Joseph was a work in progress, even after seeing God.

History 1:28). Later, the very first revelations he allowed to be published included stark admonitions from the Lord, making it clear that he needed to repent and continue to grow spiritually. "And behold," declared the Lord to His young prophet, "how oft you have transgressed the commandments and the laws of God, and have gone on in the persuasions of men" (D&C 3:6). Thus, like Abraham, Moses, and Peter, on a personal level Joseph was a work in progress, even after seeing God.

Second, even as we are careful not to claim more for Church leaders or scriptures than they claim for themselves, we commit a much graver error if we claim too little for them. Miriam and Aaron appear to have made this very mistake with their brother Moses, whose fallibility they knew all too well. When their brother married an Ethiopian woman, "Miriam and Aaron spake against [him]. . . .

Hath the Lord indeed spoken only by Moses? Hath he not spoken also by us?" (Numbers 12:1–2).

The next line in the Numbers narrative is a beautiful piece of understatement: "And the Lord heard it." The Lord hears everything, of course, including when we murmur against His anointed servants. The Lord then demanded that Miriam, Aaron, and Moses meet Him at the tabernacle of the congregation, where He appeared in a cloud and "called Aaron and Miriam: and they both came forth." Typically, He told Miriam and Aaron, He communicates with prophets through visions and dreams, but that wasn't the case with Moses: "With him will I speak mouth to mouth . . . : wherefore then were ye not afraid to speak against my servant Moses? And the anger of the Lord was kindled against them" (Numbers 12:5–9). So angry was the Lord that He smote Miriam with leprosy, although He later healed her at Moses' request.

Surely Moses included this episode as a cautionary illustration of the dangers of speaking against those whom the Lord has chosen. Years ago when I was shopping for a law school, a friend and I attended a ward close to one of the nation's premier universities. Elders quorum was packed with law students, including a third-year student who taught the class that day. A national magazine had just featured the Church in its cover story, which included a quote from Elder Oaks about not criticizing Church leaders. Leaning against the table with the magazine and no manual, the instructor shared the quote, stroked his beard, and said something like, "So here's the question I submit to you today for discussion: Is he right?" We then proceeded to debate the wisdom of Elder Oaks's statement—with the irony completely lost on the instructor.

At one point in the class I swallowed hard and raised my undergraduate hand. I suggested that we might be able to learn from David's example in refusing to take the life of the fallen and murderous King Saul, because he had been the Lord's anointed. "Interesting thought," mused the instructor, as if citing scripture were a quaint novelty, and the discussion rolled on.

As I reflect on David's story, it occurs to me that it beautifully illustrates not only the importance of being slow to criticize the Lord's anointed servants, but also how having a generous view of the Lord's anointed makes such deference possible. Many would have allowed their faith to be undermined by the fact that the prophet Samuel had chosen and anointed a king from whom the Spirit of the Lord eventually departed because of his wickedness (see 1 Samuel 16:14). If Samuel were truly a prophet, they might have wondered, why would he have chosen a man to lead Israel who eventually fell? Moreover, Saul's apostasy was more than an abstract theological concern for David, as the king turned against his anointed heir in a jealous rage. If we imagine the confusion and doubt of an assistant whose mission president tried to kill him, we get a glimpse into how David could well have felt.

Yet none of this turned David from God. Not only was his faith unshaken, but he refused to lift his hand against the king, even in self-defense. Instead, when he came face to face with the king who was trying to kill him, "David stooped with his face to the earth, and bowed himself" (1 Samuel 24:8). While it was clear to Saul that David had obtained the strategic advantage and could have killed him, David declined, even though some of his men urged him to do so: "I will not put forth mine hand against my lord; for he is the Lord's anointed" (1 Samuel 24:10).

David knew full well that his former mentor had fallen short of God's expectations. But because the Lord had anointed him, David refused to strike out at Saul. He understood both that God uses imperfect men and that we should treat those whom God calls with great respect, despite their imperfections.

Elder Henry B. Eyring illustrated the kind of deference we will show to the Lord's anointed when we have both faith and humility. "Sometimes we will receive counsel that we cannot understand or that seems not to apply to us, even after careful prayer and thought. Don't discard the counsel, but hold it close. If someone you trusted handed you what appeared to be nothing more than sand with the promise that it contained gold, you might wisely hold it in your hand awhile, shaking it gently. Every time I have done that with counsel from a prophet, after a time the gold flakes have begun to appear and I have been grateful."³² Elder Eyring's humble approach to counterintuitive prophetic counsel reminds us of the Lord's loving caution: "All they who receive the oracles of God, let them beware how they hold them lest they are accounted as a light thing" (D&C 90:5).

Finally, I find it easier to be merciful in my judgment and deferential in my attitude toward the Lord's anointed when I remember that none of them asked to be called. Any bishop puts in numerous hours of unseen service each week in addition to his day job. Most apostles work weekends for decades beyond the age at which most men get to retire to their hobbies. Remembering this helps me become more interested in what I can learn from their examples and teachings than in finding personal flaws that might somehow excuse me from obeying their counsel. And even if, as was the case with my mission president, I may need to occasionally sift out some personal opinion from the pure and established doctrines they preach, I find myself more grateful for the nuggets of wisdom they share than irritated that I might have to sift a bit.

For me, President Packer summed up the whole matter powerfully yet humbly with this counsel:

> We who have been called to lead the Church are ordinary men and women with ordinary capacities struggling to administer a church which grows at such a pace as to astound even those who watch it closely. Some are disposed to find fault with us; surely that is easy for them to do. But they do not examine us more searchingly than we examine ourselves. A call to lead is not an exemption from the challenges of life. . . .
>
> We are sorry for our inadequacies, sorry we are not better than we are. We can feel, as you can see, the effect

of the aging process as it imposes limitations upon His leaders before your very eyes.

But this we know. There are councils and counselors and quorums to counterbalance the foibles and frailties of man. The Lord organized His church to provide for mortal men to work as mortal men, and yet He assured that the spirit of revelation would guide in all that we do in His name.

And in the end, what is given comes because the Lord has spoken it, "whether by [His] own voice or by the voice of [His] servants, it is the same." (D&C 1:38.) We know His voice when He speaks.[33]

Notes

1. Bart D. Ehrman, *Misquoting Jesus: The Story Behind Who Changed the Bible and Why* (New York: HarperCollins Publishers, 2005), 3–9.

2. See Ehrman, *Misquoting Jesus,* 47–56.

3. Ehrman, *Misquoting Jesus,* 9, 11.

4. Ehrman, *Misquoting Jesus,* 211.

5. "The Testimony of Three Witnesses," Book of Mormon.

6. Donald L. Enders, "A Snug Log House," *Ensign,* Aug. 1985, 20.

7. Jay E. Jensen, "The Power of the Word," *Ensign,* Oct. 1991, 15.

8. Boyd K. Packer, "Revelation in a Changing World," *Ensign,* Nov. 1989, 15–16.

9. Royal Skousen, "Critical Methodology and the Text of the Book of Mormon," in *Review of Books on the Book of Mormon,* 6:1 (1994), 144.

10. Although many assume the purpose of "textual criticism" is to criticize and undermine faith in the text, for faithful scholars the real purpose is to carefully examine multiple copies or editions of a book such as the Bible to ascertain the original wording of the text. See, for example, Brian Hauglid, "Searching for God's Word in New Testament Textual Criticism," *Religious Educator,* 8:2 (2007), 101.

11. Terryl L. Givens, *By the Hand of Mormon: The American Scripture that Launched a New World Religion* (New York: Oxford University Press, 2002), 83.

12. Gordon B. Hinckley, "Testimony," *Ensign,* May 1998, 71.

13. Richard L. Anderson, "Book Reviews," *BYU Studies,* 9:2 (Winter 1969), 229.

14. Spencer J. Condie, *In Perfect Balance* (Salt Lake City: Deseret Book, 1993), 189.

15. Bruce C. Hafen, *A Disciple's Life: The Biography of Neal A. Maxwell* (Salt Lake City: Deseret Book, 2002), xv.

16. I am indebted to the consultants of Senn Delaney for this insight.

17. Quoted in Russell M. Nelson, "Truth—*and More,*" *Ensign,* Jan. 1986, 71.

18. Dallin H. Oaks, "Criticism," *Ensign,* Feb. 1987, 68.

19. Oaks, "Criticism," 70.

20. George Albert Smith, in Conference Report, Apr. 1947, 24; quoted in Oaks, "Criticism," 70.

21. I am indebted to my daughter Danielle Eaton for this insight.

22. David O. McKay, *Gospel Ideals* (Salt Lake City: Improvement Era, 1953), 142–43; quoted in Oaks, "Criticism," 70.

23. In what must have been a difficult revelation to receive, the Lord told Joseph in 1830, "And in temporal labors thou shalt not have strength, for this is not thy calling" (D&C 24:9).

24. Brigham Young, in *Journal of Discourses,* 4:297; quoted in Oaks, "Criticism," 72.

25. Lorenzo Snow, quoted in Oaks, "Criticism," 72.

26. Joseph Smith, *History of The Church of Jesus Christ of Latter-day Saints,* ed. B. H. Roberts, 7 vols. (Salt Lake City: The Church of Jesus Christ of Latter-day Saints, 1978), 5:265.

27. "When Are the Writings or Sermons of Church Leaders Entitled to the Claim of Scripture?" *Church News,* 31 July 1954, 10; quoted in Boyd K. Packer, "The Twelve Apostles," *Ensign,* Nov. 1996, 6.

28. Harold B. Lee, "The Place of the Living Prophet, Seer, and Revelator," in *Charge to Religious Educators,* 2nd ed. (Salt Lake City: The Church of Jesus Christ of Latter-day Saints, 1982), 111.

29. Ezra Taft Benson, "The Gospel Teacher and His Message," in *Charge to Religious Educators,* 51–52.

30. Frankly, earlier in this dispensation Church leaders were much freer in publicly expressing their personal opinions on doctrinal matters. In recent decades, they seem to have taken great care to limit their official comments to expounding doctrines in which the Brethren are in agreement. And on those rare occasions when they do express personal opinions, they are careful to identify them as such and not as the official position of the Church. Indeed, it has become rather standard practice for General Authorities to include a disclaimer in their published works, even if they are largely a compilation of talks previously delivered in general conferences and devotionals at Church colleges, indicating that their comments should not be construed as the official position of the Church.

31. Stephen E. Robinson, *Are Mormons Christians?* (Salt Lake City: Bookcraft, 1991), 15–16.

32. Henry B. Eyring, "Finding Safety in Counsel," *Ensign,* May 1997, 26.

33. Boyd K. Packer, "Revelation in a Changing World," *Ensign,* Nov. 1989, 16.

CHAPTER 11

THE FEARFULLY TIMID AND THE BRASHLY OVERBEARING

Whether we are ministering officially or unofficially in God's kingdom, each of us frequently faces critical junctures at which we must decide just how bold to be. Should I invite my neighbors to Church now? Is this the right time to challenge the man I home teach to stop smoking and prepare to be sealed in the temple? Dare I tell that teacher how I think his class could be even better? Should I raise my concerns with my friend about the man she's dating?

If we take the wrong course of action in any of these situations, we could needlessly alienate those whom we're striving to bless—or we could pass up a golden opportunity to help them. Many of us are naturally so reserved that we fail to help people because of our fears. And a few of us are so comfortable being bold that we are occasionally clueless about how counterproductive our efforts can be when we move beyond boldness to overbearance.

I begin by exploring the dangers of the extreme that I believe is a problem for more of us than the other: being so timid that we miss opportunities to boldly help others.

The Fearfully Timid

We often discuss the great joy that will be ours if we manage to help bring even one soul unto Christ—and we should. But the Lord reminds us that there is a troublesome flipside to that principle. "But if the watchman see the sword come, and blow not the trumpet, and the people be not warned; if the sword come, and take any person from among them, he is taken away in his iniquity; but his blood will I require at the watchman's hand" (Ezekiel 33:6). In our day, President Thomas S. Monson articulated the same principle of accountability this way, quoting President John Taylor: "If great joy is the reward of saving one soul, then how terrible must be the remorse of those whose timid efforts have allowed a child of God to go unwarned or unaided so that he has to wait till a dependable servant of God comes along."[1]

The phrase that captures my attention in this sentence is "timid efforts." It's not enough that the watchman on the tower calls out meekly or that he dutifully goes through the motions of warning others of danger. Timid efforts to warn will not excuse those of us who know of dangers others cannot yet see. To escape responsibility for the sins of those we have an opportunity or obligation to help, our efforts must be more than perfunctory. For example, once Lehi partook of the fruit of the tree of life himself, he called out "with a loud voice" to beckon his family to share in the fruit of Christ's gospel (1 Nephi 8:15).

To illustrate this point, I often ask my students to consider what they would do if they got up early on a Sunday morning and discovered a fire when almost everyone else was still asleep. What steps would they take to warn others in their apartment complex and lead them to safety? How many of their fellow tenants would they try to warn? How persistent would they be? What if their friends were irritated and just wanted to go back to sleep? What if their roommates thought they were joking? How would they try to convince others to leave the burning building while there was still time?

This analogy is obviously imperfect: it would hardly do if we started shouting or throwing cold water on people who initially reject our gospel message. Still, the metaphor helps my students and me scrutinize our own efforts in bringing others to Christ. When we understand the urgency of the gospel message, we will be bolder in sharing it. I next look at a variety of situations in which we and others can be blessed by greater boldness.

BOLDNESS APPLIED

Sharing the Gospel

Shortly before my mission I went on splits with the local missionaries. I was assigned an elder who was in the last month or two of his mission, and together we visited a "callback"—a family the missionaries had never before taught but who had given the missionaries permission to drop by another time. When we knocked, the missionary introduced us and the person answering the door invited us in before my companion even gave any kind of door approach. As I recall, the missionary practically protested, thinking the people didn't understand who we really were. I finally decided to go in myself, and the full-time missionary eventually followed suit. When we left later, he said that no one had ever invited him in like that before.

Sadly, it became clear to me that this missionary had not had much success during his mission gaining entrance to people's homes to teach them. His experience led to low expectations, which in turn made him reluctant to ever ask to come in—which led to even fewer people inviting him in. On the other hand, as I later watched missionaries in my own mission, I noticed that those who were invited in the most were those who asked to be invited in the most.

The principle seems obvious, but the fact is that even for missionaries, asking to come in was often a bold step. And since most people declined the offer, it was sometimes hard to keep asking. But those missionaries who worked with greater faith usually had greater expectations. Somehow, when they acted as if it were completely

normal for them to ask if they could come in, more people were willing to let them in. "If ever there was a common characteristic among
successful missionaries," wrote Elder Spencer J. Condie, "it is the
trait of boldness, the courage to follow the Lord's oft-repeated admonition to 'open your mouths' (see D&C 24:12; 28:16; 30:5, 11;
33:8–10; 60:2)."2

Boldness helps not only full-time missionaries but member missionaries in our efforts to share the gospel. For several years, I rode
the bus almost daily to and from work, and for a few years I traveled
regularly as part of my job. It was a busy time in my life, and I'm
embarrassed to admit that I did little to share the gospel in transit
because I viewed that time as part of my workday in which I needed
to be productively engaged in other matters. I worked hard to share
the gospel with friends, neighbors, and part-member families in the
ward, but on the bus and plane I usually kept to myself and focused
on getting things done.

When we moved to Rexburg, Idaho, however, I quickly came to
miss the missionary opportunities that had surrounded me in Seattle.
Rather than a burden that perpetually hung over my head, sharing
the gospel became a privilege for which I yearned. My wife and I
have begun to view every trip away from our wonderful little LDS
enclave as an opportunity to share the gospel, and we try to prepare
accordingly—from packing pass-along cards and a Book of Mormon
to praying in advance for the chance to sit next to someone who
would be willing to hear about the gospel.

In the case of a trip to Brazil, my wife and I even studied Portuguese for several months before departing on our trip. Once in
Brazil, people initially laughed at our Portuguese (especially in a
pharmacy in Brasilia where we tried to explain with a combination
of hand gestures and our broken Portuguese that our friend needed
some ammonium). But by the end of our two weeks, we were able
to communicate on a very rudimentary level in Portuguese. Together
with the basic English skills of some of our Brazilian seatmates, we
were able to engage in several wonderful gospel discussions that

culminated in our leaving pass-along cards or copies of the Book of Mormon. Similarly, on virtually every trip I take involving air travel, I have been blessed to be able to share the gospel in some meaningful way with at least one of the people next to whom I sit during my journey.

I have come to cherish the opportunity to explain the gospel and testify of its truthfulness with those who are willing to listen. But my recent success in sharing the gospel in such situations leads me to look back on ten years of riding the bus in Seattle and three years of business travel as an executive with tremendous regret. If I had approached my daily commute in the same way as I now approach traveling, how many lives might I have blessed? Instead, I was too busy reading the newspaper, my scriptures, or materials from work to take the time to get out of my commuter comfort zone and share the gospel.

Reaching Out to the Less Active

My father is probably the best home teacher I have ever known. He specializes in working his way into the hearts of people who have not attended Church for years, people who often have not accepted home teachers in the past. He begins with conversations on doorsteps, sometimes for months, if necessary. Over time, he begins to get to know them and serve them more, dropping by things from the garden or offering to help out in different ways. But birthdays are his real calling card. He starts with a homemade birthday card, featuring his own cartoons and original greetings. Then the strikingly original design of the birthday cakes, together with the rough decorating finish, make it clear that he has not purchased the treat at any store. To top it all off, he plays "Happy Birthday" with reckless abandon on his trombone. It's no wonder that people soon started inviting him in; the whole neighborhood could hear him playing the trombone on the porch if they didn't. (One day as I played my accordion with reckless abandon on the doorstep of someone I home taught, I realized that I was simply following in my father's foot-steps.)

I once interviewed an older woman whom my father home taught for years following this basic pattern. After he'd mowed her lawn several times and given her several blessings in time of illness, my father asked if she'd be willing to come to Church. She hadn't been in nearly twenty years, but she readily agreed to come, soon returning to full activity. "I guess I just needed someone to ask me," she explained. When I interviewed her for a documentary I made for my father's seventieth birthday, it had been several years since he had been assigned to be her home teacher, but she proudly showed me some of the birthday cards he'd made her.

My father's experience with this woman shows what a great bless-ing a little boldness can be—and what a shame it is when twenty years' worth of home teachers before him failed to ask the question that could have led to her return to full activity.

Sometimes we can facilitate great changes in the lives of others with a simple invitation. In other situations, we may need to be bolder and more persistent to participate in miracles. Elder Mervyn J. Arnold tells of one such extraordinary story. Brother José de Souza Marques was a member of a branch presidency in Fortaleza, Brazil, where he focused his reactivation efforts on a young priest by the name of Fernando Araujo. Initially he visited Fernando at his home on Sunday mornings and, with permission from Fernando's mother, rousted the young man from bed. On the third Sunday, Fernando tried to slip out of his house before Brother Marques arrived—only to find Brother Marques sitting on the hood of his car studying his scriptures. Unable to shake Brother Marques after eight Sundays, Fernando finally decided to spend the night at a friend's house before heading for his surfing competition on Sunday morning. Fernando tells what happened next: "I was at the beach the next morning when I saw a man dressed in a suit and tie walking towards me. When I saw that it was Brother Marques, I ran into the water. All of a sud-den, I felt someone's hand on my shoulder. It was Brother Marques, in water up to his chest! He took me by the hand and said, 'You are late! Let's go.' When I argued that I didn't have any clothes to wear, he replied, 'They are in the car.'"

I confess that when I first heard this story of extraordinary boldness, I wondered how long Fernando remained active, having required so much effort to come back. He turned out all right, it seems—serving as bishop, stake president, mission president, and regional representative. By boldly dashing into the water in his suit, Brother Marques almost certainly ruined a suit but saved a boy.[3]

Providing Corrective Counsel in Our Callings

For most of us, corrective counsel is much needed and rarely given. As Elder Neal A. Maxwell noted, "People tend to shy away from correction even when it might be helpful."[4] I was surprised even in the corporate setting to discover that the CEOs with whom I interacted were surprisingly reluctant to provide constructive criticism. In fact, in some cases they were actually more willing to let someone go than to try to provide candid feedback along the way that might have prevented the problem.

In a disciple training class I team-taught, I observed that it was much easier for our students to talk about giving corrective counsel than it was for them to actually do it, even when just role playing. They were often full of tough advice about what should occur in a particular scenario, but when we put them on the spot and gave them a chance to implement their advice, most quickly toned down what they had to say.

As a young General Authority, Elder Boyd K. Packer once returned from a stake conference and reported a problem he'd found in the stake. "Brother Packer, what did you do about the problem?" asked President Joseph Fielding Smith. Elder Packer replied that he'd come to report it. "That doesn't do much good, does it?" President Smith replied softly. From his experience, President Packer made this resolve: "When I have found a problem and it was in my capability to resolve it, I would do so. Then it became a problem solved rather than a problem found and reported. . . . When I have received a prompting that something needed to be said, I have tried to say it as diplomatically and as wisely as possible. But I have tried to have the courage to say things that are difficult to say even though they may make some uncomfortable."[5]

Imagine how much better the teaching in the Church would be if quorum and auxiliary leaders took to heart their responsibility for teaching and regularly interviewed teachers in their organizations, providing them with specific praise, needed support, and one suggestion for improvement.

"Tell me how you feel about the level of participation in your class," an auxiliary leader might ask. In most situations, teachers who are struggling would probably admit they weren't satisfied and could use some help, but even if they didn't, a loving leader could suggest, "I wonder if you might try focusing on improving class participation for the next couple of months. I've made copies of a few pages from *Teaching, No Greater Call* that might help, and you might want to watch Sister Brown teach the Laurels sometime soon, because she's really good at involving the girls."

Imagine how much more effective we could be in building the kingdom if we developed a greater ability to give—and to receive—corrective counsel in a Christlike way.

Providing Unofficial Corrective Counsel

When I was a teenager, I often had conflicts with my younger sister, Jennifer, primarily because she was a little brat—or so I thought. My parents were very disappointed that we didn't get along better and talked to us about it often, but to no avail. I was disappointed that they could not see that Jen was largely the cause of our difficulties.

Then one day my good friend Sid Beers gave me some kind but direct advice: "You know, Rob, you probably ought to be nicer to your sister." I was taken aback. It was one thing for my parents to say such things, but when a friend who was supposed to be on my side made such a comment, I had to think twice. Soon I began treating her much better—partly as a response to Sid, and partly to show that I had always been nice—and almost immediately our relationship improved dramatically. Indeed, I soon learned that Jen was no brat at all, and she became one of my dearest friends. I cannot describe my gratitude to Sid, who saw what I could not see and who dared to tell me about it when I still had a couple of years left to change my behavior. To this day, there are few people from whom I'd rather receive a phone call than Jen.

On another occasion, I was similarly blessed by the boldness of a missionary companion and dear friend, Kevin Cook. He was telling me about another missionary whose German was the best German our mission president had ever heard a non-native speak. I'm embarrassed to admit that my reaction was that I hoped to master the language so well that our mission president could one day say that of me, and I'm even more embarrassed that I somehow shared this thought with Elder Cook.

Inspired, bold friends who are willing to tell us hard truths on occasion can be an invaluable asset.

"You know, Elder Eaton, there's always going to be someone who speaks German a little better," Kevin taught me with incredible perception, "someone who's a little smarter, someone who's a little richer. You're never going to be happy if you're always comparing yourself to others." It was profound advice—boldly given—that I have remembered long after Kevin forgot ever giving it to me.

Sid and Kevin were neither my bishop nor my parent nor my Young Men's leader—which made their advice all the more persuasive, frankly. We have more power as peers than most of us realize. As a bishop, I was eternally grateful to members who had persuaded their friends to come to see me to get the help they needed. I fully understood that such friends were often in a position to do something that neither parents nor Church leaders could have done.

Inspired, bold friends who are willing to tell us hard truths on occasion can be an invaluable asset.

Opportunities for unofficial mentoring and shepherding abound. In fact, if we are courageous, we may even see them in situations where we are neither leaders nor peers. A colleague in CES told of one of his students who was brave enough to provide such feedback to him as a teacher. It was early in his seminary career, and he was struggling in the classroom. One day after class, this teacher found a note from a young woman who succinctly shared some much needed advice: "Tell me, and I'll forget. Show me, and I might remember. Involve me, and I'll understand." It forever changed the way he taught.

Serving Others

Providing service is an area that doesn't seem to require much boldness. Yet sometimes when we see a difficult situation, we are not sure exactly how to help or how our offers to help will be received, so we do nothing at all. On the other hand, loving Saints often help in bold ways. One of the most inspiring talks I've heard at a funeral came from Cindy Phelan, a woman who had been helped in a difficult time by the deceased, Sister Cindy Stephens. A cyst had been discovered in Brother Phelan's cheek, and Sister Phelan found herself sitting at home dwelling on the frightening possibilities the cyst represented. Rather than simply ask how she could help, Sister Stephens told her friend to block out a couple of hours on a given day. When she arrived, Sister Stephens brought with her six sealed envelopes, with activities ranging from shopping to service. The envelope Sister Phelan chose contained a note indicating they would spend the morning volunteering at the bishops' storehouse—which proved to be precisely what Sister Phelan needed to help her forget about some of her worries. Her spirits were lifted in ways they never would have been had Sister Stephens simply offered, "Let me know if there's anything I can do to help." Sister Stephens's boldness in volunteering help had made it easy for her friend to receive the gift that Sister Stephens offered.

All too often, I fail to leave my comfort zone to help those in need, fearing that I might offend rather than help in my efforts to be of assistance. However, I managed to rise above such concerns when a friend in my ward was diagnosed with a terminal case of cancer. I call him a friend, and he was—in the American sense of the term, which is used quite loosely. Germans would have called us acquaintances, since we'd known each other for only a couple of years and hadn't really spent much time together. But my heart ached for Stephen, his wife, and the six children he would soon be leaving behind. At first, I was unsure of how I could help, but soon an idea came to me. I enjoy conducting interviews and making family history movies, so I offered my services. I told Stephen that I wanted to get his life history on videotape and possibly create a mini-documentary or two on specific segments of his life, drawing from the interview footage.

By interviewing Stephen for about eight hours over a period of several weeks, I came to know him rather intimately; we became friends, in the German sense of the term. The DVDs we were creating were for his children, not me, but Stephen was kind enough to speak quite candidly, despite my presence as an interviewer. I learned about his parents and grandparents, his childhood, his jobs, his courtship and marriage, his children, his struggles in life, his journey to becoming a professor at BYU–Idaho, and his love for Scouting.

In fact, as I conducted the interviews about Scouting, I had an ulterior motive that I withheld from Stephen: I planned to make one of the mini-documentaries about Stephen's love for Scouting, complete with interviews from boys he'd helped and leaders with whom he'd served through the years. As I talked with Stephen about how Scouting had blessed his life as a young man, he confided that although he'd earned the rank of Eagle Scout, because he had moved just as he earned it, he never had an Eagle Court of Honor—something he'd always regretted. I passed the information along to my Scouting friends in the ward, who soon secretly obtained official approval to hold an Eagle Court of Honor for Stephen, which they then planned.

Although his health was failing, with the help of Stephen's wife we somehow convinced him to attend a court of honor without revealing that it was for him. Many of the young men he'd shepherded years earlier as a Scoutmaster returned to honor him. Colleagues gave heartfelt tributes, and we showed my mini-documentary, complete with interview footage from him, his former Scouts, and brethren with whom he'd worked in Scouting.

I'd nearly missed out on my part in the affair—probably the most rewarding unofficial service I'd done in years—because I had worried that it would seem too forward of me to volunteer to interview Stephen for his posterity. Moreover, because of my experience in talking with Stephen, I came to know and care about his wife and children in ways I would not have otherwise. As is often the case, by going out on a limb and offering a bit of service, the door was opened to other opportunities and blessings for years to come.

Asking

As I have previously mentioned, President Boyd K. Packer taught that no "message appears in scripture more times, in more ways than, 'Ask, and ye shall receive.'"[6] Among others, the brother of Jared and Peter demonstrated spiritual chutzpah as they implemented this principle in their lives. The brother of Jared's request for the Lord to touch the stones he had molten led to one of the most extraordinary visions ever recorded (see Ether 3). And the reason Peter was able to literally walk on water, however briefly, was that he asked (see Matthew 14).

While we should always seek to submit our will to the Lord's when we pray, I have observed that people with great faith are often boldly specific in requests they make of the Lord, as was the brother of Jared. When I listen to my wife pray, for example, she rarely asks the Lord simply to bless our children. Instead, she reviews what is going on in their lives and asks Heavenly Father to bless them in very specific ways.

I was unwittingly the beneficiary of one such prayer recently when traveling to Kentucky for a reunion with Dianne's family. Because of teaching obligations, I flew out a day later than she and the children, so I rented a car at the Nashville airport when I arrived just after 10:00 P.M. Before beginning my two-hour drive, I took a quick look at the map provided me by the rental agency, even though Dianne's father had given me fairly detailed directions to the Kentucky state park where we were staying. As I followed his directions, I soon found myself on an interstate freeway heading out of Nashville. Unfortunately, the directions I'd been given specified only exit numbers and names, not the distance between turns. As I drove along the interstate looking for exit 89, then, I was momentarily confused when I saw that the exit numbers were decreasing from something like 35 to 33. Quickly realizing that I'd have to cross a state line somewhere along the way if I was going to end up in Kentucky, I assumed that exit 89 must be on the Kentucky side of the line. I pulled in to the state park just after midnight, precisely as scheduled.

When I arrived, Dianne was very relieved to see me; apparently some of her siblings had gotten lost using the directions. "So you found the place all right?" she asked.

"Oh, yeah," I replied, the confident male navigator, thinking my wife had gotten worked up over nothing. "It was no problem."

"I'm so glad," she said. "I prayed that you would think to look at a map before you left and that you'd realize the exit numbers would change after the state line." What had seemed intuitive behavior to me had actually been inspired—a direct blessing of my wife's spiritual audacity in pleading with the Lord for a very specific blessing.

In addition to asking blessings of the Lord, I have discovered great blessings by asking others for spiritual and even temporal advice. After making a couple of long trips in the car with my mission president to attend zone conferences, I realized I had a unique opportunity on my hands. Here was a man (Richard Klein) of extraordinary gospel knowledge and commitment, and he was essentially trapped in a car with me for three or four hours. "President," I began, "do you mind if I ask you some questions?"

"Not at all, Elder," he replied, and the avalanche of gospel inquiries began. I believe that he came to regret his decision and that I overplayed my hand, because hours later he said something like, "Don't you ever stop, Elder?" Still, in the months I spent working together with him as an assistant, many of the most valuable insights I gained came as he answered questions I asked.

In a temporal context, I realized as a young college student planning to attend law school that I'd never really spoken to a lawyer, which seemed rather foolish. So I called Boeing's legal department out of the blue and asked which firm handled their international legal issues. I then called that firm, asked for their international law department, and spoke with a secretary: "I'm just a college student planning to attend law school, but I'm interested in international law and was hoping an attorney there might be willing to talk with me." I ended up talking on the phone with attorneys from the top two firms in Seattle—both of whom invited me to come to their offices, where I met with each of them for an hour. To this day, I pass on some of the advice they gave me to college students who ask about how to prepare for a career in the law. And I tell all my students who have questions about choosing careers that if they will be bold enough to ask even strangers about professions that interest them, they'll be amazed at how much valuable information they'll get.

Being a Force for Good

Few people have demonstrated to me personally the righteous benefits of boldness more than my friend and former mission companion, Kevin Cook, whom I have already mentioned in this chapter. When I served in Germany, many of the stores where we'd purchase gas for our car featured nearly pornographic pictures on the laminated countertops where we paid the cashier. I was bothered by this brazen display forced on the stores' customers, including me, but it never occurred to me to do anything about it. But one day as I was with Elder Cook in such a store, after receiving his change, Kevin calmly pointed to the counter and said something along these lines, "By the way, as one of your customers, I thought you might want to know that I don't appreciate these pictures here at all." He didn't look zealous or wacky as he smiled and walked out—just confident and principled. Probably twenty-one years old at the time, he had spoken with the quiet dignity of a fifty-year-old General Authority.

His courage reminded me of the famous reprimand President Spencer W. Kimball once gave the orderly who took the Lord's name while wheeling President Kimball into surgery: "Please! Please! That is my Lord whose name you revile."[7] I am haunted by my own lack of courage that led me to ignore a prompting in a similar situation. I had been invited by one of my daughter's teachers to join him and some of his friends in their weekly game of basketball in the school gym. I was the only Church member present. The players seemed to be good guys, but some of their language wasn't. None of their profanity was new to me, but I bristled when I heard one of the players repeatedly shout the Lord's name in vain as part of a stream of profanity.

I played on several occasions with this group, and at some point the thought came to me that I should say something like this between games: "I know that I'm a guest here, and I appreciate you letting me play with you. But if it's not asking too much, I was wondering if you wouldn't mind choosing some name other than Jesus Christ's to shout when you get angry—heck, use mine if you like. It's just that His name is sacred to me, that's all." If I had done that, some of the guys might have thought I was a prude. But I can't help but wonder what most of them would have said years later when asked if Mormons were Christians, had I only heeded the prompting. "I don't know about all that theology stuff," I can imagine them saying, "but yeah, I'm pretty sure that Jesus is a big deal to them."

But I said nothing. Worried about how I would come across as a newcomer to the group, I just tried to close my ears and bite my tongue. I allowed fear to prevent me from being a force for good.

OVERCOMING FEAR

One day near the end of the ski season, I'd taken my nine-year-old son, Jonathan, skiing. Trying to get the most out of the day, I promised him that if we kept going, we'd take a break at 2:00 and get some of the wonderful waffle fries they served at this ski resort. But when we walked into the cafeteria at 2:00 with visions of warm french fries in our heads, we were disappointed to find that the cafeteria had been closed. No more than 15 feet away from us, I could see that one last order of waffle fries remained under the heat lamp. Seeing an employee cleaning the floor inside the roped-off area, I decided to do what I could to keep my promise. "Excuse me, ma'am," I called out. "I'd pay you whatever it took if there was any way we could get that last order of fries."

She stopped her cleaning and walked toward the fries. "They're pretty soggy—they've been here for a while."

"We wouldn't mind that at all," I assured her.

"Well," she said, picking up the basket of fried goodness, "they're just going to go to waste. Here you go—enjoy."

As Jonathan and I sat down to a mound of free waffle fries that tasted better than ever, I asked, "What did you learn from what just happened?" Jonathan is the most reserved of our children by far, and I was hoping he'd learned something about the benefits of boldness.

"I learned that I'm never going to get french fries that way," he said simply and took another bite of fries. I laughed out loud at his candor.

President Howard W. Hunter observed that fear is "a principal weapon in the arsenal which Satan uses to make mankind unhappy. . . . A timid, fearing people cannot do their work well, and they cannot do God's work at all. The Latter-day Saints have a divinely assigned mission to fulfill that simply must not be dissipated in fear and anxiety."[8]

A friend and former ward member, Jan Penny, once said something in a talk that helped me understand a connection I'd never before noticed in Matthew 25. In the second parable in the chapter, the Savior condemns the temerity of the servant who did not increase his talents out of fear. In the final segment of the chapter, the Savior promises that those who have helped the hungry, naked, poor, and afflicted—the least of His brethren—would be rewarded with the kingdom of God. Jan connected the two segments of the chapter with this profound question, which I've written in the margin of my Bible: "What good am I not doing because I'm afraid?"

What good am I not doing because I am afraid?

Jonathan has plenty of time to overcome his fears, and he may never need to ask for french fries after the cafeteria is closed. But if he and we are going to play our part in moving forward the work of the kingdom, we cannot be a "timid, fearing people" who are overly inhibited by our anxieties. So how can we overcome our fears to be bolder in doing God's work?

Embracing the Moment

I once listened to a captivating speech by a former astronaut, Dr. Jerry M. Linenger, who documented his experience in *Off the Planet: Surviving Five Perilous Months Aboard the Space Station Mir.* On one occasion, he was assigned to undertake a space walk to help repair the space station—for five hours. Initially, the knowledge that he was traveling outside the spacecraft at a speed of 18,000 miles an hour was mortifying. Dangling from the end of a pole, as he moved farther and farther from his host vessel, Linenger eventually reached a point where he suddenly experienced an "overpowering sense of speed" and an "overwhelming sensation of falling. I felt as if I were falling off the station and catapulting toward the earth."

"My heart raced. I wanted to close my eyes in an effort to escape this dreadful and persistent sensation of falling. White-knuckled, I gripped the handrail on the end of the pole, holding on for dear life." Linenger began to analyze his situation, realizing that he had felt just fine inside the space station going precisely the same speed. But it is one thing to freefall inside the space station and along with it, and quite another to do so outside the station, attached by a cord. Inside the station with everything moving together with him, it was easy to trick himself into forgetting how fast he was moving. But not now. "I *was* going 18,000 mph. I *was* freefalling." The physician-astronaut finally began to calm himself by noting this salient fact: despite the exceptional speed at which he was traveling, he had not hit bottom. Indeed, there was no bottom to hit. "I convinced myself that it was okay to fall and fall and fall, as long as I would never hit the bottom."

Once Linenger got past the sheer panic, he began to embrace the extraordinary nature of the experience. Two hours later, as he moved back along the same pole, his attitude was altogether different. "Swinging back on the pole was the ride of a lifetime, pure thrill, pure joy. . . . I was spacewalking, hanging out like a satellite. I was having an experience few others would ever share. 'Yahoo!' I found myself shouting to [my colleague]. This was great. What a view! What a ride!"[9]

Almost none of us will ever go through what this astronaut experienced physically. But many of us have felt overwhelmed by tasks God has given us officially or unofficially, and our instinct is to clutch at something, white-knuckled, holding on for dear life, and hoping for the moment to be over soon. But if we realize that the moment will be over all *too* soon and that the moment itself is actually quite a blessing, we may find ourselves relishing the opportunity instead of merely enduring the moment. For example, most missionaries will never again wear a name tag in the full-time service of the Lord. Never again will it be as easy and appropriate for them to talk with complete strangers on the street or in their homes.

President Gordon B. Hinckley made a similar point to bishops in a leadership address: "This is a strenuous season in your lives. But there is great joy and satisfaction also. The time will come when you will be released, and at that time a deep and poignant sadness will come into your hearts. You will realize then that the Lord has been with you, that you have had a rich and wonderful experience, that you have exceeded your natural capacity because of the Lord's help, and that this was one of the most joyous experiences of your entire life."[10] President Hinckley's analysis can apply in numerous other callings and in life itself—any opportunity that can seem overwhelming at times but is, in reality, all too fleeting. Relishing such opportunities can help us overcome our fears.

Faith Born of Experience

When David volunteered to fight Goliath, his confidence that God would deliver him was grounded in his own past experience. God had helped him defeat a bear and a lion, so why not Goliath? (1 Samuel 17:34–35). "David had made his previous foul shots," commented Bishop Richard C. Edgley, "and he saw the basket as very large."[11] Recognizing how God has helped us in the past helps give us the faith to believe that God will be with us when we act on soul-stretching promptings and commandments in the future. When we remember how good God's track record is with us, it buoys our confidence to face our own Goliaths.

When he was called to the First Presidency, the Lord helped President Henry B. Eyring take courage by using just this kind of analysis with him: "As I prayed in these last few nights, those and other memories flooded back with an assurance something like this: 'Haven't I always looked after you? Think of the times I have led you beside the still waters. Remember the times I have set a table before you in the presence of your enemies. Remember, and fear no evil.'"[12]

We can gain faith from looking not only at our own past experience, but the past experience of others as well. Indeed, the scriptures themselves provide such a collective database of spiritual memories, enlarging the memories of those who study them (see Alma 37:8). Thus, Elder M. Russell Ballard promised:

> Our faith can help us be equally bold and fearless during the course of our respective journeys, whether we are parents working with a troubled child, a single parent trying to raise a worthy family, young people struggling to find a place in a wicked and confusing world, or a single person trying to make the journey through life alone. No matter how difficult the trail, and regardless of how heavy our load, we can take comfort in knowing that others before us have borne life's most grievous trials and tragedies by looking to heaven for peace, comfort, and hopeful assurance.[13]

Keeping an Eternal Perspective

One of the benefits for my students of imagining what they would do to warn roommates about a fire is that it's easy for them to see that, despite whatever short-term resistance their roommates put up, they would be grateful in the end for anything their roommate did to try to warn them. For me, one of the best ways to overcome my fears in sharing the gospel and building the kingdom is to realize that in the long run, the same is true for our efforts to help others. "The danger may be hard to see," taught Elder Eyring,

> but it is real, both for them and for us. For instance, at some moment in the world to come, everyone you will ever meet will know what you know now. They will know that the only way to live forever in association with our families and in the presence of our Heavenly Father and His Son, Jesus Christ, was to choose to enter into the gate by baptism at the hands of those with authority from God. They will know that the only way families can be together forever is to accept and keep sacred covenants offered in the temples of God on this earth. And they will

know that you knew. And they will remember whether you offered them what someone had offered you.[14]

Paul kept precisely this eternal perspective when he proclaimed, "For I am not ashamed of the gospel of Jesus Christ: for it is the power of God unto salvation to every one that believeth; to the Jew first, and also to the Greek" (Romans 1:16). Why wasn't he afraid to boldly share the gospel of Jesus Christ? Because he knew that it was the way God would save anyone who came to believe in it. Such conviction-fueled perspective enabled Paul and can enable us to endure affliction and withstand mockery.

Seeking the Spirit

When the resurrected Savior appeared to the eleven remaining apostles, it is worth noting that they were huddled together behind closed doors "for fear of the Jews" rather than preaching the gospel in the streets of Jerusalem (John 20:19). Their fears were hardly unjustified: their leader had just been crucified for teaching the same doctrines they espoused. Their lives were definitely at risk. Yet only a few weeks later, Peter and John testified with such boldness before the assembled Jewish leaders that those leaders marveled. What was the source of such boldness? Surely the knowledge of the Savior's resurrection was a boost to their confidence, but Luke's account suggests another source of Peter's power. "Then Peter, *filled with the Holy Ghost*, said unto them," Luke began (Acts 4:8).

How did Peter come to be filled with the Holy Ghost? To be sure, Peter and his brethren had now received the gift of the Holy Ghost, but the account in Acts helps us understand how they took advantage of this gift. After being grilled and released, Peter and John returned "to their own company," which offered a prayer that included this plea for strength: "And now, Lord, behold their threatenings: and grant unto thy servants, that with all boldness they may speak thy word." Their prayer was answered dramatically and directly: "And when they had prayed, the place was shaken where they were together; and they were all filled with the Holy Ghost, and they spake the word of God with boldness" (Acts 4:23, 29–31). Surely the Lord answers such prayers today, filling us with the Holy Ghost and enabling us to speak with boldness, despite the things that threaten us, whether we are Sunday School teachers, parents, friends, missionaries, auxiliary presidents, or priesthood leaders.

Move Forward

Perhaps Peter and John also gained strength in the very act of testifying. President Hinckley promised prospective missionaries, "Your fears will fade as you stand boldly in testimony of the truth."[15]

Whether we're seeking to comfort a friend who mourns, to warn a ward member who is straying, or to share the gospel with a neighbor, we may hesitate to act on our promptings because we don't know exactly what to say. Indeed, my experience has been that the prompting to do something usually precedes the instructions about precisely what to say. Yet when we move forward, "led by the Spirit, not knowing beforehand" just what we will be saying (1 Nephi 4:6), the Lord always delivers. Indeed, He has been clear that this is His model: "Neither take ye thought beforehand what ye shall say; but treasure up in your minds continually the words of life, and it shall be given you in the very hour that portion that shall be meted unto every man" (D&C 84:85). As Elder Eyring promised: "With daily study of the scriptures, we can count on this blessing even in casual conversations or in a class when we may be asked by a teacher to respond to a question."[16]

The prompting to do something usually precedes the instructions about precisely what to say.

THE BRASHLY OVERBEARING

As a second-year law student, I learned an important lesson about advocacy when I sat on the moot-court board. One of my responsibilities was to read and score the briefs submitted by each team in the competition; I also watched many of their oral arguments. The students were talented, but because it was their first exercise in advocacy, many of them made a simple but sometimes fatal tactical mistake: they pushed hard on every argument they made, and they seemed to make every argument that came into their mind. In addition, they often refused to acknowledge any weakness in any aspect of their case, as if doing so would result in an automatic loss for their fictional client. Worst of all, some of them ratcheted up the rhetorical volume so high that it was almost difficult to hear the logic of what they were saying. On the other hand, the students who prevailed in the competition sounded much more measured and reasonable in their approach. They focused their efforts on their strongest arguments, realizing that they often needed to prevail with only a single argument in order to win an issue.

A former solicitor general of the United States later spoke to our school and confirmed some of the conclusions I had formulated while watching my peers. He said that as he argued before the United States Supreme Court, he occasionally faced opposing counsel who were more accustomed to arguing before juries than before appellate judges. Such attorneys often used bluster before the court, when carefully reasoned argument would have been much more effective. Bluster does not go over well with Supreme Court justices, apparently.

All of which reminds me of great running backs in football. Really. Some less-seasoned running backs seem to rush constantly at full speed. If a play is designed to run between the right tackle and the right guard, they hit that hole at full throttle, whether or not an opening has been created there. But great running backs often look like they're running at half speed—until they see their hole. They may make their way on a sweep behind a lead blocker with what looks like almost foolish patience. But once they see the hole, they explode through it.

If we are not careful, some of us make the same kind of mistakes in building God's kingdom that my classmates and brash running backs make. Having been inspired to make a rather blunt comment to a straying friend on one occasion, we may believe we now have license or even an obligation to candidly speak our minds with all our friends on every issue—only to learn that we've done far more emotional harm than good with our efforts. Having successfully challenged a friend to hear the gospel, we may decide the best way to move the work forward in the kingdom is to now boldly challenge every friend to hear the gospel in exactly the same way—only to alienate a number of friends who weren't yet ready for such a challenge. "There are many who are bold in declaring the gospel," observed Elder Condie, "but their boldness carried to the extreme can readily offend rather than instill a desire to learn more of the restored gospel."[17] Hence Alma's caution to his son Shiblon: "Use boldness, but not overbearance" (Alma 38:12).

Announcing Truth Is Not Enough

Whether we are friends, missionaries, teachers, or Church leaders, it's sometimes easy to notice when and how others are straying from the path. Unfortunately, we sometimes confuse this first diagnostic step with the entire analysis of how to help them. "I had to say it," a local priesthood leader once explained in defense of calling out his ward on some issue, "because it was the truth." Having discovered others' errors, we may be tempted to simply announce our discovery, perhaps together with a prescription: "That boy you're dating would never make a good husband. You should stop dating him." "You don't involve your students enough in your lesson; you should have more participation." "You won't be able to enjoy eternity with your family unless you're sealed to them. You should stop smoking now and go to the temple."

My friend Henry J. Eyring uses this marvelous metaphor to describe a better approach. He notes that we are sometimes tempted to simply beckon others to join us on Mount Sinai. But if we are going to be effective in getting them there, we must do more than demand that they make the upward trek. To help them climb to where they need to be, we must go to the foot of the mountain, seek to understand what the mountain looks like from where they are and what parts of the path may be hardest for them, and figure out the best way to persuade them to join us.

When we're keenly aware of our weaknesses, having others point them out to us isn't particularly helpful.

In other words, it may be true that our ward or quorum isn't doing a good enough job of home teaching. But simply announcing that fact probably isn't any more effective in improving home teaching than telling someone they are overweight is in getting them to lose weight. Often, we already know that we need to make certain changes in our lives. When we're keenly aware of our weaknesses, having others point them out to us isn't particularly helpful. What we often need is simply encouragement, support, inspiration, and sometimes even instruction on how best to make the change.

Timing Matters

To see how timing matters, we need only to consider the case of a new neighbor family who moves in. What if we promptly introduced ourselves and boldly challenged them to baptism? Surely, such an extreme approach would make these new neighbors less likely to join the Church rather than more.

So what about helping them move and then casually inviting them to attend Church with us on Sunday? That's a much safer approach, but it could still be too fast for some neighbors. Our Heavenly Father knows which people would respond best to which kinds of invitations, so only when we seek to know His will can we be most effective in bringing others unto Christ. For some neighbors, the next step might be a Book of Mormon, but for others it might well be a loaf of bread or a listening ear.

I'm grateful for the wise counsel of Elder Dallin H. Oaks when it comes to sharing the gospel:

All of us have family members or friends who need the gospel but are not now interested. To be effective, our efforts with them must be directed by the Lord so that we act in the way and at the time when they will be most receptive. We must pray for the Lord's help and directions so we can be instruments in His hands for one who is now ready—one He would have us help today. Then, we must be alert to hear and heed the promptings of His Spirit in how we proceed.[18]

To my knowledge, in my extraordinary neighborhood in Rexburg, only two families are not members of the Church. Those two families are literally surrounded by members of the Church—and have been for some time. In addition to my usual desire to share the restored gospel with those who have not yet received it, I am concerned that these families feel welcome in our neighborhood and our town. Thus, my approach to sharing the gospel with them is altogether different than when I am able to engage someone in gospel conversation on a flight. "Part of the quest in striking the balance between meekness and boldness," wrote Elder Condie, "lies in determining not only *when* to be bold but also with *whom* we are to be bold."[19] In other words, what could be an inspired thought to share with someone on the plane is not necessarily the right thing to say to my Rexburg neighbors.

"It is not enough that we are going in the right direction," Elder Oaks taught. "The timing must be right, and if the time is not right, our actions should be adjusted to the Lord's timetable as revealed by His servants. . . . Proclaiming the gospel is His work, not ours, and therefore it must be done on His timing, not ours."[20]

Milk before Meat

When I think of timing in sharing gospel truths, I am reminded of the Sunday School teacher who was asked a question about whether Adam and Eve had navels. Somehow, this question prompted him to diagram the reproductive process in graphic detail on the blackboard for his class of astonished twelve and thirteen year olds. What he taught was true—but not helpful.

"Teaching some things that are true, prematurely or at the wrong time, can invite sorrow and heartbreak instead of the joy intended to accompany learning, . . ." Elder Packer once explained. "It matters very much not only *what* we are told but *when* we are told it. Be careful that you build faith rather than destroy it."[21] There is wisdom in following Paul's advice and not sharing meat before milk, lest those we are trying to help cannot bear it (see 1 Corinthians 3:2).

It is so hard for some of us not to share all the gospel knowledge we have on a subject when someone asks. As I was teaching this principle to my Missionary Preparation students this year, the Spirit whispered to me that I had committed precisely this mistake in one of my own recent conversations. I had been asked a direct gospel question by someone who was less active. I hesitated in responding and tried to answer diplomatically, but ultimately I shared a fair amount of doctrine and information. I believe that everything I said was doctrinally accurate, but the Spirit taught me that I had gone too far. Even though I had taught truth, I had not been helpful because I had shared more than this individual needed to hear at that time.

Stewardship Matters

When we serve as parents and in any calling in the Church, our stewardship gives us license to say and do certain things that would be presumptuous for others to do. How often have we heard a member in his zeal call a ward to repentance during fast and testimony meeting? Such remarks would be appropriate if delivered by the bishop—and if he were prompted by the Spirit—but not when given by a member of the ward as part of a testimony. When we are sensitive to the limited scope of our callings, we can more easily avoid saying things that are inappropriately forward.

This can include situations where, in our enthusiasm, we wish others would do something more quickly than they are. We may even be right about what needs to be done—but not if we jump the gun.

I served as a missionary during a brief period when we taught about the Savior in the first discussion and the plan of salvation in the second; we did not mention anything about the Restoration until the third. I came to love the discussions we were assigned to teach, but early in my mission, I felt frustrated at times that we weren't introducing the Book of Mormon sooner. So my companion and I began introducing the Book of Mormon very briefly at the end of the first discussion with a simple explanation like this: "We've talked today about the importance of faith in Jesus Christ and His atoning sacrifice. To prepare for our next discussion, we'd like you to read three wonderful chapters about faith and the Atonement in the Book of Mormon—Another Testament of Jesus Christ. We consider this book to be scripture, like the Bible, and we'll tell you more about it later. But for now we'd ask you to read Alma 32–34 to help you understand what we've discussed today."

Fortunately, we did notify our mission president in our weekly letter of what we were doing. It wasn't long before our phone rang. I can't remember exactly what our mission president said, but it probably went something like this: "Bless your hearts, Elders, but you can't do that. The Brethren have asked us to wait to introduce the Book of Mormon until the third discussion, so that's what we're going to do."

Roughly one year later, that same companion and I were working together again, but this time as assistants. A General Authority who visited our area expressed some concerns about the drop in the number of copies of the Book of Mormon that had been distributed in the Church in the last year, and I can only assume that his conversations with our mission president alerted President Klein to changes that would soon be made in the order of the discussions. Accordingly, our mission president felt that he now had license to have the missionaries introduce the Book of Mormon at the end of the first discussion. He asked Elder Cook and me to write up the very approach we had proposed almost a year before.

But for us, the moral of the story was not that we had been right. In fact, we had been wrong in jumping the gun. "I taught three different sets of discussions over the course of my mission," President Klein explained. "The right set of discussions to teach was the set the Brethren were asking us to teach us at that point in time."

"We prepare in the way the Lord has directed," advised Elder Oaks. "We hold ourselves in readiness to act on the Lord's timing. He will tell us when the time is right to take the next step. For now, we simply concentrate on our own assignments and on what we have been asked to do today."[22]

Style matters. Even when giving corrective counsel is within our stewardship and the timing is inspired, wise shepherds still prayerfully ponder how best to deliver the news so that it will help rather than hinder the progress of those in their care. For example, a bishop or father might be inspired to get an overweight young man to lose weight so that he'll be allowed to serve a mission. He could just blurt out the news: "Look, you're way overweight. If you don't shed some pounds, you won't be allowed to go on a mission. So go lose some weight." But consider how much more effective it would be if he said, "You know, I've been meaning to lose some weight, and it's not too early for you to start getting in shape for your mission. Would you be willing to start an exercise program with me?"

When I first became a bishop, I heard another more seasoned bishop give some advice that puzzled me at the time but made great sense later on. "Don't chew out the ward," he counseled. "I've tried it a couple of times, just getting some things off my chest and telling them how it is, but it doesn't work. I felt horrible afterwards." He had learned that no matter how frustrated he became with members of his ward, railing on them out of frustration was counterproductive.

Piling on Doesn't Help

One of the many shortcomings I have as a parent is that when I do finally get around to giving corrective counsel to my children, I don't know when to stop. If their response does not immediately show that they have taken my advice to heart, I keep repeating my advice, trying to approach it from different angles. More than once they have told me that piling on such advice is not helpful. By contrast, after exhorting Laman and Lemuel "with all the feeling of a tender parent," Lehi wisely "did cease speaking unto them" (1 Nephi 8:37–38).[23] Lehi undoubtedly understood this teaching from Elder Maxwell: "We are cautioned by Paul, interestingly enough, not to reprove others too much, causing them to 'be swallowed up with overmuch sorrow' (2 Cor. 2:7). President Brigham Young, ever practical as well as spiritual, said we should never reprove beyond the capacity of our healing balm to reach out to the person reproved."[24]

STRIKING THE BALANCE

So how do we strike the balance? When should we boldly challenge someone and when should we patiently befriend them? When should we address an issue and when should we bide our time? Let me suggest two final factors that may help us when facing such dilemmas.

Motives Matter

When we refrain from boldly sharing the gospel with friends, neighbors, and strangers, we sometimes say we are doing it to avoid alienating them—and we often are. But are we occasionally silent or slow in bringing others to Christ not because we are concerned that bold action would be bad for them but because we fear it could be hard for us? Are we actually more concerned about avoiding rejection and embarrassment for ourselves than we are about helping them come to Christ?

Similarly, when we are tempted to speak the truth boldly to others, is our directness born of genuine concern for others—or are we merely venting our frustrations? Just as we should never spank our children simply to make ourselves feel better, we should never boldly give corrective counsel simply because the conduct in question has been bugging us. (One way for me to tell when I've succumbed to such lesser motives is that my style in presenting the information is, well, more embarrassing.)

Another motive against which those of us who are more naturally bold must guard is pride: are we taking bold action so that we can boast of what we did, or because it really is the best avenue for helping those we serve? Do we use a bold retort in a gospel conversation with someone not of our faith because we think it will go the farthest in helping them understand our view—or because it scores the most points in a sort of virtual debating match about which we can tell our friends later? On the other hand, when our true motives are to genuinely aid the other person, we are much less likely to speak sharply or give corrective counsel imprudently.

Love Really Matters

Love is like the duct tape of virtues—it can fix almost any problem. In this context, pure love can help us both to overcome timidity and to avoid overbearance.

"Perfect love," taught John, "casteth out fear" (1 John 4:18). When I imagine the post-mortal scene President Eyring's warning brings to mind—when my friends remember whether I shared the gospel with them—I can easily imagine those with whom I didn't share the gospel asking this: "So were you not as certain about these truths as you claimed to be, or did you just not care for me that much? I'm just working through this and trying to understand why you didn't bother letting me in on the secret."

My imagined replies are feeble. "I just . . . I didn't want to offend you. I was worried that I might come across as self-righteous—you know, kind of ethnocentric."

"So you were worried more about how you would come across," I imagine my friend replying, "than how my life would be? Thanks, pal."

It's simply not a pleasant conversation to contemplate. And I can envision such conversations not just with friends with whom I didn't share the gospel, but with members of the Church for whom I had stewardships that I only timidly fulfilled. When we come to genuinely understand certain eternal truths and to genuinely care about certain people, our love for them will drive out our fears for ourselves. Love trumps timidity.

Love also helps ensure that when we do act boldly in our ministering efforts, we will act wisely and more effectively. When I look at the list of people whose bold counsel has helped me, the common denominator they share is that they love me—and I know it. Elder Maxwell observed the importance of "speaking truth in love," as Paul admonished (Ephesians 4:15).

Love is like the duct tape of virtues—it can fix almost any problem.

> There is something about others' knowing that we love them which . . . helps something to get through. . . . If we speak the truth in love, . . . there is a much greater chance that what we say will find its mark in the hearts and the minds of other people.[25]

Of course, loving others doesn't excuse us from scrutinizing our motives, improving our style, and following the Lord's timing. But having love in the bank with others gives us spiritual capital—the goodwill that we will certainly need if we are prompted to reach out to them in boldness.

Ultimately, as I strive to find the balance between these two extremes in my life, nothing better captures the image of the ideal for me than this counsel from President Hinckley: "Walk boldly, quietly, but with confidence and assurance."[26]

Notes

1. Thomas S. Monson, "To Learn, To Do, To Be," *Ensign,* May 1992, 48.

2. Spencer J. Condie, *In Perfect Balance* (Salt Lake City: Deseret Book, 1993), 182.

3. Mervyn J. Arnold, "Strengthen Thy Brethren," *Ensign,* May 2004, 46–47.

4. Neal A. Maxwell, "Jesus, the Perfect Mentor," *Ensign,* Feb. 2001, 12.

5. Boyd K. Packer, *That All May Be Edified* (Salt Lake City: Bookcraft, 1982), 249.

6. Boyd K. Packer, "Reverence Invites Revelation," *Ensign,* Nov. 1991, 21.

7. Spencer W. Kimball, *The Teachings of Spencer W. Kimball,* ed. Edward L. Kimball (Salt Lake City: Bookcraft, 1982), 198.

8. Howard W. Hunter, "An Anchor to the Souls of Men," *Ensign,* Oct. 1993, 73.

9. Jerry M. Linenger, *Off the Planet: Surviving Five Perilous Months Aboard the Space Station Mir* (Secaucus, New Jersey: Carol Publishing Group, 1999), 205–7.

10. Gordon B. Hinckley, "To the Bishops of the Church," in *Worldwide Leadership Training Meeting: The Bishopric and Aaronic Priesthood,* June 19, 2004 (Salt Lake City: The Church of Jesus Christ of Latter-day Saints, 2004), 28.

11. Richard C. Edgley, "That Thy Confidence Wax Strong," *Ensign,* Nov. 1994, 40–41.

12. Henry B. Eyring, "God Helps the Faithful Priesthood Holder," *Ensign,* Nov. 2007, 56–57, citing Psalm 23.

13. M. Russell Ballard, "'You Have Nothing to Fear from the Journey,'" *Ensign,* May 1997, 60–61.

14. Henry B. Eyring, "A Voice of Warning," *Ensign,* Nov. 1998, 33.

15. Gordon B. Hinckley, "Converts and Young Men," *Ensign,* May 1997, 50.

16. Henry B. Eyring, "'Feed My Lambs,'" *Ensign,* Nov. 1997, 83–84.

17. Condie, *In Perfect Balance,* 185.

18. Dallin H. Oaks, "Sharing the Gospel," *Ensign,* Nov. 2001, 8.

19. Condie, *In Perfect Balance,* 191.

20. Dallin H. Oaks, "Timing," *Ensign,* Oct. 2003, 13.

21. Boyd K. Packer, "The Mantle Is Far, Far Greater Than the Intellect," address to religious educators, Brigham Young University, Aug. 22, 1981, in Church Educational System, *Charge to Religious Educators,* 3rd ed. (Salt Lake City: The Church of Jesus Christ of Latter-day Saints, 1994), 65.

22. Oaks, "Timing," 12.

23. I am indebted to Steve Dennis for this insight.

24. Maxwell, "Jesus, the Perfect Mentor," 14.

25. Maxwell, "Jesus, the Perfect Mentor," 13.

26. "News of the Church," *Ensign,* Sept. 1998, 77.

CHAPTER 12

THE POWER TO BECOME

Enough already, my children might say. *They get the point.* The difficulty in ending this book is that I keep seeing more potential applications of the principle that virtues can become vices if we aren't careful. In fact, it's evidence to me of the principle's usefulness that my children will sometimes point out additional applications of the principle to me. But my aim in writing this book never was to create a comprehensive list of spiritual extremes. Instead, it was to heighten readers' awareness of the notion that many of these extremes come in countervailing pairs so that they can better recognize their own dangerous tendencies. Writing this book has certainly done this for me.

But that's not all I hoped to accomplish. Several years ago I participated in what has become almost a ritual in the corporate world: together with other managerial employees, I was required to submit to a personality test. Afterwards, I foolishly complained about the test because the questions it presented seemed like a list of false dichotomies. "Do you consider yourself to be thoughtful or funny?" the test would ask. Why couldn't a person be thoughtfully funny or humorously thoughtful? Were these mutually exclusive traits? After

I vented, the woman who had administered the test smiled and said knowingly, without any intentional irony, "Oh, we know your kind—you're one of those who thinks he can't be categorized." They had actually created an informal category for those of us who thought human personalities were so complex as to defy pigeon-holing billions of people into four or five slots.

In defense of the test and the woman who administered it, I must concede that most of my fellow workers felt quite comfortable with the labels they were given to better understand themselves. And as I recognized some of the personality types in my colleagues, it did enable me to interact more effectively with some of them. For example, while a few superiors preferred detailed and lengthy analysis, others wouldn't read anything over a page, if that. They wanted conclusions delivered clearly and quickly. So I must confess that there was some benefit in simply understanding people's natural styles a little better.

But I had another more fundamental concern with the whole personality-analysis exercise, which later became the heart of an entire executive retreat I attended. This particular brand of personality evaluation emphasized strengths and weaknesses of various personality types. But it stopped short of suggesting we could do anything about them other than be aware of them. As I listened to the presentations, I had to concede that some of my colleagues were so hooked on analysis that they became bogged down in an analytical quagmire and never got anywhere—while others were so eager to take action that they were frequently sprinting off in what ended up being the wrong direction altogether.

So why not take the next step? Why not encourage people who are naturally analytical—perhaps to a fault—to realize the benefits of limiting the time for analysis and then moving forward with a decision? Why not persuade people who are naturally drivers, movers, and shakers to pause to ask some tough questions and engage in some rigorous thinking before taking action? Perhaps it was because some of the proponents of dissecting personalities doubt our ability to change. (Incidentally, I realize that my exposure to personality analysis is quite limited and that it's entirely possible that some consultants or self-help experts take precisely this approach.)

With the gospel of Jesus Christ, though, we see things differently. For us, improving ourselves is not merely a self-help exercise. Changing the way we view things is at the heart of the gospel itself—with repentance itself denoting "a change of mind, i.e., a fresh view about God, about oneself, and about the world."[1] When we read the Sermon on the Mount, Christians do not think, "Too bad I wasn't born with the meekness personality type. Guess I'll never get to inherit the earth." Instead, we see the Savior's sermon as a soaring invitation to become things we may not already be.

And if transforming ourselves from natural men and women into Saints who are simultaneously bold but not overbearing, organized but spontaneously compassionate, hard-working but not workaholics—if achieving that kind of spiritual metamorphosis on our own seems impossible, that's because it is. It's not self-help we're after. Again, at the heart of King Benjamin's charge to put off the natural man and become Saints is a phrase that is at the core of the gospel of Jesus Christ: the natural man will remain an enemy to God "unless he yields to the enticings of the Holy Spirit, and putteth off the natural man and becometh a saint *through the atonement of Christ the Lord*" (Mosiah 3:19; emphasis added). Through the Holy Spirit, the Lord will bless us with enticings—perhaps even enticings that show just where our weaknesses lie and why they need to be changed—and then He will give us the ability to transcend them, through the enabling power of the Atonement. As followers of Christ, our aim is change, but it is divinely guided and divinely assisted transformation we seek.

This book is intended to be merely a diagnostic tool to help us recognize what might be some "weak things" in our lives. It's the gospel of Jesus Christ that then gives us power to do something about those weak things, "for if they humble themselves before me, and have faith in me," the Lord explained to Moroni, "then will I make weak things become strong unto them" (Ether 12:27). For years I overlooked a phrase at the outset of the gospel of John that announces a theme of that book and, for me, helps capture the essence of the gospel of Jesus Christ: "But as many as received him, to them gave he *power to become* the sons [and daughters] of God" in the most profound sense of that phrase (John 1:12; emphasis added).

Can we change ourselves? Not enough to warrant salvation. But Christ can truly change us, taught President Ezra Taft Benson, "and changed men [and women] can change the world."[2]

Notes

1. LDS Bible Dictionary, "Repentance," 760.
2. Ezra Taft Benson, "Born of God," *Ensign,* Nov. 1985, 6.

INDEX

About the Author

Robert Eaton, a professor of religious education at BYU-Idaho and a regular speaker at BYU Education Week, is a graduate of BYU and Stanford Law School. Prior to teaching religion full-time, he worked as a research assistant for FARMS, an attorney, and a corporate vice president. He is the author of *Digging Deeper* and co-author of *Becoming a Great Gospel Teacher*. He and his wife, Dianne, live in Rexburg, Idaho, and are the parents of four children.